See You at the Summit

Randy contemplates the world from atop Mt. Kilimanjaro

See You at the Summit:

My Blind Journey
from the Depths of Loss to the
Heights of Achievement

Randy Pierce

with Tracy Pierce

Editor: Gene LeJeune

Cover Illustrator: Greg Neault
Cover Photographer: Justin Sylvester

Dedication

I dedicate this journey to each and every one of you choosing to read my story, for you are ultimately the reason I wrote this book. It is in appreciation of you who seek to learn, grow and climb towards something better. I like to believe I am in your company.

It is written in honor of my parents and pups. My mom, Georgia, and dad, "Buddy" were the first to guide my steps. They taught me love, kindness and an appreciation for my next essential guides. Modi, Ostend and Quinn are my three boys and these delightful dogs were the closest, dearest friends imaginable. They each guided me, often literally, through the most essential paths of my life and deliver me to the story revealed within See You at the Summit.

Printed in the United States of America

First Printing, 2018

ISBN: 9781720296799

Imprint: Independently published

Contents

Foreward

When I first met Randy Pierce, in 1984 in the halls of Phi
Kappa Theta at the University of New Hampshire, he was tall,
lanky, sighted, smart, and — from what I observed — perpetually
injured. He was always freshly sutured, wrapped in a bandage, or
sporting a new cast. Sometimes this was from pushing himself too
hard, often it seemed like bad luck. As an outdoor education major
beginning to lead backpacking trips, I made a mental note to
NEVER, for the sake of sound risk management, take Randy
Pierce on a hiking trip.

And yet, in 2010, I forgot and I invited Randy to join a class of
UNH students I was teaching on a five-day backpacking trip in the
Pemigewasset Wilderness Area of the White Mountains, despite the
fact that in the intervening two decades, his now-total blindness
had increased his potential for injury.

We avoided medical excitement on that trip, but let me be clear:
It was hard. Our first big day, 6.3 miles of hiking from the bottom
of Bondcliff trail to the remote Guyot shelter, took 20 hours on the
trail, moving so slowly that we ran out of water, daylight, energy
and, even humor. Anyone who's backpacked knows that just
standing still in a backpack for 20 hours is exhausting, let alone

climbing the rocky slopes of Bondcliff. When his guide dog The Mighty Quinn refused to guide Randy through a part of the trail, deeming a section of washing machine-sized boulders as unsafe, we adapted to the ankle-twisting terrain using a human guiding system, with Randy's hand on the backpack of a hiker in front of him, while The Mighty Quinn looked at us in protest.

Two years and many hikes later, Randy had joined me again for a trip, this time with a group of first-year students who were backpacking in the Kinsman section of the White Mountains the week before UNH started its fall semester. On the final day of the backpacking trip, the students' excitement of first-year move-in was upon us: We had a van to meet, mandatory on-campus meetings they needed to attend, parents waiting in Durham, *and* we were behind schedule. But two years of practice in human guiding made me and Randy a backpacking team to be reckoned with. With his left hand on my pack and his right on his walking stick, Randy could anticipate his next steps with confidence. I accentuated my pack movements to help keep him on the trail and he provided steady feedback that helped fine-tune my guiding. We developed some simple communication: When I said "highway," Randy knew the trail ahead was smooth and pushed into my pack to signal me to accelerate. "Sloper" indicated an angled rock that Randy would investigate with his foot. "Tight behind" signaled the path was so narrow he should follow directly behind me to avoid jutting rocks, impaling branches or other non-ADA-compliant obstacles mountain trails serve up with frequency. ("Tight behind" almost always prompted an adolescent joke.)

We flew down that challenging trail in the Kinsmans at more than three miles per hour — a blistering pace for any backpacker, and three times faster than our earlier attempt — and met our van with time to spare. But what makes that experience one of my fondest memories of our many, many adventures was the triumph of our teamwork and problem-solving over the situation that, just a few years earlier, challenged us to tears. Randy and I have felt this joy of being in synch with each other repeatedly, on hikes and also skiing and cycling. Without Randy, I may never have realized that overcoming adversity is not only incredibly satisfying, it's also a lot of fun. Working in such terrific partnership with my friend, in the mountains, on a beautiful day, and just *nailing it* is one of my many cherished memories of our teamwork and trust.

I didn't just include Randy on my backpacking trips to show him a good time (as this book illustrates, he's quite capable of finding adventures on his own). I brought Randy along not for Randy's sake but for that of my students. On those trips — and in this book — Randy offers an honest look at loss and a story that people can identify with. We all grieve loss in our life. We all have challenges. Even though the vast majority are sighted, I believe you will identify with Randy in his story. Hopefully you will also be inspired to join with him in finding your peak potential. Randy helps us understand that a blind guy hiking at a breakneck pace on some of the gnarliest trails in the White Mountains is possible not because he is especially gifted but because he has worked hard at communication, trust, practice, problem-solving and flat-out effort to master the adversity life throws his way. Randy's talent is his approach to adversity. It's a message the college students on those trips are fortunate to have lived, and one so powerful several of those students continued to be inspired by Randy's approach to adversity in the way they live their lives.

Even though this book shares Randy's many responses to adversity, what Randy would want you to know is how average he is. He's taller and faster and more analytical than most of us and he definitely drives worse than nearly all of us, but on balance his accomplishments are less about talent and more about tenacity. And in that way, Randy invites us to make his story *our* story. Any of us can, with a problem-solving mindset and a tenacious perspective, build a team, take risks, and overcome our own adversities. Hopefully in the process you make some dear friends and create wonderful memories.

Brent J. Bell, Ph.D.
Associate Professor of Outdoor Education
University of New Hampshire

Acknowledgement

Tracy and I agreed I get to take the lead on acknowledgements and this means I choose to put my first and foremost thanks to my amazing wife Tracy. All the best turns of phrase and many sentences which would have sprawled at your feet in a tangled heap were saved by her talented efforts. As my ever attentive, loving partner in the journey of life, she patiently encouraged and inspired me over the three years in which this book has been at some stage of development. Actively working beside me for the last intense year, she not only ensured the book could happen but enabled life's disruptions to be managed, talking me down from a ledge or two along the way. Thank you will never say enough but I hope our life always conveys the love, respect, admiration and appreciation I hold for you.

My sweet Autumn has the unenviable task of guiding in the footsteps of a legend but undaunted she infused our hearts and home with a joyous, affectionate burst of energy. She has brought me to many summits, literal and figurative as well. During the writing of this book she has nudged my arm off the keyboard a time or 54 as a reminder I should attend our work and needs beyond the book.

She also tolerantly curled into an impossibly small ball at my feet, particularly after being fed, to allow me the time to acknowledge she is "Awesome Autumn!" Every single day our journeys remind me that she is the gift of freedom and independence to explore this world I love, and I love her all the more for the attentive choice she makes in being my Guide Dog.

My love of history and literature which quintessentially captures moments of deepest human experience led to an easy admiration of my friend Gene Lejeune. Throughout our many diverse adventures and discussions, he seemingly knows every reference and provides exactly the right quotation to place me in the moment. He offers the back story which gives insight and depth to these tales. He also happens to have all the skills of a talented editor and an eager willingness to not only edit the words but also draw forth the full measure of the story with the right question at precisely the right time. Thank you for the gift of your craft and even more for the friendship which made this book and our time shared so much more rewarding.

Any book with a chance to be good needs a reader who will ruthlessly challenge every aspect. No matter that my personal life is exposed and vulnerable, I needed to hear what is irrelevant, uninteresting, selfish, arrogant, mitigated, cruel, confusing, and hopefully some good things too. Chris Woods gave me the harsh candor and fortunately the encouraging praise when warranted. He also did it with a clear kind intent our years of friendship and trust encourage. I am astounded by the level of detail and quality he gave to me. We'd talk through his reactions and suggestions for hours and he sent detailed notes I used to revise my many drafts. He singlehandedly caused chapter reordering and significant restructure of the flow but only because it made this a better book much as he helps me always evaluate how to improve as a person. When it was most difficult for me to write because of the many distractions on my time he shared a quote which is ultimately his own though he loosely derived it from Stephen King: "When you really want to write, nothing will stop you. When you don't, you probably shouldn't anyhow!" When the writing was finished he was most directly responsible for the subtitle which correctly assessed the real journey in the book, "from the depths of loss of the heights of achievement."

Justin Sylvester is yet another in a long list of incredible people I'm fortunate to have in my world. Included in his lengthy list of ludicrous talents is generosity, gracious humility and an artistic eye for photography. He took the picture of Quinn guiding me to the summit of Mt. Monroe which not only adorns the cover of this book but has been the signature image for our 2020 Vision Quest charity since Justin took the photo and gave us full permission to use it anywhere we chose. The image has been shown to thousands around the world and featured prominently because it captures so much. I want to capture an appreciation for the other side of the photo, my friend behind the lens.

As I express my appreciation for the many friends who played a direct and significant role in this book, I feel overwhelmed by the sheer volume of effort towards this project. Why are so many friends so kind and generous of their time and talents? Greg Neault is the perfect example as I cannot imagine anyone more giving of so many hours and such impressive creativity. His artistic skills for the cover design are the obvious initial example, thank you Greg. His clever creations in the author series and other social media marketing is part of what lifts the book up towards its summit and without Greg I would have been less likely to achieve many of my favorite peaks. So why are my friends so kind and generous? Perhaps their life story may share that insight, I will just acknowledge how fortunate I am to have friends like Greg who make life fun, adventurous, meaningful and at the same time successful.

Another of my readers stands out for the encouragement he has gifted me in a host of diverse adventures from hiking, skiing, cycling and even some roots of running. When Professor Brent Bell reconnected with me many years after our college friendship together, I had no idea how many pivotal experiences we would share. He's experienced some of my worst choices and moments, yet our friendship has endured in strength, love and respect for each other. Fortunately, we've had many summits of success as well and he shared kind commentary on the book which is extra important since I asked him to write the Forward for See You at the Summit. We all likely experience triumph and tragedy along our path and Brent's kind approach to guiding me through both is just a small measure of my appreciation for a person I admire greatly.

The Best man! Rob Webber had this role at my wedding and certainly contends for it throughout my life, including in my appreciation for his technology contribution for three years of connecting our Peak Potential Auction readers to the book blog. I learn from him consistently, celebrate adventures with him frequently, and find inspiration in him constantly. He's probably twice saved my life, so without him there would be no book! In fact, without him I might still be trapped on Mt. Kilimanjaro. Since we met in college in 1985 I have never had to consider a time without Rob and that is what I appreciate most of all.

In evaluating the various publishing options, Matt Landry turned out to be a tremendous guide. Always willing to give his time, wisdom and stories of his experiences Matt made our decision-making journey easier. It may have been difficult to limit reminiscing about the White Mountains we both love so well or philosophizing on the merits of a more positive world, but I'm tremendously grateful he chose to be such a fantastic friend and resource along the path.

Dave Chartier seems to have landed on my virtual speed dial setting for when I need to "phone a friend' for assistance. Numerous times in life and again several times in the creation of this book I leaned on his thoughtful, albeit humor laden, approach to problem solving. He reviewed a key point or two in the book and loaned me his visual acumen for review and adjustments of cover designs along the way. It's a wonder he hasn't changed his number yet!

I do not wish to imagine my life's different course if I did not have the gifts of my guide dogs, Autumn, Quinn and Ostend. I have these incredible gifts because of the choice made by "Puppy Raisers" to dedicate months and months of their lives in loving devotion to the care and training of the young puppies who are on the path towards becoming Guide Dogs. Puppy Raisers are the heart and soul of the Guide Dog programs. Beyond the energy, time and love invested comes the incredible sacrifice of giving their dog away so it can be matched with a blind person, like me, who's life will be changed forever. They are my heroes and I wish to acknowledge their work, character and choice with my full awe and admiration.

Future In Sight (formerly known as the NH Association for the Blind), Guide Dogs for the Blind and Guiding Eyes for the Blind are organizations which have been exceptionally positive influences in my journey. The path to living independently and savoring life was not obvious to me after going blind, but with the right guidance it became clear. This is why I will always strive to ensure their work continues for others and why 2020 Vision Quest proudly supports both Future In Sight and Guide Dogs for the Blind.

Lastly, I would not be writing this final acknowledgment if an incredible community of people did not consistently encourage me. In emails, social media and most especially at my many presentations I am inspired to believe in the story I shared on these pages. In fact, many times people requested that I share the story in a book and this idea took time to germinate fully within me. I had doubts, but a strong community of continued reinforcement led me to deliver what you requested. Along the way I discovered writing this book was a tremendous gift to myself. As such my final thank you is for those who choose to believe and encourage others and certainly did so for me. On our journey to achieve our peak potential, the ripples of influence of the right words at the right time are how we best climb. It is thanks to all of you I am climbing still and may sincerely wish for your success that I might "See You at The Summit!"

Introduction: A Leap of Faith

"To finish the moment, to find the journey's end in every step of the road, to live the greatest number of good hours, is wisdom."
Ralph Waldo Emerson

I stood atop a 25-foot platform with the muddied waters of a daunting Tough Mudder obstacle beneath me, sightless eyes shut to better focus on the angle of my toes pointing me in the right direction. A crowd of several hundred competitors surrounded the obstacle shouting my name in a cacophony of support: "Randy! Rand-dee! Ran-Dee!" I held my hand to my ears to inspire them to shout a little louder, so I could draw strength and encouragement from their emotions.

Despite the swell of emotional support, I hesitated as doubt began to rise within me. I had lost my focus, my mental image and a fair bit of my nerve. I needed the reassurance of repeating our initial approach, in which I leaned precariously over the edge of the platform while my friend Jose held onto my shirt to anchor me. Extending to the absolute limit of my reach so I could graze the T-

14

bar with my blind cane, all to confirm the target I was likely already marking with my toes.

Faltering and overwhelmed, I told Jose "I think I need my cane again." His words were final if not entirely reassuring "It's gone!" He said. "We passed it down and can't get it back now. You've got this, trust yourself and jump!"

Confronted with the finality of Jose's statement I felt a bit trapped. Did any of them actually believe I would succeed in leaping 9 feet out, catching a trapeze T-bar, swinging the full arc, launching up and out to ring the hanging bell before plunging down into the muddy water below? "Positive adversity" I reminded myself.

My heart pounded to the rhythm of the crowd. I bent my legs deeply and launched upward and outward with all the strength and confidence of my willful decision, sweeping my arms into an exaggerated bear hug motion, to connect with the vertical bar allowing me to slide down to the tiny T-bar handle. I more than covered the distance: I was shocked by the force as my chest, face and upper arms connected hard with the bar. "One Mississippi, two Mississippi..." I counted to myself to measure the timing of my swing, which would arc me to the high point on the far side of this massive obstacle. My arms seemed impossibly slow in their slide towards the handle which I needed. As my momentum began to slow I switched to a hand only grip for the mere moments of that final comfort.

Time had quickly run out and I needed to release my final connection and launch myself blindly into the vast unknown where somewhere hung a suspended bell, seemingly impossibly beyond reach. I'd like to suggest there was any thought of grace as I flailed my arm towards the highest and furthest point possible. I doubt that was the case, however, and I relied on the length of my arms and focus in my mind of where the highest and furthest point of my flight would reach.

I was both surprised and delighted as, just by the barest bit, I felt my fingertips connect enough to ring the bell, bringing the sweet sound of success to my ears mere moments before the crowd's screams confirmed my victory. Adrenaline surged through me as I plummeted towards the water. Plunging into the depths, I was an arrow straight to the bottom, where my feet struck, and legs bent to absorb the force of my fall. Those legs sprang up with the powerful intensity of the moment and as I thrust my fist into the air I cleared the surface of the water with an exultation matched by the hundreds still cheering wildly.

As the scene above demonstrates, I relish the opportunity to live in the moment. This is just one glimpse from the many adventures I intend to share ahead. These experiences support my appreciation of the phrase that life is more about the journey than the destination. This emphasizes appreciation for the process and not just the final result. My many adventures have prompted some to label me an adrenaline junkie or to suggest I have a reckless exuberance. I quite disagree. There is a process behind my approach to these moments and a method I have developed throughout my life which guides the incredible journey I am about to share.

The arrival of legal and eventually total blindness after a rather ordinary 22 years of life had a tremendous effect on me. But in a steady progression, the influence of my blindness diminished surprisingly and incredibly as the adventures and experiences gathered into a foundation from which I climbed to what many consider impossible heights. The Tough Mudder bell ringing moment stands out as one of several poignant demonstrations of that experience and achievement, though disguised perhaps in the reckless guise perceived by some. When viewed alone I fully understand the ease of that presumption. The many steps involved in my choices paint a much clearer picture of the problem-solving approach through which I manipulate physical, social and emotional risks to better my experience in all the wonders of my journey through life.

My Tough Mudder leap represents one moment of unique success. It is surrounded by many vastly different moments which include athletic achievements, personal triumphs, and professional accomplishment, which ultimately have one common aspect. They are moments surrounded by a base of learning to believe in personal possibility. Yes, there are many setbacks and shortcomings along the journey. These too involve the confidence to pursue my goals and reach for a destination with a clarity of vision necessary to guide me.

My life and choices have led to a vast number of experiences starting with the stories of the essential moments in the making of the man I am today. I will share with you highlights of meaningful adventures, practical takeaways from those experiences, as well as an insight into my life background. Each of these enabled me to make the choices necessary to appreciate and find value in all of my experiences, setbacks and successes. I hope we'll find together the process through which my personal frustrations and failings transformed obstacles into stepping stones for the heights to which I would climb. I believe this will be relevant as a methodology in your own world, as you choose to strive for your own version of peak potential.

I find tremendous value in having a destination to ensure life is a journey worth appreciating. While the ultimate ending point of any particular journey can and likely will change many times along the path, each goal I choose provides a framework, a map of sorts, to help guide and ensure the right ratio of marvels along the way. Certainly, I always wish to remain open and able to savor serendipity. I've found my own journey in life to be laden with numerous peaks which are the result of deliberate choices and planning for those destinations.

In contrast, John Lennon gifted us with the notion, "Life is what happens while you are busy making other plans." I strive to sustain sufficient flexibility to ensure my plans are not so rigid that I fail to appreciate the possibilities around me. This includes appreciating all the positive gifts that surprise us along the way and reacting as well as possible to unexpected challenges.

My journey from fully sighted through "legal blindness" to total blindness was very different than I would have ever guessed. When confronted with the stark reality of going blind my initial responses were, not surprisingly, extremely poor. I was angry, depressed and even in a bit of denial.

Somehow, I found the ways to transition from believing everything fun and meaningful in my world was no longer possible. I discovered methods to believe in myself and celebrate the ability awareness which resulted. I trained for and achieved my second-degree black belt in Shaolin Kenpo Karate, I climbed mountains with some historic results, I ran marathons, founded a charity and in ever more profound ways, learned to reach for and achieve my peak potential personally, professionally and philanthropically.

I feel incredibly fortunate in reflecting upon my multitude of experiences and even more so how those events steadily developed into the philosophy and methodology with which I live this astoundingly rewarding life. This is not to suggest there are not any low points along the way or that I do not continue to find my fair share of struggles. It is simply my good fortune to have found the real value in how to make choices for both planning and responding to events in my life.

I invite you to join me in this sharing of my journey. Along the way there's a bit of adventure, humorous anecdotes, some triumph and tragedy as well as several captivating stories of love and loss. Together they provide the foundation of how I developed the approach and attitude many have asked me to share.

Whether they have value for your personal approach is something you'll have to determine. When asked for advice I'm often more eager to share my opinions and my experiences, though I strongly believe that each of us is ultimately responsible and accountable for the choices we make in our life. I believe you will likely find entertainment in a myriad of cathartic emotions and should they resonate for you then I support your choice to use them to improve your own life.

In my own journey of accountability, I have come to understand how the risks and rewards of my choices affect me. I have also learned the weight of influence we all have, deliberately or inadvertently, on others around us. Mindfulness of our influence on others is an ethical attentiveness, a form of social responsibility. I'm certainly well aware of this, particularly as I set out to write a book at the encouragement of many within my community. This community is in part a development of my drive to build teams as one of the positive responses to my sight loss. Collaboration is an essential element of my approach to success. It is a balance of celebrating both independence and teamwork. Both are vital means of enhancing our ability to stride forward in a positive fashion.

A second and perhaps more significant aspect of my means to achievement, and this book, involve my approach to setting goals. I contend that a lack of goals will lead to stagnation. My life feels most enriched and positive when I use goals to direct my choices. Those who attend my presentations likely know goals are a crucial point and I refer to them as "positive adversity".

There are three very significant benefits to goal setting. The first is that since we are choosing to set the goal we may presume it's something positive we wish to achieve. By creating a direction for our efforts, it becomes far more likely that we will reach these achievements. This is not to suggest the goal will be easily obtained, only that in setting it we provide focus, taking the first steps in our ability to reach the goal. There's far more involved in reaching most goals but it begins with this first and critical step.

A second important benefit to setting goals is simply that in working towards them we begin to develop the skills which may be used to reach future achievements. I relate this to the old adage "Practice makes perfect." I've never fully believed in the perfection side of that quote, but I do believe practice makes progress. As such, the skills needed to reach future goals are developed. We refine these skills and ultimately this imparts the tools we need to achieve still more goals in the future.

The third and final benefit to this positive adversity approach is a simple but powerful realization. By reaching for goals and developing skills needed to achieve them we become more confident of our ability to manage positive adversity and consequentially negative adversity. This confidence prepares us to live our lives with less fear of the challenges our choices may create. In so doing, we provide a freedom of decision and action capable of enhancing our lives tremendously!

We will all undoubtedly face challenge throughout our lives and experience varying levels of anticipatory trepidation. The more we familiarize ourselves with adversity, emphasizing the positive over the negative, the more we become comfortable and confident with how to respond. I believe my response to varying challenges developed into a map guiding me to some incredible summits, literal and figurative. I hope to illustrate this throughout the pages ahead.

One additional aspect of goal setting is my belief there is a bonus benefit created by living in the experiences resulting from the goals we set. Whether it's the gray jay landing in my hand on a mountain climb or the tear-invoking drawing of a school child; I found those unexpected rewards enrich my life immeasurably. I often refer to this as the magic on the path. These treasures seem most likely to occur when we are more invested in the myriad opportunities life has to offer. Thus, it is that we arrive here - this book is one of the goals I created to challenge myself. I set the goal to write this book knowing full well it would involve learning many new skills and require a significant amount of time and resources amidst my already challenging schedule.

I want to reach beyond my comfort zone finding the way to share deeply of my life experiences and the effect on myself and the world around me. Perhaps for some of you it is a little positive adversity to work through these pages with me. From our brief start of my early years we'll leap quickly into the defining moments, experiences, and adventures which are my life. I look forward to sharing the journey with you, see you at the summit!

Pictured Randy prepares to take the leap at the California Tough Mudder

Start at the Beginning

"Let's start at the very beginning. A very good place to start."
The Sound of Music

When we reflect on our lives there are so many moments which might mark the true start of our journey. I've dedicated considerable introspection into evaluating just when I became the person I am today. I wonder at what point I effectively became the person who I accept as me. I don't think it was those earliest infancy moments when adventures were dangerous diapers and learning to crawl away from my parents who shared those faded tales. Nor do I have strong enough memories of my toddler years, including my exploration of the bottom of our swimming pool. I do vividly recall the quaver in my Mom's voice as she recounted her fearful discovery of me unfazed and fully submerged for unknown minutes! I do see some roots in my childhood and through my school years with David Killiam, our music teacher, challenging us to expand our minds as well as our voices. There are still stronger roots in William Schomburg's English classes prodding me to believe William Wordsworth's "the child is father of the man." There are certainly many influences on the person I've become in the journeys I took as a child.

In the early years of our lives we burst with energy in so many seemingly chaotic directions, only to halt dramatically and repeat the process again and again. In my life there was the energized and frenzied drive of my mischievous boyhood. There was also the comforting stability of my first decade living in our home on Fordham Drive in Nashua, NH. I was the youngest of three or technically, four children and that technicality was significant to our family dynamic. The first child born was the only girl, Cindy-Lou. I knew her only through a photograph I still recall vividly though she died at only 11 months, of spinal meningitis, 11 years before I was born. Her death had tremendous influence on my parents. The signs of that pain and how it fractured their relationship was always evident to me. I think my Mom always sought a justification for her loss as often, anger and blame can be protective measures we use to shield us from grief. My Mom did not live an angry life, but she did harbor some blame towards my father for their loss despite it being entirely the fault of the ugly and unexpected spinal infection. Another consequence of the tragedy was my Mom's tendency to over-protect her living children. This would ease a little by my arrival, but would have tremendous effect on my eldest brother, Daniel.

Dan preceded me by ten years and as such my youthful memories of him are few and far between. But there was a magical afternoon, when returning from high school he stepped into the living room, put on his new album with the song "The Locomotion" and proceeded to dance. Hearing this new, strange and different sound coming from the formal living room where I was not supposed to play, I snuck cautiously to the edge of the entranceway and peaked in on him, uncertain if I was allowed to witness his antics. Normally if he was assigned to babysit me, I'd keep to myself and he'd encourage this behavior! Never the less, I peered around the corner to watch his dance steps never expecting to be caught. I was surprised by the immediate warmth and welcome in his smile as he saw me. He motioned me into the room to join him. I froze for a moment of indecision and he danced right up to me, took my wrists and guided me encouragingly into the room and taught me the locomotion. We laughed and caught the best moment of pure joy together I ever recall with my now deceased brother.

Both of my parents had fulltime jobs and an assortment of daycare options form the core recollection of many hours spent accompanied by my brother, Richard. Being six years older than me provided enough responsibility in those days and gave him enough worldly experience in my eyes to provide a significant amount of direction. We shared a bedroom, as our home was small and most nights he would read me bedtime stories. At times he may have chosen tales more suited to my age, but more often I recall the stories challenging me and him helping to talk me through them. I developed a love for books and appreciated the inflections he used for the characters, even at his relatively young age.

Pictured: Randy (right) and Rick visit Santa 1969.

We also had a respectable stockpile of board games. Rick was always willing to join me in these games, patiently taking the time to teach me how to play, and due to his years of advantage, help me learn to lose. I was a terrible loser. To my chagrin, I'd cry and even throw a temper tantrum. Somehow Rick found the way to overlook those outbursts and still be willing to play again. He was a constant source of inspiration, friendship and fun throughout my childhood. The real bonds of friendship would need some time to develop but his patience with his immature and slightly wild-child little brother made it possible. This is not to suggest he lacked behavioral challenges of his own! I well recall how his angelic reputation with my parents, which was not entirely accurate, gave him credibility and power over his younger and more mischievously inclined brother. To be clear he was better at getting away with things than I was and happily would sell me out or leverage false reports of my behavior for a little extra work from me. Many times, he had me take on his dish washing chore during the summer, with the threat of telling Mom and Dad I was bad if I didn't. I'd protest that I hadn't misbehaved, and he'd point out they would believe him, and I'd still be punished. My summers of play were important enough I'd mostly accede to his demands and he usually didn't push too far.

Our backyard bordered with undeveloped land which went on for what seemed forever, to my youthful eyes. The vacant "lot 26" which was our side yard had a major trail into those woods, as well as, an enormous boulder in the shape of a sleeping giant. My friends and I often met on the giant to discuss the adventures ahead or the injustices of our parental overlords. Shared excursions into the woods launched from the giant although our fenced yard also had a secret back gate to our own private trail. My summers were filled with exploring and adventuring on Blueberry Hill, the Forgotten Path, the Birches, Kite Meadow and far beyond the dark forest which had trails through which the entire world could be found someday. I don't know how many hundreds of acres were back there, I only know that to me, Christopher Robin's woods had no advantage over my own wilderness. I suppose I lacked a Tigger, Eeyore and Pooh but I had Planet of the Apes and a dinosaur world well before Jurassic Park. My imagination filled those woods with adventures and companions aplenty.

My woods did have some borders as the single-track old farm road marked the limits of what I was allowed to travel alone. Beyond that was the dark forest but there was space enough inside this limit. It held mysteries and treasures such as a Forgotten Path which went unknown for years until scavenging for more blueberries. I scrambled under some brush and found this hidden path which paralleled our most commonly hiked trail. Both led to a small meadow below a rise where the trio of white birch trees provided our favorite climbing opportunity. No matter who joined me for the climb up those trees it always seemed our talks were more meaningful and our friendship closer because of the shared experience of being in the trees together. It was from this hill we could look down to the main road which marked another border on the far side of Kite Meadow. That stretch was exposed enough to allow the winds to blow up the gentle rise. It was a large field, ideal for unstringing our kites without fear of entanglement. This natural treasure was where my kite, my imagination and many of my dreams took flight.

My adventurous nature did, on occasion, get me into trouble and put a few extra reasons for worry into my parents' minds. Within a few months of learning to ride my bicycle I started doing tricks to match some of the older boys. Standing on my seat and rounding a corner I took a hard fall, badly bloodying my knee and earning my first significant scar. It wasn't just in adventures that I added worry to my parents and injury to myself. Helping my friend crush and remove a rock from their land, I was pulling out pieces as he smashed the rock with the mini-sledge hammer. We lost our timing and my left-hand ring finger earned my first collection of stitches and broken bones as the hammer crashed down on it. We actually decided for a short few minutes to hide it, but the severity was clearly a problem. Shock had numbed my pain enough, so I was calm and patient when I should have been more urgent on my return home. When I called out to my Mom, she announced that she was in the bathroom changing into her bathing suit. She stepped out and without fanfare I showed her my injured hand. She screamed and slammed the door as she thought to change again, stopped, opened the door to wrap my hand in a towel and then slammed it again to change for our first emergency room visit. There would be many more injuries, surgeries and hospital visits ahead, some due to my pushing limits, and most managed with the love and support of my family.

I was a few years younger than the other boys in the neighborhood. I drove myself to be competitively competent subconsciously attempting to overcome the advantage of their years as they tended to be physically larger, faster and more mature. Mostly I didn't much mind or consciously notice. I did have to work harder to succeed, often thinking strategically to accommodate for their advantages. I constantly pushed my limits. Mostly it was just enjoying life, playing games and if not entirely staying out of trouble, doing our best to not get caught! I always expected, as a young boy might, our friendships would last forever. They would not and while those first ten years from 1966 until 1976 would provide a foundation of some form for the person I would become, there were more significant formative points for me still ahead.

Both of my parents were hard working laborers often seeking as many overtime hours as possible. As a result, their time outside of work was very important to them, albeit in different ways. My father had a love of fishing and hunting which was his primary form for relaxation. Whether to escape from work, return to his youth or simply for the love of the hobby my father would head north to the deeper woods for as many weekends as possible. My mother had no interest in either of those hobbies, which was a point of contention between them far too many times. My mom loved gardening and landscaping and could happily spend an entire weekend with an assortment of yard projects shared as a family. They were vastly different from each other in many ways beyond their pastime pursuits.

I have no doubt that my parents loved each other, just as I know how well they loved all of us children. Unfortunately, due to the various differences and stressors they separated and reunited several times in my first ten years. These were traumatic episodes with many of the details hidden from me due to my age. I always stayed with my Mom at the home on Fordham Drive but not without significant challenges. The disruption of missing my dad, watching my mom's sadness, anger and confusion over our broken family all took their toll. In an era of one car, which my father kept, there were other difficulties. To continue playing in my basketball league mom would frequently walk with me in the winter for the nearly three miles necessary to get me to practice or games and repeat it to return home. When I think of the resolve in this gesture, her determination to keep my life as close to normal despite the unreasonable sacrifice involved, I marvel at her strength. I can only imagine the other similar sacrifices she made for my two brothers and the essential needs for our home. My parents' separations always seemed to last several months and occurred a handful of times in my young life. I delighted in their reunions even as the stressful buildup of arguments before the separations always frightened me

Pictured: The Pierce family 1970
Front L-R Rick, cousin La'ra, Bud, Randy Back L-R Dan & Georgia

I strongly believe my parents gave their best efforts towards their marriage. They did so with the same determination with which they attempted to make a better life for us and that showed in every decision they ever made. There are many, many examples throughout my years of this effort, perhaps none as significant as the decision for us to move to Colebrook, NH. This little town nestled in the shadow of Vermont's Mt. Monadnock was the rural retreat where my Dad could have his hobbies so close to hand that it would allow my parents, hypothetically anyhow, to spend significantly more quality time together. It was going to bring our entire family closer together. I felt a blend of excitement and dread. I could feel the joy in my father's approach and the hopeful resignation of my mother, who chose a sacrifice she thought would unite her family which was always most important to her.

My brother Dan, then aged 20, determined he would not be making the journey and would set out on his own, renting a room from the neighbors across the street. That shock hurt my mother and resonated with me as I began to fully realize the drastic nature of this change. When a ten-year-old boy learns that he is leaving all of his friends behind, leaving the only home he has ever known and travelling 200 miles north to a town on the border with Canada; it likely is going to stir some impressive pre-teen angst. I'm proud to say that I did not disappoint.

There were so many changes wrought by this move that only in hindsight do I fully appreciate the benefits it ultimately brought for me. At a critical point of my development I learned several important skills. Most directly I met an entirely new community, fostering friendships and positive relationships along the way. I acquired an ease and comfort with meeting people and making connections. The difficulty of handling such a significant life change provided a foundation for my management of adversity. I succeeded in many ways, as well as, stumbling into a few mistakes with both results serving me well in life's obstacles ahead.

Living in this rural town also provided many opportunities to be involved in virtually any activity which enticed me. Because of some initial isolation I would learn to lean on my brother Rick as a friend and role model. The latter was amongst the best benefits of this transition and one which to this day I celebrate.

Colebrook still has some important stories to share. However, I consider those experiences to be less at the heart of who I am today. While all of those are a part of my identity, my most significant life's catalyst took place in May of 1989 when at 21 years of age my life changed dramatically.

I was still celebrating my recent graduation from the University of New Hampshire and working as a Hardware Design Engineer at Digital Equipment Corporation, a job I enjoyed and at which I excelled. My friend Sean Griffin had suggested we learn fencing together. I eagerly accepted, full of enthusiasm for the new experience.

Just a few lessons into the training, my instructor, Chris Pullo, noticed a problem. Our small class had paired off for drills and I was working with him directly. The drill was a simple series of basic parries and before my right arm moved across to block his attack he caught my eyes shifting to his foil. He instructed me to keep my eyes on him and to use my peripheral vision to see his weapon. When I told him, I couldn't see his blade without the glance

I could hear a little frustration in his voice as he had me lock my eyes on him and asked if I could see his blade now. I told him no and was thinking about whether the wire mesh of the fencing mask was somehow interfering, as I hadn't fully adjusted to it yet. His disbelief became incredulity, which progressed to concern as he began to work with me to explore the extent of the problem with my left eye.

Because fencing relies so heavily on eye movements and peripheral vision he could detect that my "blind spot" seemed unreasonably enlarged. He quickly used the tip of his foil to map out a disconcerting discovery: my sight contained an unexpected and expansive void.

We all have blind spots which correspond to the point where the nerve attaches to the retina in the back of each eye. They are a small area in the upper left of our left eye field and upper right of the right eye field. In a matter of moments, he had discerned that my left eye had a blind spot three times larger than normal.

Surprisingly, his concern had very little emotional impact on me. I didn't feel at all anxious, simply curious. Everything about my sight seemed normal to me, but I believed the conflicting information he had just demonstrated. I just couldn't understand why it was a big deal. Chris on the other hand seemed sufficiently distraught to give me pause. He urged, effectively demanded, that I visit my doctor immediately. I called my Doctor for an emergency appointment from the health club office and went there directly. I can scarcely imagine how such a subtle aspect caused Chris's alarm. He may very well have played an integral part in saving some useful sight for me over the next eleven years.

By that very evening, I had escalated from my primary care doctor to an ophthalmologist, Dr. John Dagianis, who would play a significant role in my sight loss management. His quick diagnosis of the severity of my case, and thorough determination, moved me that same night into the hospital at the University of Massachusetts Medical Center under the care of a neural ophthalmologist, Dr. John Gittenger, Jr. My optic nerve was swollen, which was causing it to die from the outside inward. I would spend nearly two months in the facility undergoing every test with even a hint of relevance; it took just two weeks for this first episode to run its course.

At the end of those two weeks, despite a high dosing of a catabolic steroid to reduce the inflammation and suppress my potentially compromised immune system, all of the sight in my right eye was gone as well as roughly half of the sight in my left eye. As the nerve had died from the outside inward, my left eye was reduced to a constricted visual field or "tunnel vision". A biopsy of the right optic nerve provided no better understanding of why the nerve trauma was taking place.

From here, I would enter a period of intensely frustrating medical evaluation, but the fundamental catalyst had arrived. I was now legally blind and above all other aspects of this change, I was doubtless depressed. I now thought everything fun or meaningful in my life was no longer possible. I would need a radical transformation or rebirth of myself to survive this experience and become the person I am today.

First Struggles with Blindness

"In order to carry a positive action, we must develop here a positive vision." Dalai Lama

Doctor Dagianis finished his emergency examination and with a few simple words demolished the nonchalance of my reactions thus far. His tone was so somber the words almost didn't matter. They conveyed to me his fears for whatever was happening to me. He began "Randy" and I remember that single word vividly it seemed he was speaking to me person to person with empathy as if deliberately breaking the clinical barrier. I remember him removing his thick glasses, wiping his brow and looking at me with such earnest concern it was hard to fathom this was our very first visit.

Dr. Dagianis sent me directly to the University of Massachusetts Medical Center in Worcester. He called ahead to ensure the medical team, including Neural Ophthalmologist, Dr. John Gittenger Jr, were ready and waiting for me despite extending beyond their normal hours. Upon arrival I was taken immediately into the emergency room. Almost before I realized an IV was inserted into my arm.

The stark and sterile clinical backdrop did nothing to abate my emotional overload. Dr. Gittenger reiterated the serious and bleak reality: my vision was in jeopardy. His candor was clinical, not cold, as he explained they simply did not know the cause of my swollen optic nerve. Standard procedure required treating the symptom while they began an all-out search for the cause. The treatment plan involved a "mega-dose" of a catabolic steroid known as Solu-Medrol. The negative side effects were significant both in the short and long term. Dr. Gittenger told me it was the maximum dosage they were allowed to give me and that in itself filled me with concern. What happens if you exceed the maximum dosage?

How exactly does one process the abundance of possible side-effects? I could barely discern which I was likely to suffer as they read a list longer than anyone could hope to memorize let alone consider. What I could reasonably gather is that it could cause hallucinations, heart concerns, liver and organ damage, weight gain, stomach ulcers and muscle deterioration. It could enhance feelings of anxiety at a time when I would be in emotional overload from the potential vision impact. I barely wanted to sign the form, but my medical team thought it was the best chance of preserving my sight and from what I could imagine of being blind that was something I wanted to attempt at virtually any cost. A flurry of legal signings later and suddenly the translucent bag was hung on the pole, dripping its potent drug drop by dour drop into my arm.

Despite those deleterious effects, the doctors' goal in prescribing Solu-Medrol was first and foremost to reduce the swelling of my optic nerves. They also hoped it would shut down my immune system which was a minor suspect in the root cause of the inflammation. Thus, with some reluctance, I accepted the first step in a long process as the Solu-Medrol was administered in the emergency room that night.

With my initial treatment complete it was time to depart the emergency room and enter into the depths of this enormous hospital complex. I was taken by stretcher down long dark hallways feeling as if I was being wheeled into a prison. Feeling the lurching of the stretcher as we rolled into an elevator, I couldn't help but think perhaps it was actually a dungeon. This would be my new home for the next unknown number of days or possibly weeks, though I was assured of at least five days of this detrimental dosage. While hopeful it would resolve my sight concerns, I could not shake the feeling of certainty that the cure was worse than the disorder.

Those first days of exploration at the hospital were dark, ominous and difficult. The complete course of medication seemingly did nothing to halt the death of my optic nerve tissue. I suffered the heightened anxiety of the drug side effect which exacerbated the harsh reality of my condition. My medical team struggled to understand why my optic nerves were so grossly affected. For my part I struggled with so much of the overwhelming experience, as each moment brought a barrage of new concerns, tests and explorations. I feared each test might reveal some new and more sinister reality, while doing nothing to help us understand or prevent my physical and emotional descent into total darkness. While most of the tests ultimately were not challenging, they certainly failed to give us any actual answers to why this was happening to my nerves. Some of these tests were administered frequently which distressed me physically and emotionally.

Twice each day I was placed in front of a Humphrey-Zeiss and Goldman perimetry visual field test. I still recall the discomfort of my chin placed awkwardly on the hard-plastic holder while the technician painstakingly adjusted that holder for optimum alignment. I used a clicker to denote when I observed spots of light randomly flashed around my peripheral vision. A laser was aligned on my pupil such that it could detect if my eye moved off center. If my eye moved it invalidated that particular data point.

Keeping a central focus despite the flashing peripheral events took a surprising amount of concentration each time. Harshly, the final results were an instantaneous print-out highlighting how much peripheral vision had been lost in the short hours since the prior test. Not only did I dread the energy spent on this test but as each printout filled with more black ink indicating lost vision it also filled me with despair.

Several distressing details intensified my anguish. This device used a dot-matrix printer and when it passed over the parts of my field where there was no sight loss it simply did not print and made no noise. When the print heads crashed down upon the paper with their mechanical "kzzsssh" it was jarring for the noise and more so for the blacked-out sight it was reporting. This new print-out would be added to my chart which I would take every opportunity to examine for any shred of information I might glean. The ever-growing stack of these print-outs were stored sequentially, and I would flip them quickly to see a slow-motion version of the tide of blindness washing over my sight. There was cruelness to the day my left eye saw the complete loss of the right eye field and the confirmation that eye's test wouldn't be necessary any longer. The cruelty was compounded as my remaining eye put the shrinking focus on its own fate losing as much as 10 degrees of field in a single afternoon. Both eyes shed tears of despair for the loss.

It was a full two weeks before the first bit of good news arrived: the swelling had begun to reduce for my left optic nerve. While this meant that my sight had stabilized, the entire right optic nerve was now dead and roughly half of the left optic nerve was similarly dead. This means I was totally blind in my right eye and had extreme tunnel vision in my left eye. I was now "legally blind". Those words resonated with me along with words like "disabled", "crippled" and a host of other derogatory terms which ultimately made real my fear of being inadequate. Additionally, I slowly began to accept the awful realization my nerve death was irreversible. I would not be getting better but could only hope to stop the vision loss and preserve my remaining sight.

Meanwhile the barrage of tests did not slow or stop. I underwent a very painful surgery performed on my right eye to remove a slice of the now-defunct optic nerve for more detailed analysis. To this day one of the most painful moments in my life was both the needle inserted into my eyeball and the intense burning pain of the local anesthesia it delivered! Unfortunately, this biopsy ultimately did not provide any useful answers or explanations.

Nearly every morning and afternoon saw me transported to a nearby facility for the relatively new Magnetic Resonance Imaging (MRI) scans. My medical team was searching for the tumor they thought the most likely source. These early units required absolutely no motion by the patient: I was tightly strapped onto an uncomfortably hard sliding table and slid snugly into the incredibly tight tube for an hour at a time. The pounding sounds of its operation were more like a jackhammer than any medical test I'd ever experienced. No tumors were ever found, and every supplemental test and procedure indicated that aside from the mysterious nerve trauma and death, I was in excellent health. It seemed to me that I was indeed broken in ways their exhaustive tests simply couldn't discern.

This new reality had a tremendous negative effect on my mental and emotional well-being. My first reaction was the shock of realizing my condition was something they could not fix. I'd always thought that a hospital or perhaps an eventual high-end facility would be able to diagnose and repair my injury or sickness. Invincibility is all too often the perception of our younger years and I was no exception. Learning that my legal blindness was likely permanent devastated me.

In my pre-teen years, I watched from a distance as a neighborhood boy slowly deteriorated from leukemia. When he died I was sheltered enough to not fully understand its meaning. For me, he simply stopped being around as if he had moved away although his family remained. My mom's explanation helped me to glean there were diseases from which some people might never recover. Soon afterwards I had a much closer and more powerful experience. My young cousin Brenda had died suddenly and unexpectedly from a rare heart condition. At her funeral I saw my first dead body and recall asking my Mom if Brenda couldn't just wake up. In a macabre moment my Mother encouraged me to touch her and as my fingers barely grazed her arm the experience was burned into my memory. Her skin was cold and hard like stone. That memory haunted many of my dreams for years to come. I understood the permanence of the transition out of life from that moment forward.

Obviously, I understood that I wasn't dead or dying at this point but my understanding of the nature of death reinforced the permanence of my condition. Frustratingly though, I didn't have any disease or condition the doctors could explain. They were clear I wasn't going to get my sight back and that seemed incomprehensible to me. I felt unreasonably poked and prodded with little effective result and deeply isolated as well.

Since the problem was with my optic nerve, the hospital placed me in a neurological ward. In the weeks I was at the hospital every roommate I can recall was experiencing conditions such that not one of them could speak or interact with me. This provided me with a couple of important perspectives. During moments of mental and emotional struggle I rarely had a person with whom I could talk and commiserate. I also experienced a little guilt in the middle of my various pity parties because, to my mind, their struggles were more pronounced than I could reasonably fathom. How dare I feel badly for myself when I could clearly observe others facing much worse challenges? This rhetorical question did not prevent my anguish and frustration. It very much fed the resulting guilt for those reactions.

I was further isolated from support as visitors were rare, since the facility was a significant drive from my home. As a part of my denial approach, I attempted to act normally to my friends and family on the phone and in person. I provided the accurate medical information but tried to hide and even misrepresent the emotional impact. I simply put on the best show I could. I did this in part to reduce the depressing impact on them. Undoubtedly my choice was mainly to hide from my own painful emotions. This was an easy trap for me and left me more sullen and gloomy during the long periods when friends and family were unavailable.

One significant impact was on my relationship with my girlfriend. As college was out for the summer she was at her parent's home, hours away and without a car. My first call from the hospital was likely a significant shock for her at the young age of 19. I don't remember all of the words we shared in that first call, but I do recall her sadness and empathy. I was too engrossed in my own emotions to fully appreciate the magnitude of this change for her. I have little doubt it was difficult and no doubt part of the reason she seemingly began evading all further contact with me. Unfortunately, I didn't understand, at the time, her challenges with the news of my blindness. She didn't call or visit and was never able to take the calls I made to her home. This frustrated me, hurt me and as often is the case with defense mechanisms, angered me as well. Although, she and I would reconnect finding our peace and closure late that summer, her initial absence significantly deepened my intense loneliness and feelings of rejection and inadequacy during those critical first months.

All of this isolation could have provided a tremendous time for introspection, but I spent more of my time trying to hide. I'm a little ashamed of the countless hours I spent staring at the ceiling. The tiles of my hospital room were the type to have hundreds of neat circular holes in a somewhat chaotic pattern across the tile. This pattern made it difficult to count them and yet that's exactly what I spent hours attempting to accomplish. I'd often lose my place or be interrupted, sometimes by something as simple as breaking down in frustration and sadness over the change in my life. In one instance I was nearly through the task when a nurse came into the room to check my vitals. I remember determining I would not lose my place. I kept counting in my head and staring at the ceiling while giving her access to my arms for the tests but having no interactions with her. Even then I was aware it wasn't fair treatment of her, but I stubbornly held to the evasion my senseless distraction allowed.

This is only one small example of a tragic choice on my part. I was foolishly distancing myself from all the nurses and staff. These fine people represented my primary source of regular interaction. They were the very people with whom I had initially built friendly and fun relationships. Looking back, it is clear that I began to withdraw further, increasing my isolation, as my medical news became more disconcerting to me.

The key conversation which began to shake my self-imposed isolation took place due to the well-meaning kindness of one particular nurse to whom I am so very grateful. I'm sad to say her identity is lost to me due to the overwhelming challenges of my health. Her message did not reach me effectively in the moment though I believe she anticipated my reaction which is why she chose an unusual approach. She acquired a day pass out of the hospital for me to enjoy the beautiful weather provided by Memorial Day weekend 1989. Despite the IV in my arm, I was released for a very special treat: to join her and her husband on their small sailboat in the waterway directly behind the hospital. This released us from the clinical environment and provided freedom for a personal conversation that proved to be vitally important to my future.

The day was warm, sunny and beautiful and lifted, at least a little, my sour spirits. As she began to have her frank discussion with me I was initially taken aback. Normally I respect and thrive on direct and earnest conversation though her words strangely irritated me. She told me the nurses had all loved the energetic and gregarious presence I brought with me into the hospital. They appreciated my initial resiliency and were eagerly working hard to help me in all aspects of my medical care. They had noticed my withdrawing from them and while I was not in any way unkind, rude or inappropriate; I was no longer the person who had captured their enthusiasm and support. They would absolutely continue to give me the best service possible. Yet, she had to wonder if the nurses would have developed the strong connections and desire to give so much of themselves if I had arrived acting as the person I had now become.

This was a lot to absorb. I knew my irritation was unfair and the emotional and mental dissonance was a much-needed catalyst for change in my life. Her words steadily worked deep within my introspective mind. In fact, her candor provided focus for my thoughts, reducing the time I spent in idle pursuits such as counting holes in ceiling tiles. The full measure of benefit took weeks or perhaps even months to become prominent in my thoughts. It was longer still until they blossomed in my actions and reactions to the world around me.

The clinician/patient relationship aside, she was wisely reminding me that the person I had become would more likely drive future people away rather than gather them together. Ultimately, she was my source for the philosophy of friendliness and outreach with people around me, despite my challenges. I am eternally grateful for her encouragement to find the energetic and positive version of myself. Her simple reminder helped me resume an approach to life which built and enhanced friendships and teamwork. This would be fundamental in my ability to face challenges and fully enjoy all that life has to offer. I only wish she could know just how much higher she helped me climb with her choice to have such a candid and significant conversation with me.

My time at the University of Massachusetts Medical Center came to a fairly abrupt end after more than a month of adapting to the routine of explorations. My sight loss had seemingly stabilized, albeit at this vastly inhibited state of legal blindness. Dr. Gittenger shared the frustrating and disappointing news they were no closer to understanding why my nerves had been impacted so traumatically than when I first arrived. They were fairly clear the lost sight would not return and entirely uncertain if subsequent episodes of loss might occur. They had exhausted all reasonable explorations and it was time for me to return home with a plan to follow up regularly to monitor for possible reoccurrence of the optic nerve swelling and deterioration. This was an ominous medical reality and yet did not compare to the trepidation I felt regarding what life would be like at home.

When the time came for me to leave the hospital I did not believe I could return to the room I rented from two friends in our bachelor pad era. Rob Webber and Paul Albino had been understanding and supportive throughout my medical uncertainties and likely would have done much to try and help me adapt to my challenges. My brother, Rick, and his wife Monique generously opened their home to me instead as the better fit. They modified their basement into an in-law apartment, rushing the process to ensure I would have a place from which to begin exploring what legal blindness would mean going forward.

Rick had been concerned and supportive throughout my time away. One particular discussion stands out beyond all others. With emotion palpable and voice quavering he asked me if they could take one of his eyes and give it to me. While this was not the nature of my challenge nor a medical possibility at the time, the depth of love in that offer speaks to the character of Rick and to my great fortune in our relationship. Despite his altruistic offer I would need to explore life with the limited sight of my own eye.

The early times were difficult as I, all too frequently, failed in my attempts to use my limited sight for navigating myself around the house. I hit my head, banged my shins or bumped my arms into a variety of objects heavy, pointy or messy. The resulting pain, injury, frustration and embarrassment resulted in my feeling tremendously awkward virtually everywhere. I was at my worst when trying to walk indoors or when there were people moving around me. I tried to put up a good show during social interactions, while simultaneously trying to withdraw from people to silently hide the emotional meltdown I felt inside. My family was supportive, understanding and encouraging, as well as incredibly patient with me. I was the one driving most of my anguish and surprisingly given my present approach, contributing very little to the solution in those early times.

Fortunately, someone, still unknown to me today, helped make a vital connection which was, and remains, one of the most important steps forward in my struggle with blindness. It might have been a family member, a work contact or a friend, I was too distraught at the time to remember, but I remain grateful for their guidance to someone with an understanding of blindness. At their suggestion, I made a call to the New Hampshire Association for the Blind or Future In Sight, as they are known today. Their social worker directed me towards many resources for the blind. This began the process of training so essential to creating hope lifting me from the seemingly helpless feeling in which I was immersed. I began orientation and mobility training which helped me understand how to use the white cane as a mobility tool, along with a host of other practical approaches to navigate my environments successfully. A Low Vision Rehabilitation expert provided instruction and options for daily living adaptation, making appliances more readily usable and facilitating personal care needs.

I learned much from all of these lessons, yet the most impactful and vital aspect was the realization that I no longer had to be on a downward spiral. I was now starting to glimpse the possibility of a normal future. I could see that blindness would be a challenge and a struggle, but also that there may be light at the end of the proverbial tunnel, even for someone going blind. Despite all of this, one of my biggest problems was, at the heart of it, I didn't want the trainer's solutions. I wanted to have my normal sight back. Even though I understood that was unlikely at best I harbored a deep-seated resentment for any other solution.

My trainers encouraged me to accept that the skills they offered would enable me to accomplish all of the things I did with sight, in a slightly different way. It is a credit to their coaching they managed to gain my intellectual acceptance of this process. To my regret, I was not yet prepared to emotionally commit to their solutions. For now, it was enough to dedicate myself to the work and accountability involved in becoming more independent. This I could do, and it would distract me a little from how I felt about my blindness as I was still very much wanting distraction from a reality I did not welcome.

Nero Be All You Can't Be

"We are what we imagine ourselves to be." Kurt Vonnegut Jr.

Emerging from the hospital in late June I had some considerable time at home to reflect on much of my life. While on Short Term Disability from work, ostensibly to develop all the skills necessary to manage the challenges of someone new to legal blindness, I thought much about how, exactly, my time would be spent. Human Resources told me that I qualified for Long Term Disability coverage and that it would be my choice whether to ever return to work or take the disability option. The very notion that I might make a choice to never work again felt ludicrous to me. What would I do with each day? What would give meaning to my life? Was it even possible for my life to have meaning?

At just 22 years old I was simply overwhelmed: how would I physically get to work? How would I read my computer screen, or the many schematics required for my job? There was just so much uncertainty! Fortunately, I was not yet prepared to give up the career so newly begun. The initial adaptive training suggested I might not have to give up my career and my immediate managers were all willing to work with me towards a return. Given the encouragement of the New Hampshire Association for the Blind, I wanted to develop the skills to return to work as soon as possible.

Simultaneously, I was trying to determine what hobbies and entertainment might be possible for me. Initially I assumed that most of the sports which previously were my primary diversion would no longer be possible. Before ready access to searches and communities through the internet, it was difficult to find information on what other visually impaired people did for entertainment. I made this search more difficult by choosing to identify as neither sighted nor blind I caused myself to feel trapped. I was in limbo, unable to do many things because of my blindness and unwilling to accept help because of my existing sight. The additional denial and isolation were further limiting and damaging to me and I did not entirely understand what I was doing for many years.

My short-term disability left me many hours in the day to explore my new limitations and challenges. Mostly I secluded myself at home and practiced moving around with my cane while using my limited field of sight as best possible. My family and peers were at work during the day and various low vision therapists, social workers and mobility instructors made up only a few visitor hours each week. My world was a riot of emotions, I was in denial, afraid, ashamed and entirely uncertain of my future. I was determined to try to find sufficient skills to at least seem normal again. I applied myself diligently to truly improve primarily, because I wanted anything to help minimize the isolation and incompetence which I felt so powerfully.

On weekends and some evenings, friends came to visit, and we discussed what we imagined my restrictions might allow. I needed my friends to help motivate me to try anything, because a large part of me wanted to just quit. I believe focusing on what my sight limitations seemingly prevented was ultimately the wrong approach. It took time for experience to allow me to see that it is better to focus on goals and solutions rather than restrictions. This discovery has shaped my life ever since.

My family and friends, knowing my passion for books encouraged me to resume reading. I found that while I could still read it required a lot more focus and concentration than when I was fully sighted. This was too much mental strain for any appreciable enjoyment. Outside of sports, reading had been my top pastime; the exercise for my mind that sports were for my body. Suddenly I felt deprived of the two most important aspects of my world. The two things which most relaxed and refreshed me were gone at a time when I needed them more than ever.

My friend Sean Griffin encouraged me to remember the enthusiasm with which I invited him to consider joining me in an experiential opportunity called NERO. Just a few months earlier, this brand-new venture New England Role-Playing Organization (NERO) began holding weekend long L.A.R.P. (live action role playing) events which captured my imagination.

Their product was a live action game which allowed players to create and assume the roles of characters, much as a writer and actor. These roles would be unscripted allowing the player character to make their decisions and choose their own responses throughout the events. NERO was effectively a live version of the popular table-top game Dungeons & Dragons. I spent much of my youth playing that game and loved the blend of creativity, imagination, story-telling and social interaction. Now NERO seemed a means to take this form of recreation to a much higher level!

I first learned of the game in April of 1989 by reading a computer posting at Digital Equipment. A colleague provided a vivid description of his weekend experience and I was immediately enticed. He traveled to Camp Kiwanee in Hanson, MA where the staff and players simulated the adventurous happenings of the imaginary town of Ravenholt for the next 40 hours of the weekend. Players maintained their character's persona while interacting with other players and an assortment of staff characters. He shared the story from the perspective of his character and I felt like I was reading a novel. He, or rather his character, was the hero I was following. I immediately knew that I wanted to create my own hero within this story.

I eagerly learned all the details I could about NERO, which provided staff that acted as non-player characters (NPC's). These npc's acted as allies or villains, advancing the storyline through a variety of means from clues to combat. It was in fact a rather elaborate undertaking in which a multi-acre summer camp was transformed through theatrical props, costumes and a fair bit of imagination into a medieval fantasy town in which the events of the weekend would take place.

A simple set of rules helped players understand how to appropriately interact with others. These rules focused less on the improvisational theater and much more on how players and npc's would fight each other with padded replica weapons and a simulated magic system using thrown packets. Each player had significant influence as to their level of involvement with any particular aspect of the game. Much as in a great fantasy novel, there were mysteries and adventures to be discovered and explored. The games ranged from the overarching weekend plots, mini-adventures throughout the day or night and even slowly unveiling the rich histories of fellow players. Whether you chose to be directly involved with various activities or not, there was always a chance that another player or npc might take actions which directly affected you. This meant that the entire time spent playing the game had a considerable amount of uncertainty and excitement.

Some of the NPC villains or monsters roamed just to combat characters. You literally could be attacked at any point within the game! You had to be on guard at all times. With no predetermined results there was a competitive component which further enhanced the atmosphere of suspense and danger.

For me, the appeal was far more than the physical aspects of game combat. The idea captured my excitement as I pondered the many avenues my intrigue-loving mind could follow to resolve the diverse mysteries carefully created by the staff. Improvisational moments of public speaking enabled players to vastly change the direction of the plot-line or to incite others to join in their plans and schemes. It could be as simple as creatively crafting entertainment in the flavor of the game, in words, song, music or playful banter. All in all, the diverse environment would challenge the mind and body in a very untypical fashion.

By the design of the game rules, each player has reasonable freedom to determine the nature of the character they want to create for themselves. They assume the personality of their character and like many actors, the more they invested themselves into the role the more believable the results. The live action part of this game resulted in an element of player limitation. For example, someone who is naturally a slow runner would have difficulty in portraying a quick character. While the rules provided ways to augment skills beyond a player's natural restrictions there were some reasonable limitations.

As a young, healthy, fully sighted and rather athletic person I didn't see many physical restrictions ahead for me.

Inspired by those first exciting descriptions, I called the founder and owner of NERO, Ford Ivey. He very pleasantly provided me the basics I would need to attend an event and I began assembling some friends to join me for that May of 1989. My sudden sight loss arrived at just this time and I had to forego attending the event. The reality is that the intriguing potential of NERO was entirely lost to me because of my overwhelming medical struggles.

That is, until, Sean reminded me of my prior enthusiasm declaring he was still excited to try the NERO game. Better still, Sean was willing and eager to help me try to determine how I might take part. After all, as he pointed out, many stories abounded where blind characters have pivotal roles. I reached out once again to Ford Ivey and explained why I had vanished after my initial inquiry. I told him I had become suddenly and very unexpectedly blind and asked him if he thought I could still play his game. There was only a very short pause before he responded candidly that while he didn't know, he was willing to give it a try. I'm not sure either of us understood how pivotal a part of my life that decision would become.

I doubted my abilities to do most things and it would prove challenging for me to overcome this belief. Fortunately, the very nature of NERO encourages people to live NERO's slogan: "Be All you Can't Be!" With that, and given Ford's approval, I decided to make the attempt. I wanted to ensure it was our best effort and discussed approaches with Sean and Ford extensively. Instead of being the warrior which appealed to my inner athlete, I reluctantly created a support character less likely to engage in combat of any type. My character history explained my blindness and how and why he was a healer.

We attended our first training day event in August of 1989 and it was every bit as enjoyable as I had envisioned. Our day held a pair of short adventures for each new group to undertake together. Our group was small which meant each of us needed to play a significant role. While walking along a path in the woods we were ambushed by a group of npc's wearing the masks and make-up of goblins and orcs. As the team healer I had only a padded, six-foot-long staff intended to be used for me to defend against attacks until someone could come to my aid. I soon found to our surprise that my athleticism combined with long reach, quick reflexes and strategic mind helped me to be more effective than we initially expected. Instead of needing others to come to my aid, I quickly came up alongside my companions and provided them aid by flanking our opponents. I was surprised and pleased by my initial success. As we resumed our trek through the woods I was quickly brought to earth, almost literally, by the challenge of the terrain. I stumbled over downed branched and rolled my ankles on rocks and roots with surprising regularity. Almost immediately doubt returned to my psyche. Had I been lucky? Were they just distracted? Those questions were answered, almost immediately, during our next fight where I tested a new skill, "magic" with very good success.

As a healer I had access to a very limited form of magic combat. To cast a spell, I would throw a small cloth packet of birdseed while shouting a phrase to help the 'victim' understand the effect if the packet struck them. I had always shown a tendency for a strong arm and keen throwing accuracy, which allowed me to have greater range than many expected. I found my tunnel vision was limiting but not as much as I had anticipated. At distance the tight angle of vision opened enough that I could reasonably determine a target. Since the acuity of my vision in that field was good I could differentiate targets well. While my sight impairment definitely had an impact, the more I practiced interacting with the world the better I became at building an enhanced mental image to supplement my limited sight. Moving objects, like running people, would always challenge me but practice steadily increased my effectiveness. Strategically I learned how well I could use a wall or even a tree on my blind side as a stationary safe area to reduce the mental tracking required and enhance my comfort and safety.

Some may wonder how a game can be life changing. Let me try to explain an interesting psychological effect. The fantasy nature of NERO made it easier for me to attempt virtually anything, despite the risk of failure. My character "Alaric the blind" was a part I played. When I tried something while playing the game it was easy for me to justify that if it didn't work it wasn't my failure, but Alaric's. It may seem a subtle difference but the freedom that psychological twist allowed provided me with comfort in the new challenges of sight restriction. It's simply a form of risk management. NERO reduced my emotional risk because the failure wasn't directly attributed to my own ineptitude or blindness but that of my character.

This created a freedom I was able to take beyond physical actions. At a time when I was feeling significant insecurity, I chose to define Alaric as the opposite: exuding confidence. In retrospect this wasn't so much a conscious decision to challenge my current self as it was a subconscious attempt to grasp for fragments of my former self. Whatever the ultimate motivation, I quickly found that at each event I would relish the development of Alaric as a character and my own personal journey of growth and discovery. Specifically, I began to marvel at the benefits of focusing on my abilities more than my disability.

From the first experience of my sudden sight loss I had associated myself strongly with disability. Blindness encapsulated an inordinate amount of negativity upon my psyche. But each time someone referred to my character as "Alaric the Blind" I began to build a little comfort with that nefarious word: blind. I hadn't yet really differentiated the terms visually impaired, legally blind and blind. In fact, I'm not sure I was even exposed to the allegedly more politically correct phrase: visually impaired. I was aware that blind was a label which for me and many others came with a lot of additional baggage. To be perfectly clear the baggage mostly involved assumptions of inability, incompetence, isolation and often ignorance. The stereotypical perspective on blind people was ultimately far from flattering and also far from reality. Fortunately, NERO was a game not based in reality but rather in the fantasy world it expected us all to create together. My new community didn't seem to hold these stereotypes, or at least never seemed to inflict this belief upon me.

September of 1989 brought my first full weekend event. I, like most attendees, immersed myself fully into the persona I had created. The boundless energy of my youth helped bolster my eager involvement in many diverse experiences during the weekend. My bed assignment for the weekend put me with the Healer's Guild at a central location. This was more a group of individuals rather than any particular team, although they were supported by a staff designed character who maternal ways did much to encourage everyone to find an active and involved role. I was isolated from the friends with whom I had come to the game and so found some good initial comfort and direction from this motherly character.

Learning new environments with limited sight is always an additional challenge. I arrived early to memorize the layout of the various indoor and outdoor spaces across the large site. I also practiced using my padded staff as I might use a blind cane to help me navigate safely. This was intimidating but I felt a thrill at exploring unknown environments, something I'd have thought impossible a few months prior. In trying to express the excessive confidence of my character I suppressed the feelings of intimidation and began my outreach to all of the characters, both player and staff. This is very much the approach I would have taken in the real world prior to my sight loss though I did so with the crutch of trying to portray a character concept.

There is a theatrical methodology known as Stanislavsky Method Acting which effectively suggests that by acting a part you may feel the part. With the immersive nature of an entire weekend spent trying to emphasize Alaric's boldness, it is not completely surprising I began to internalize that same confidence. This was buoyed by my discovery that I was one of the more athletic of the people who chose to play a healer. Interestingly there were many who presumed my blindness was not actual but a role-playing decision for my character. For the most part, people were generally eager to understand my lack of sight and to assist when possible. It was an early ice breaker and my natural comfort at meeting new people made it easy for me to begin connecting pleasantly with people before the game and as my character once the game began.

As there was no clear way to differentiate between an npc and a player character, it was natural for people to seek resolutions to the game's mysteries and challenges from the characters all around. This was part of the reason a significant opportunity presented itself. A group of players slightly younger than me had discovered an adventure with some mythological background. They had found a 'cave' which contained a Medusa and the results had gone poorly for them. Mythology suggests that to look upon a Medusa turns you to stone. Naturally, not looking made it very difficult to defend themselves. As we had crossed paths a few times earlier, they began to think that a blind person might make the ideal hero to help them retrieve what they lost and defeat the Medusa. They sought me out at the Healer's Guild as someone to aid them in returning to that abandoned and failed first encounter with the Medusa. I joined them, and our success began an in-game friendship. This fortunate circumstance became the foundation of a team which I would ultimately lead for many years. Real world friendships developed more slowly but surely, and many of those team members remain friends to this day and several have had significant roles in encouraging me to continue and manage each subsequent stage of sight loss.

At another early event I was attending, one of the game's more influential teams, the Barony of Westmarch, held a recruitment competition. I decided to undertake the challenge and was amused to discover that after a few playful rounds of witty banter, mental puzzles which I always enjoyed, they had a dagger fight with a little twist. They blindfolded both combatants. While the New Hampshire Association for the Blind certainly had not included blind dagger fighting in my initial training, they had helped me understand the value of using all my senses, as well as methods of moving more safely with my restricted sight. I used this knowledge to my advantage to win the competition. I'd noticed most people tended to crouch and use sweeping low swings to try and strike their opponent. I'd also noticed that there were exposed rafter beams within reach of my long arms. As my final fight began I jumped up to hold the rafter with my left hand thus removing all the low attack areas. I pulled myself up and hung upside down listening. As I heard the swoosh of the padded dagger I made the mental image of where the person swinging would need to be and slowly reached out and tapped him with my own dagger. This was, I think, the very early start of my acknowledgement to myself that I was developing new and different skills because of my blindness. It was a start to my eventual realization that *going* blind is much harder than *being* blind because of the incredible human ability to learn and adapt.

Heidi Hooper and Donna Asbornsen were leading the team of Westmarch at that time and both took a chance with their decision to add me to the team. It was still far too early for any of us to really understand if someone blind could be an effective player in this game. It is so easy for many to view a blind person as a burden and certainly in such an ever-changing environment as NERO, this reality was true during both the game itself, and logistical aspects outside of game play. Donna and Heidi each made me feel completely welcome and comfortable and seemingly had more confidence in my ability than I did myself, perhaps because they had only interacted with the confidence of my character choices. Whatever the reasons behind their decision, it helped me take yet another step along my journey to feeling worthwhile.

As part of the Barony of Westmarch my initial role was "Court Healer." I had to learn methods of expressing the things I could do reasonably despite my blindness when confronted with others' doubt. Conversely it became helpful to communicate the realistic challenges which suggested when another individual might be better suited to a particular task. Better still I was attempting to inform and educate with the self-assurance expected of Alaric. Learning to work with leadership in this capacity was a valuable skill I'd continue to develop outside of the game with a similar confidence I maintained in the game. My effectiveness at weapon combat continued to improve dramatically, and to my surprise I found even with the rules disadvantages for a healer in weapons combat, I was at least an equal match for most fighters in the game. In-game I chose to identify as a Warrior, and in another surprise and bold move, Heidi elevated me to a Knight in her Barony. As the first non-fighter Knight it only encouraged me to work all the more on my combat skills to be equal to any challenge.

At the same time, I began to develop my own core team. This provided comfort with leadership roles I had embraced prior to blindness and had believed lost to me. I took the initiative to lead naturally in most situation. When we met new characters, I would step forward first and introduce myself and the team as well as begin our own polite questions of them. It certainly helped that I have a strong voice and a natural aptitude for thinking quickly on my feet. As the game often had intrigue hidden in these meetings it was important to assess the various characters you were meeting quickly to understand if they might be friend or foe. I took responsibility for this task, gaining the confidence that my team would back my decisions. On a deeper level, as the game continued for multiple events over many months, years and eventually decades, there was value in learning how to build alliances. It is always beneficial to learn to work harmoniously towards common goals.

A more challenging goal was the political maneuvering which ensnared or eliminated a rival. Our team would meet often, and I would lead the discussions of our reactions, plans and schemes. All this intrigue as well as the subtle plans to help identify and build resources quickly captured my enthusiasm. I spent enough energy with those aspects that I slowly began to think less and less of my blindness and the occasional awkward moments it provided. Yes, I missed an extended hand for a handshake now and then, leaning on

Alaric's confident nature I'd simply remind others that I couldn't always see as they might expect.

Pictured: Randy at a NERO event in the mid-1990's

Sometimes a visual cue would escape me that might be essential, and my team learned helpful methods to ensure I was aware of the cues in ways which became increasingly more natural. We all began to believe that the limitations of my eyes only affected my sight and perhaps very little else, if we found ways to work around those challenges. Ultimately, I found comfort that vision-induced mistakes were not a fault of mine but an aspect of my blindness which simply needed to be explained to educate those around me.

As time progressed my character took more clear definition and while it is not customary to share insight into a character outside of the game, I do so here because those choices had such profound impact on me and the direction of my life. I chose to have Alaric show his outward image differently than his inner motivations.

Those he shared rarely, and with only the closest of confidants. He was a hard-edged force for goodly causes who believed the ends justified the means. He masked this as best as possible by acting outwardly a fierce dedication to law and order. He would give every effort to ensure true justice took place according to his definition, though attempting to orchestrate it such that all would be more likely to presume his chivalry, purity and goodness. I share a little of this detail because it highlights that in-game my character used deception to build a façade even as I too was putting on a show, out of game, in pretending so much acceptance of blindness well beyond my actual comfort. I was surprised both in and out of game to discover how many people were eager to lean on the strength they perceived both in-game and out of game as a result.

All through this time I continued to practice many skills, especially weapons training. At home I took up studying Shaolin Kempo Karate to help me improve my focus and orientation. I took every opportunity to spar improving my technique and strategy. I had enough natural aptitude and work ethic to stand out in NERO weapons combat, which began to bolster my own confidence in and out of the game itself. Between leadership, combat and the chivalrous qualities I attempted to portray through Alaric, I was soon promoted to a higher Knight status. As a Bannerett Knight and a member of the "Circle of Companions" I was charged with presiding in judgment over other nobles. This was an upwardly mobile version of success in the game and it soon led beyond the game for me.

My increased focus on leadership in the game inspired me to be more involved by volunteering on all levels. Writing story lines and running events for others to experience provided me with a great deal of pride and satisfaction and gave me another outlet for my creativity. It also enhanced my organizational skills as coordinating events for NERO was a hybrid of creativity and project management. NERO was an interesting business model in that it relied heavily upon volunteer labor to play roles, write parts, manage logistics, props and a host of things for which they would be hard pressed to reasonably pay a staff. Volunteering for NERO let me enhance many useful skills while allowing me to express my appreciation for all that I'd gained through playing the game.

I accepted many administrative roles which placed me in positions of leadership in managing and running the game. As people interacted with me in a myriad of ways, I began to see that although

I was certainly still legally blind, for most it was as if I had no disability at all. In fact, there were many who simply assumed I was fully sighted. Perhaps one of the most potent demonstrations of this was when a player, having lost to me in a tournament fight, stepped out of game to register a formal complaint with the people running the event that I simply wasn't role-playing a blind person very well! I'm not sure he understood how to respond when he learned that it wasn't a role-playing decision for me but that I was, in-fact, legally blind.

This may suggest that NERO was an entirely positive learning and growing experience. I would however, be remiss to exclude a potential significant detriment with my experience. In the escapism and entertainment of the game, I had begun to subconsciously lose my own connection to my blindness. I was in denial because I no longer felt blind. In fact, I felt less blind and less disabled when playing NERO than I did when trying to manage many things in the real world. The feeling of wishing for time in a game more than time in the real world ought to have raised concerns about hiding from reality. Fortunately, introspection and time with friends outside of the game helped me realize the possible risks. This awareness allowed me to manage and mostly avoid excessive dependence on the game. It was simply an incredibly enjoyable and rewarding time to be playing Nero.

As for my feeling less blind, that wasn't necessarily inappropriate except in my choice to hide from the realities of my blindness. I harbored inner shame at being blind and in some ways chose to pretend I simply wasn't blind. I stopped using my cane in the real world to escape from strangers' reaction to it. I was good enough scanning with my remaining sight to mostly get away without incident, but it was only a matter of time before the mostly part caught up with me. I had moments of concentration failure when I'd knock over a display at the supermarket or bump into someone who didn't have any means to be aware of my sight impairment.

The ultimate incident which shook me from the mix of shame and vanity that had me hiding from my cane took place outside of the game. I was in a grocery store walking down an aisle confidently. I was scanning down and ahead to ensure I wouldn't walk into anything when suddenly my left knee slammed solidly into the soft shoulder of a very small child. He had stepped out from behind a shopping cart after I had scanned and so entirely out of my small field of vision. If I were normally sighted I would have seen him. If I had been using a cane it would have caught him first and saved the collision or alerted his parents to my blindness which would have suggested greater caution. Instead he was knocked to the ground hard and while, ultimately not hurt, it highlighted to me the risk I was choosing for others by avoiding my cane. This incident made me reconsider the reasons why I wasn't using my cane and resulted in a significant step towards my acceptance of blindness. It's a step I think I might have reached a little sooner if I hadn't developed over-confidence through my NERO experiences.

Back in the game, my team became steadily more competent, earning accolades in various ways and before very long I was elevated to lead my own Barony. With a limited number of higher leadership positions available and with the game growing steadily in popularity, the organizers of the game began to place trusted high valued leaders into positions where they would have tremendous influence over the entertainment of other players within the game. These positions were initially held by staff characters and the transition was intended to help expand the ability to entertain the vast numbers of players coming to experience the game. It suggested confidence that players taking these positions would be attentive to the enjoyment of others while competently enhancing the overall atmosphere of the game. It was a privilege and an honor to be selected as one of the early players in this position

In September of 1991, the nationally renowned Dragon Magazine featured a story about NERO and suddenly the game's popularity grew exponentially. Players were joining and attending from all over the country and at their peak, events had 500 players and 300 staff. In this environment I built a team of 80 dedicated players who all reported to my character. The logistics of coordinating such things began to enhance our out of game connection time. It was necessary for me to lead and coordinate our massive team in many ways and I found myself very comfortable in that role.

My out of game responsibility to ensure every person was able to enjoy the game required a surprising amount of attention. Certainly, I made many mistakes in the process of learning how to lead and coordinate people, but I had many more successful moments and established many long-term friendships. I leaned on these heavily as episodes of increased sight loss would ultimately bring me to the total blindness. In the worst transitions I took some time away from the game to develop skills but, even totally blind, I found my way to being an effective influence and leader within the game. Later, when my neurological condition also put me into a wheelchair I still demonstrated that I could participate and have tremendous positive and enjoyable influence. Those were not easy times and I owe much gratitude to the friends and family who supported my efforts to navigate campgrounds and woods without the ability to see or walk.

NERO was a significant part of my life for many years, though never so much as for that first decade. I still maintain some peripheral connections to it presently. Many similar business ventures evolved from NERO. Even that process taught me other aspects of business competition, mergers and acquisitions. I enjoyed several other systems at various times and for some part of my life established myself as one of the authorities on LARP rules, plot approaches and even business methods. These games have transformed and adapted significantly and while I still occasionally enjoy a limited amount of time attending one, they are a key part of my history.

Overall NERO has given me several lifetimes of stories. Far beyond these tales, it is the gift of personal growth at the heart of my NERO experience. I learned to see my blindness more clearly, accept it, and more importantly see beyond it. This has left a very real and pertinent impression on my approach to believing in possibility.

Modi Norse Dog of Courage

"I hope to be the kind of person my dog thinks I am."
Anonymous

While I made many strides towards independence after my initial vision loss, my heart and spirit were still deeply wounded. I returned to my job at Digital Equipment Corporation in Merrimack, NH. With very few modifications I resumed my former work as a Hardware Support Engineer working on Local Area Network products. I also resumed various hobbies and activities with moderate success and finally moved away from the comfort and support my Brother Rick and his wife Monique had so kindly provided for me.

Living in my own condominium in Nashua had brought both an independence and freedom which I used for another major life step. I entered into a long-term relationship with Sharon Taubenfeld, who I had met through both Digital and the NERO game. Our work group relocated to a facility in Tewksbury, MA and the challenges of not being able to drive made that commute difficult. Sharon and I decided to lease half of a duplex in Chelmsford, Massachusetts. We shared several months living together as a family leading up to our first Christmas together. Seeing Sharon's connection to the three cats who kept her as a pet reminded me of my own yearnings for the connections to my boyhood dogs Puppy, Tippy and Regal. I hoped perhaps to add the companionship of a dog for the Christmas season.

Right after Christmas we began calling and visiting various animal shelters to look for the right match. Many places were low, as Christmas gifts often empty the shelters at least briefly, but we were willing to travel a bit. On December 28, 1991, we found ourselves at the Sterling Animal Shelter. An allegedly two-year-old "Dobi-shepherd" mix named Jackie was sitting by himself and I felt an immediate attachment. He seemed so eager to please me and so desperate for attention I was hopeful we might make it happen immediately. I don't know if I can ever give Sharon enough appreciation for her patience and open mindedness in supporting my strong wish for a dog despite all the significant responsibilities involved. Similarly, I cannot give her enough credit for the sacrifice involved in bringing this stray dog home to her beloved and unsuspecting cats.

While the shelter offered a form claiming he was good with cats we also understood there was uncertainty and risk, but his demeanor was encouragingly attentive and friendly. We suspected he was older than they suggested. He had some impressive scars on his muzzle which almost seemed as if he'd been struck by a bicycle chain or similar. I cannot fathom the malice of a person who would lash out in this fashion. We wanted very much to give him a loving home to atone for some of the cruelty in his past and to build the relationship I cherish between dog and human.

We knew that Jackie was a name they had randomly assigned and that it wasn't what we would call him. Sharon named her cats after various gods from mythology and it seemed a reasonable place to start the name search. I thought the blend of brown, black, tan and some small white on this sturdy pup made him look a little like a bear. He seemed so gentle that I wanted a name that playfully suggested qualities of courage and ferocity. Thus, when I came across Modi the Norse god of courage and berserker rage whose symbol was the bear; I had my name. Modi quickly adapted to his name and to our approach to life.

This was even more impressive as I was unfortunately ill-prepared for the responsibilities of being an appropriate dog owner. I had grown up with many different dogs, but my parents ensured all the proper aspects of care. I had a series of follies which Modi patiently endured. My only saving grace was a very real affection and desire to learn. I didn't have the internet as a resource and reading was difficult. I'm ashamed that shouting "No!" and "Bad dog" were part of my approach at times. He loved me through these unnecessary and unacceptable approaches to our communication. Far too slowly I began to understand that it was my responsibility to find effective means of letting him know what I wanted and praising and rewarding him for the eager fashion in which he would try to please me. More quickly I began to step outside of my own contemplations and try to understand the thoughts and reasons behind his actions. In this I soon found that as much as I believed I was ready to dedicate myself to him, he was even more ready to dedicate himself to me.

Pictured: Modi enjoys a little snow.

As is the case with many dogs, Modi loved walking adventures. He encouraged me to take up the leash and walk the quarter of a mile to the Mill Pond Park which abutted a wetland wood where I took him off leash and we would play together. As he explored around us he kept vigilant watch on my location and always returned quickly when called. I made a game of trying to hide from him and this enabled him to show off just how much more advanced his sense of smell and hearing were than my own. I left sight off that list in part because dogs do not have particularly good sight but because in some ways I was still hiding from my legal blindness. In fact, during the hiding sessions I'd often use the excuse of his finding me for a good scratching of his fur coat and the chance to talk. While I spoke to him and he listened to every word as if intent on understanding all the nuances of my meaning, the reality is that I was speaking to myself; broaching the subject of my blindness.

I had accepted the medical details of my sight loss but in many ways, I was evading the emotional distress. I still felt inadequate, less than my peers in some way I couldn't describe. I felt angry this had happened to me, fearful it would continue to get worse and ashamed that I couldn't admit to these feelings even to myself. Modi may not have understood my words, but this only meant he wasn't judgmental. He absolutely could understand my emotions and he somehow knew when to lean into me, when to paw at me and when to bound backwards enticing me to let it go and get up and just run with him. In our walks and the introspective subtlety of our conversations I began to heal and accept more of my responses for the understandable and reasonable reactions they were

The dichotomy of the time for me was that amidst the insecurities which Modi consoled I was also experiencing success and growing confidence in various ways. I continued to play basketball, softball and darts with enough effectiveness to have many suspect I wasn't blind at all. I was both proud of this response from others and frustrated as I thought they didn't understand how much effort it took for me to compensate so well for the vision loss.

I did not simply flip a switch of responsibility and fall into being the ideal dog owner. Too many times I allowed some activity or event to entice me away and while I generally ensured his needs were met, I did sometimes shirk my responsibilities to him. The hard part for me in this realization is that I traded away opportunities to explore the woods, or simply spend time together. Despite this he was always eager to join me when I was ready and never gave indication of any disappointment for my not having been there for him. Each time I returned home he greeted me with an enthusiasm which made clear to me how much I was loved and there's a lesson there for certain. I think all of us should learn to ensure that loved ones in our lives know how much they are loved and appreciated.

This can be as simple as the enthusiasm we show in our greetings or the simple task of putting aside any distraction to give them the attention they deserve.

That lesson and many others were lacking in my personal approach at that time. Perhaps as a result I began another transition. Sharon and I ended our romantic relationship and began to plan our departure from our Chelmsford home of three years. Once again Modi was by my side listening without judgment, playfully distracting as necessary and giving the love and comfort which lifted my spirits.

Modi and I landed in Lowell, Massachusetts on a quiet little road. Our new Victorian home was located more residentially but it was closer to my work and still offered several wooded parks I hoped we would explore together. Early in our stay, I received a distressing call to my work office. Modi had been let out into the side yard to relieve and for the first time ever, had taken flight. I came home immediately and began searching for him. I spent hours that night walking the neighborhood and calling him without response. I was devastated as the wee hours of the morning forced me into my vacant feeling home, where no sleep would come to me. I woke the next morning and repeated the calls and searching, street after street. I imagined the worst as a fairly busy road was near. I made a flyer with his picture and offered a reward for any information. I spread them for one mile in every direction and continued my searches throughout the day. I placed an advertisement in the local paper and called the animal control officers in all four of the towns adjacent to our home. Days turned into a week and I despaired for my poor boy's fate. I was beside myself with grief, frustration and blame. I had so much love for Modi and very few skills to cope with this additional loss in my life.

While I hadn't lost hope entirely it was a frail and fleeting wish as I returned to my work routines without him. Near the end of my second week without Modi, I returned home and found the blinking message indicator on our answering machine and pressed play almost mechanically. The stranger's voice suggesting they thought they might have my dog sent my spirits soaring. I called their number and they gave me an address. Despite the eye strain involved with my limited vision, I broke out a book of maps and found their home just a few miles away.

My loyal and loving Modi was halfway between our present home and our former home in Chelmsford. A quick call ensured a friend would meet me there as soon as possible with his car but I could not wait one moment. I still rode a bicycle at this time despite the significant risks and I made my way speedily to find him. Stepping up to their screened porch entry I saw him lying on his side on a couch. He barely could lift his head, but his tail was wagging powerfully. I was torn as my joy at finding him was overshadowed by concern at his obviously injured state. The home owners stepped out and told me they had found him on their lawn more than a week earlier and he had clearly been hit by a car though it was a quiet neighborhood.

His tags had been torn off his collar, most likely by the accident. I just held him tenderly and cried tears of love and concern into his shoulder. Once my friend arrived with the car we took him directly to the veterinarian. He was hurt but with their care was expected to recover fully. Our reunion was complete though I held much guilt. Of course, he was heading to our old home, not for the home itself, but to find Sharon as he was always the most loyal of companions.

He never ran away again and when with me he would stay by my side whether on a leash or not. We did get to explore the parks in the area. Many an impromptu Modi swim took place as he chased the swans while I walked the bridge to an island where I'd sip coffee and reflect upon the solitude of our wooded retreat on the edge of the city. These moments would become critically important for my coping skills as a significant life event drew near; the final days of my working career. Ironic that while Modi never ran away again I felt in some ways I was preparing to run away. Even though logically I knew that wasn't true, it was how I felt emotionally, and it stung me with shame.

My second episode of sight loss took place in 1994. This was the loss which caused me to give up reading for pleasure. It was also the loss which transformed my job at Digital Equipment because suddenly reading schematic diagrams was unreasonable. Attempting to read my computer screen was becoming almost impossible. I began working with an early computer screen reader to see if it might be feasible to convert my vocation to software engineering.

I found a company named Henter-Joyce that produced a promising new blind access program called J.A.W.S. (Job Access with Speech). This relatively new and not fully functional reading technology made a transition possible though not ideal. Willing to pioneer this approach, I officially made the move even as my division of Digital was experiencing several rounds of layoffs. My performance reviews had been excellent, and I was assured significant safety by my immediate managers. Several conversations with upper management helped me to realize the most recent vision loss was going to make things very challenging for me.

Since my first onset of blindness I was fully eligible for the Long-Term Disability Insurance which had been part of my initial hiring contract. The fact I had worked beyond my transition to legal blindness and excelled was a testament to my drive and determination. I think it was also a testament to the support of my managers. I'm incredibly grateful one of my managers found a delicate way to discuss several important work details. Unfortunately, Digital was a slowly failing company. If my entire division folded, as some managers anticipated, it would have been incredibly difficult for me to compete in the hiring world with my fully sighted peers. One of the most challenging decisions I would make was to accept the LTD plan and depart from the work force.

My decision immediately raised feelings of inadequacy even as I understood logically that my base salary and health benefits were going to be critical. This was especially true given the recurring nature of my mysterious neurological disorder. It was one of those decisions which feels like jumping off a tall perch, higher than your comfort zone. You can think it through and logically understand it is a reasonable choice, but your emotions still violently disagree. It's a leap of faith; jumping from that perch and then being forced to deal with the consequences of the decision. Despite feeling as if I was running away I forged ahead and was now unemployed for the first time in my adult life.

My first two weeks at home were a glorious vacation. I slept late, and Modi and I took a daily late morning stroll to our seemingly private park. I would sit and sip a travel mug of coffee while he explored the woods around me, always within quick recall and frequently checking in with me. I find a solace in nature and often recall the poem Thanatopsis by William Conant Bryant: "To him who in the love of nature holds communion with her visible forms, she speaks a various language." There were clear boundaries to my nature enthusiasm as each of these stops were predicated on a fresh hot coffee and chocolate croissant from Dunkin Donuts. My ties to creature comforts were pretty strong as well!

Those few weeks did have me wondering how long I might still appreciate the visible forms of the world around me, and what I needed to do in order to prepare, after my most recent loss of vision. I had grown complacent with stable vision and begun to accept that I would simply be at that level of legal blindness for my entire life. But now I began to believe it was simply a race against time until complete blindness. While this was a difficult realization, it no longer carried the overwhelming dismay or denial of my initial loss. Modi had helped me find acceptance, strength and courage during our years together. Once again, I took counsel with his silent wisdom and once again his non-judgmental but rapt attention allowed me to dig deeply within myself. Those two weeks of vacation steadily slid into a drive to find meaning and purpose for my life.

Now, though, Modi was by my side nearly all of the time. Our bond deepened in a way I had not known with my childhood pets. My subtle emotional shift, with his patient guidance, gifted me with an appreciation for this essential bond. I learned to understand him better than any other being in my life up until that point. I was so very close to emotionally ready when Modi came into my world, needing only his loyal and loving devotion to ease me through those final steps to embrace the emotional bond.

My friends and growing social circle became his social circle and he began to build friendships which he shared with me, something I don't think I ever understood was possible for a dog. This life of symbiosis was strong and helped give me the courage to make another major decision. I had moved to Massachusetts to follow my job. I'd gone from living alone to sharing a leased home with various friends and it had worked well enough. But I felt a little unfulfilled, as if my life was too much built around those social worlds. I was nearing my 30th birthday and perhaps that maturing had me yearning for a different phase of my life. So, in 1996 Modi and I packed up our many belongings and rented a small home on Nevada Street back in Nashua, NH.

It was close enough to downtown that I could afford it reasonably on my own and yet it had an incredibly private backyard. Modi was getting a little older, but we delighted in our explorations for all the reasonably nearby parks. It seemed wherever we lived we quickly sought out and found places of wooded seclusion for our contemplative times together. I underwent another vision loss and was using my cane all the time. Modi seemed to naturally understand that need and he eased his leash presence back so as to never interfere with my using the cane to explore the obstacles along the way. My life with Modi was the classic "boy and his dog' story, and we were most comfortable in our time together during the 1996-1998 years living on Nevada Street. We had one more move together as a bit of serendipity created an opportunity for us.

My LTD pay benefits from Digital were supposed to be 100% of my salary as an insurance payment each week. I had noticed they were significantly lower by more than a couple of hundred dollars per week. My inquiry to the human resources group had yielded a complex explanation about FICA offsets along with assurances that the amount was correct. I pushed back several times but made no progress and ultimately counted myself fortunate that such an option as LTD existed for me. When Compaq computer purchased Digital Equipment, they acquired me in the process, as legally I remained an employee on disability. They located the mistake I had suspected during their records review. Suddenly a significant amount of money was deposited into my bank account to cover the weekly shortage that had occurred over the four years I'd been away from full time work. This unexpected savings allowed me to seek out and purchase my first home on September 30, 1998. This is the home in which I still live today. It had a fenced in backyard specifically for Modi and we entered yet another new phase of our lives. A long-wooded stretch adjacent to the Merrimack River gave us trails and woods to explore once again. Still, having moved away from the downtown and into a real home of our own was an entirely new experience for us both.

In hindsight it amazes me how my time with Modi spanned so many diverse aspects of my life. While I'll cover many of those in separate and specific chapters he was my companion through so much of a renaissance-styled life. Unfortunately, our time together was slowly drawing to a close. His hips gave him some trouble from age and we began treating them with a medication which helped the hips but was a little rough on his stomach. Our walks became necessarily shorter. Several times his hips wouldn't allow him to get up and I had to either help him or in some cases carry him. We increased the dosage of his medication but the impact on the rest of his system was growing unacceptable. A very real challenge and heartache was coming more quickly than I could bear.

One snowy evening in late fall of 1999 I let him out the back door to relieve and watched as he slowly walked to the corner of the yard, eased himself down under a shrub in the farthest corner and rolled to his side and lay unmoving. I watched him giving up on his life and remembered some animals sense when their time has arrived and go quietly to find their peace. But I was not at all ready for this choice and inside my head screamed "No, no, no, no, no..." while tears again streamed down my cheeks. I rushed outside and lifted him into my arms and carried him into our home.

My brave boy accepted my selfishness and roused himself to stay with me a little longer. I knew I could not remain selfish indefinitely and I resolved to share with him a season of farewell. Spring came early and in April of 2000 with the help of my Mom we went to visit each of the parks and woods which had been a part of our lives together. Mom had bonded with Modi tremendously and her heart was as heavy as my own, but we took a bittersweet journey. Stopping at each home in which we had lived, I eased my boy out for the short walks which were all he could handle. At the Mill Pond Land Trust, he found a little more energy, almost as if the recollections brought a little youth into his limbs. We took a little private time to talk and to be close to each other at each stop on this tour and while it stretched out the painful emotions for me, I took some solace in his reactions to our travels. I took even more in realizing just how much we two had shared. On the morning of April 19, I took him into our backyard and planted a Ms. Kim lilac bush which was given to me by Rick and Monique in honor of my boy's life. I planted it in a prominent location outside the bay window so that it would always be there to remind me of my boy. I love the scent of lilacs during their too-short blooming season. I loved Modi with all of my heart and his season was also far too short.

I had taken away his choice of timing for our parting. Now the timing was my responsibility, and it stung me to my core. He was so very ill and, in such pain, there was no question it was the right decision yet as we drove to the vet for our final ride together it felt entirely cruel and unfair that anyone should ever have to make this choice. I held him in my arms as the vet administered the dose which would end his pain, giving him the peace and freedom, he deserved.

This was the first loss of life so very close to me, so deeply personal that part of me departed this world with him. There would

Pictured: Modi's farewell in the Nashua home.

never be another Modi in my life and I not only grieved for days, weeks and months; I am grieving today more than eighteen years later. Yet, I have learned that as painful as the loss feels, even greater is the love felt, coupled with the joy and rewards of experiences shared. I can drive away the tears by reflecting on some of the thousands of moments in which our time together made my life markedly better.

I learned many lessons of life from Modi. Ultimately, in his death I grew in my understanding and connection with our world. It took his patient and loving manner to teach me how to be a proper dog owner clearing the path for some of the most significant and essential relationships in my life. Modi provided the foundation for success with Ostend, Quinn and Autumn and taught me to live my life as a better person. He was my first dog as an adult and he guided me through some of my most difficult challenges. While a part of me left this world with him, a much greater part of him remains with me for all my journey ahead.

I love you Modi, my very good boy. Thank you for your patience, loyalty, love, and the courage you imparted to me as well. I am a better human because of you.

Losing Sight of the World

"The only thing worse than being blind is having sight but no vision." Helen Keller

From the first realization of my becoming legally blind, I spent more time than I would have preferred imagining how my life would change when I became totally blind. Initially I thought my complete loss of sight was unavoidable. I only briefly developed hope my situation had stabilized several years after the first episode of sight loss. My initial sight loss took place in 1989 and it wasn't until 1994 that a second occurrence brought the harsh reality back to me once again. With subsequent episodes I returned to the feeling of inevitability. I did so with the belief I would be ready to handle it physically and emotionally. In this belief I perhaps underestimated the full impact the moment of total sight loss would have on me. Fortunately, there was a tremendous benefit arriving to my life at nearly the same time to help offset the difficulties I would experience.

With the loss of my beloved Modi, the time was right for me to pursue being matched with a Seeing Eye Dog. At least that is the term I had always used for a service dog assisting the blind. This was only one of my misconceptions. There are quite a few different charities that provide service dogs to the visually impaired. Each of these schools may have subtle variations but they generally support a very similar mission. Several have trademarked their school name such that the official generic term is "Dog Guide" Candidly I find the semantics of this more annoying than valuable. I have overcome the awkwardness of that name, but I may never overcome the powerful transformation these dog guides bring to my life.

Another of my misconceptions was the notion that they were only for use by those who were fully blind. It's common for many who have some amount of useable sight to mitigate their acceptance of vision loss. I frequently thought I wasn't really blind and so avoided many of the simple practices and opportunities which might have helped me be more efficient at managing my low vision. For some it's an actual aversion to the very term "blind" as suggestive of a dark reality at the end of their journey through vision loss. It takes the right mindset to understand blindness encompasses a range of low vision through no vision realities.

It is simply a term which was given a legal definition for when and where the threshold for various types of services and classifications is set. It was certainly true that a dog guide would have been of tremendous assistance for me many years before I realized I was sufficiently low vision to qualify. The sad part is that I could have reached out to any of the schools for an evaluation and they likely would have made that clear to me, while starting the process sooner in my life. Ultimately, I don't begrudge the delay too much because my time with my rescue dog Modi was so valuable to me. I was appreciative I could dedicate my time with him entirely without the distraction of another dog in our lives. Even though a guide might have been a significant benefit in my many activities, Modi might have felt the negative impact of adding another dog who suddenly was allowed to go everywhere with me while Modi was left home. That isn't something I was prepared to have done to such a loyal and loving companion. So, it was that only after his departure could I turn my full focus on the process necessary to partner with a dog guide.

It is essential to have a foundation of mobility training prior to learning to work with a dog guide. For some this is the entire motivation to undergo the training. My instruction began in 1989 shortly after my initial sight loss. Sue Bergeron provided that training and patiently worked with a somewhat resistant and embittered young man. She helped both teach me the skills and coach me through the emotional challenges. I was never quite ready in that first year to embrace the cane as a positive part of my life. I was able to begrudgingly accept it as a tool that might provide a little extra safety. I learned the various techniques of sliding or tapping the cane one step ahead of each foot's stride. I learned to use my ears and the tactile response of the cane to get information about the surface or obstacles encountered. I readily found the balance between my usable sight for navigation and the cane to explore the regions outside of my vision. Sadly, I chose to learn the minimum necessary for my sight at the time.

As each episode of nerve inflammation and additional sight loss took place, it was necessary for me to adjust my approach to travel. In actuality these episodes caused me to adjust many of my life skills and common activities and each time I was glad there were experts in helping me learn new low vision therapy techniques to manage the new challenges. I experienced episodes in 1994, 1996, 1998, 1999 and ultimately twice in 2000. Glenn Gunn of the New Hampshire Association for the Blind had provided my final rounds of mobility training with my blind cane in 1998. At that point my vision was sufficiently negligible we did much of my training with occlusion such that I could have the skills to navigate around my neighborhood and the entire city of Nashua with no sight at all. I began to learn and understand how to feel the air shadows when in proximity to large objects like buildings. I started to hear the sound changes in my environment which alerted me to my location. I even began to understand how much information my nose might share about where I was traveling. Mostly though, I learned how to utilize the object detection aspects of the cane to prevent me from walking into things. I also practiced techniques to help me find specific desired items such as doors, chairs or curbs. These cane skills were necessary for my traveling and my environmental awareness which would be required when I began to work with a dog guide.

After Modi's death in April of 2000, Glenn provided me with a list of possible dog guide schools and said he had more familiarity with Guide Dogs for the Blind which was based out of San Raphael, California. Thus, it was I sent them my application and was surprised at the many in-depth questions about my daily routines, favorite activities and even my personality. They did not take just my report but had forms for friends and family to fill out as part of the broader profile of who I am. It was quickly apparent how much effort is put into understanding all the details for the right match between handler and guide. They sent a trainer to my home and we took a walk with me using my cane to demonstrate my mobility skills and to showcase some of the environments in which my dog and I might work regularly. The trainer then introduced me to my first taste of what it's like to work with a dog guide.

They call it "Juno" training. I put my hand on the harness handle much like I would use with a dog but in this case the other end is attached to a handle held by the human trainer. I received brief instructions on how to give verbal commands to my pretend dog, Juno. Using these commands allowed the instructor' to simulate the dog guide response. This allowed me to experience the smooth and natural flow at the heart of how a dog guide works by object avoidance and straight-line targeting. A cane typically involves probing and searching while a dog sees the desired target or destination and walks a clean straight line to it. Suddenly I was walking faster and with more confidence. Instead of being forced to put so much focus into the cane, I was free to simply trust the harness and put my focus on experiencing the world around me. It was liberating and somewhat magical to so dramatically change my interaction with the world.

I must consciously evaluate with every step when using just a cane. By comparison there is a partnership and teamwork which immediately begins to deliver freedom even with the human trainer version. I was excited, and the trainer informed me he thought I was an ideal candidate. All that was left was to wait several months for my official approval and for the school to identify the right class for me to attend. That was August of 2000 and the 28-day process would have me returning home in September. I was accepted to the division of their school in the town of Boring, Oregon. The plane tickets, my accommodations and meals would all be provided. I was told to expect a rigorous seven full day training schedule for all four weeks.

When the day arrived, I was filled with nervous anticipation. I was so eager for the benefits a dog guide would bring to my life but many, many, times more powerfully I was eager for the companionship of a dog. I had been without one of the most positive parts of my life for nearly four months. While no dog would ever replace Modi, I knew the loneliness and empty home would soon be filled with the love and friendship I find in sharing my life with a dog.

The flight to Portland, Oregon was the longest I'd ever undertaken. I still recall looking out the window with my tiny field of vision and finding the stark contrast of the volcanic cone shaped mountains which thrust out of their surroundings so vastly different and more isolated than our New England mountain ranges. Looking back on that moment holds so much irony, for they would ultimately be the last mountains I saw with my eyes. At that time mountains had far less significance in my life and yet they had stood out to me in that moment.

I was met at the airport by Trisch Wentz who would be my trainer. Our group of roughly twelve students was assembled and heard the introductory comments telling us that we were situated on the largest fault line in the United States, located at the base of a semi-active volcano. Where was that in the brochure!?! But we were not there for the geography lessons, the tours of their impressive facilities or the slow camaraderie which we students began to build. For most of us blindness was the primary commonality, although for many the desire to have our lives changed by a dog was close behind. We endured three grueling days of lessons before we earned, albeit impatiently, the right to be matched with our dogs. This ensured we were prepared for the responsibility of tending all the needs of our new guide as well as the basic rules around which our relationship would be based.

The key to the relationship is the bond. The trainers carefully create an approach which will unite us with our new dog dramatically and provide us immediate quality time. We each wait quietly and privately in our rooms for the arrival of our future guide which the instructors have determined match our pace and life needs appropriately. They usher the dog into our room with an enthusiastic fanfare designed to have the dogs energized for the meeting. Each dog has spent the last several months in a kennel environment vastly different from the caring and attentive puppy raising process. This moment of greeting marks a return to one to one contact for them, and we quickly become the target for all of their loving focus and attention.

A handsome Golden Retriever named Ostend was led into my room and immediately began working his way into my heart. He pranced into the room with his front paws playfully arcing high into the air as an obvious invitation to play. I mirrored that, and we tousled with a joyful exuberance. After a few rounds of overly rambunctious jostling of the furniture, we settled into the more appropriate behavior of two weary friends comfortable with each other's zest for fun and life. It was then I first learned of his propensity to duck his head under my hand and entreat the petting he constantly craved. This is a trait of many Golden Retrievers and Ostend had it mastered.

We were left alone for roughly half an hour to just spend time getting acquainted. Ostend was happy to guide me through the process of understanding how much he loved to be gently stroked from head to haunch. He would sit directly in front of me tall and proud. When I sat on the floor in front of him he would lean forward and place his chin on my shoulder in a hug I can still feel to this day. At the time I didn't understand how much the trainers do to prepare the dogs to begin bonding so quickly and strongly to each of us. I did understand the bond was the key to a dog guide's motivation towards all the incredible work involved in partnership with a human handler. Ultimately with food rewards almost any animal can be trained to perform virtually any task. The beauty of the dog relationship is their bond and desire to please us is all the incentive needed. Of course, this doesn't mean a little treat therapy isn't helpful along the way!

Each day brought new learning and different explorations together. We learned how to ignore distractions and pay attention to the subtle signals necessary for us to navigate a complex pattern of streets, sidewalks, curbs, doors, stores and more. Our work was progressing fantastically, and we had all the basic commands, footwork, hand signals and rewards well understood. Things were progressing so seamlessly with our trainer Trisch walking behind or beside us and steadily providing less and less instruction as we grasped more of our own communication.

Every time some new experience had me a bit curious on why Ostend might be choosing a particular action, Trisch would speak in a voice intended to convey she was pretending to give me an answer Ostend might provide if he could speak. I often hear her voice in my head to this day when I ponder what might be going through the mind of my guide. Her method no doubt enhanced the anthropomorphizing approach I take to training and playing with my dogs to this very day. She was patient, informative, consistent and always caring. We both loved language, laughter and our dogs so an easy friendship developed. The three of us were a team yet she selflessly withdrew herself from that team leaving Ostend and I together with the strongest partnership I had ever known in just a couple of weeks of training.

At the end of those first two weeks we faced a very significant challenge. I felt the "wrongness" in my head which usually signaled another vision loss was starting. My last episode was just eight months earlier, January 2000, and I had so little vision remaining I had decided to forego the difficulty of solu-medrol treatments. Before actually facing the decision, I thought to simply accept the likely end of my sight. Now faced with the reality of that permanent and total loss of sight I agreed to have the nurse at least evaluate me. She looked for the tell-tale sign of a swollen optic nerve and confirmed my suspicion. She encouraged me to visit a local neural ophthalmologist before making any final decisions. A cross country consult helped us evaluate the options and with the full support of the school administration I chose to undergo the Solu-medrol treatments. This was predicated on their confirmation that I would still be allowed to continue my training with Ostend.

His addition to my life was so important to me I would rather have gone blind than risk losing him. My only requirement was to not miss any training and if the medication made me too sick I might have to reconsider returning home early. I had enough experience to believe I would manage the illness caused by the medication and continue to focus on my training. Unspoken, but definitely in my mind, was that I would endure the hardship silently and push through any amount of discomfort to keep us progressing towards our graduation day.

On the fourth day of my treatments our training required we take a bus ride out to a location where we could board a train back to our starting point. This was designed to give us experience and practice working on both forms of public transit. While riding the bus I settled Ostend beneath me as we were trained, and I turned to talk with Trisch who was seated across from me. My limited vision allowed me to mostly see her face as we were talking. While I looked at her the narrow field of vision closed in completely and there was simply nothing in my sight. I surged with emotions of sadness, fear and resignation to the finality of my sight. As the drug caused anxiety to feel overly exaggerated, these feelings were overwhelming, and my eyes began to fill with tears at the final loss. Ostend, sensing the emotional overload, sat up and faced me putting his head onto my left knee as he looked up at me with love and concern. I pointed my eyes at the spot on my leg where I could feel the pressure of his head. Still my eyes saw nothing and as a tear fell onto my lap the field of vision opened up to a tunnel similar to the sight I'd had moments before. I could see the outline of his face, the various tones of golden fur and those deep adoring brown eyes that were studying me intently. It was not a clear image as my eyes had only allowed blurred partial vision since the previous episode, but it was enough to fill my heart with the warmth and love he was sending to me in his look. The sight faded out once again as if someone had squeezed the field closed. More tears fell from my eyes, but Ostend's head didn't move and neither did the direction of my sightless eyes. Once more the vision opened up to that tiny field allowing only his gentle muzzle and beautiful, soulful, loving eyes. It faded out more quickly this time and has never returned again. This was the last sight my eyes would ever reveal to me, my final visual interaction with the world.

Certainly, the overwhelming sadness and impression of loss was difficult for me. Yet even in the midst of that difficulty I could not help but realize what a gift I had been given. The world is rife with mundane things likely to capture that final glance. I hadn't captured anything inane or meaningless. My final look was into loving and caring eyes. My final sight was of a beloved and beautiful companion. It remains the single easiest vision for me to pull into my imagination at any moment. It is the most lasting and powerful sight which I will forever treasure. I might wish many times throughout my life for the chance to see again. I might wish to better view some wonder of the world, some splendid scene now hidden from me. I would never choose to change that final sight which was gifted to me in Ostend's loving face. I'll wish only to always cherish that precious gift and understand that as I learn more and more about vision as something similar but different from sight; my gift of sight was one in which I can and do feel truly fulfilled.

Ostend Summit to Surrender

"Do not judge me by my successes, judge me by how many times I fell down and got back up again." Nelson Mandela

My cross-country flight home from guide school with Ostend was nerve wracking. On our very first flight things went painfully awry, starting with well-intentioned but misguided advice of the flight attendant, who suggested I settle him under my seat rather than the seat in front of me as we had been taught. She thought to give my long legs extra room but instead it wedged Ostend and his harness under a section not intended for that purpose. A scream from the passenger behind me intensified the stress. Ostend couldn't back out or crawl forward, I was struggling to dislodge his stuck harness, and the plane was now piling up with passengers trying to rush aboard the red-eye to Boston. The anxiety inducing medications were coursing through my system bringing me closer to a full-out panic. But I forced myself to take deep calming breaths and politely asked the flight attendant to step the dog-fearing passenger away long enough for me to coax Ostend the rest of the way forward so that I could reset us as originally intended.

It felt brutally ironic that my trip to Oregon for the independence of a guide dog match had me returning with what was, for now at least, an unexpected loss of freedom. I felt overwhelmed and tipping towards the helplessness of my first struggles with blindness. I was grateful it was such a long flight, providing the time I would need to absorb and find perspective. Ostend soon slept soundly at my feet, earning praise for his behavior and beauty from an apologetic flight crew. I did not sleep at all as my mind raced, analyzing the choices I had made to allow things to go wrong in our boarding the plane. I resolved to trust our training to manage future situations. I saw how well Ostend and I worked together in the week after my total loss of sight. I knew we could manage everything we'd face once settled into routines at home. This wasn't our first challenge, nor did I expect it to be our last, I simply wanted to become better at handling them.

Our actual first challenge had come mere moments after my total loss of sight. We had been on a route to practice techniques for bus and train travel. Our training required us to take the bus to a train station and the train back to our starting point, allowing exposure to both modes of travel. The bus was, however, running late and as it was Oregon, a light rain had begun to cascade down upon us as we hastily stepped down the stairs and off the bus. Urged by our trainer Trisch to hurry the process I gave "Oz" the 'hup-pup" command and we sped into a brisk walk. I was scant minutes into my total blindness, sadness and confusion surging through me all intensified by the medication's influence on my emotions. What I noticed most was the total lack of any reference point to help guide me. Sounds seemed to bounce and shift all around me, making every step even more uncertain. The need to rush elevated my fear that each step might go awry. I was telling myself to trust Ostend, but my doubts were drowning me out. Ostend had been accustomed to my responding very well to his guidance, in part because my very limited sight enabled me some ability to understand the world he was showing me. Now he stopped abruptly on the edge of the train platform, directly in front of the gap between platform and train, but my lack of sight had reduced my reaction times slightly. This slower stop on my part and the slippery rain-wet metal caused my foot to slide off the edge, plunging my leg into the gap. I slid down to my thigh as the two metal sides ground against my widening leg until I was scraped to a painful halt and awkwardly wedged at an awful angle. I screamed out in anguish born equally of pain, frustration and fear. Amidst my own struggles, I felt the urgent press of Ostend against me with quivers of distress racking his body in what I believe was concern and guilt. My instructors rallied quickly to help slowly and carefully extract me. My frustration, confusion, embarrassment and fear had elevated me beyond a rational and thoughtful state, but I remember Trisch giving decisive instructions for me and those around me, a cracking edge of fear and concern in her voice. She had me stand, step onto the train and pick up the harness handle to use Ostend again immediately to "find a seat." We needed to get our whole class onto the train before it departed, and she needed me to start building confidence in Ostend right away. He was cautious, crisp and perfect. Ostend didn't round at an angle towards the seat, rather he made a precise 90-degree turn facing me directly towards it. Previously he had allowed his nose to be merely near the seat, expecting me to use my limited sight to find it. But now the tip of his nose was precisely on the edge of the seat to guide my hand perfectly. This change in his demeanor was clear and captivating to

Pictured: Ostend in a photo taken by Randy while at Guide Dogs for the Blind

my mind. I forgot for a time how much my leg hurt as I began to think about his mindset, trying to fully understand what had happened and why.

Ostend had received a clear wake-up call to my blindness in that moment. Empathically he already understood the emotional experience which was overwhelming me. Now, with incredible efficiency he began to conceive and study the physical impact this brought to our teamwork. We would spend the rest of the class striding forward from that low to surprisingly smooth and confident efficiency.

At the airport in Boston I was greeted warmly by both my mother and girlfriend. This first connection held an air of awkwardness as both were unable to mask their concern for me. It was a brusque reminder there were differences ahead in all my interactions with friends and family. I resigned myself to an arduous journey of education for the many well-meaning and caring people for whom my now-total blindness was also daunting. I found that I still held some resentment that I needed to take on more effort to help others acclimate to my newest transition. Even as I realized and desired to change my reaction, I wanted at times to wallow a little in my selfish moments of mourning. I would find those times, alone with Ostend's understanding albeit persistent nuzzling of his head under my hand. In the meanwhile, though, I would strengthen my resolve for my interactions with my friends, drop my hand to caress Ostend's feather soft ears and draw strength from our partnership.

Returning to the relative safety of my home of just two short years, I fumbled and stumbled my way into learning all the insidious details I simply did not know as well as I might have hoped. Ostend was the success story in a storm of many frustrations. I'd sit on the floor beside him and he'd quickly rotate in front of me to rest his chin on my shoulder as I gently ran my fingers through the wavy fur along his back. This would help me to relax and ease the disheartening failures of search after search when I could not remember where I'd put the bin of sweatshirts, replacement razor blades, the egg slicer, the hard yard rake or any of a myriad other items I found myself wanting on a particular day. My home was something I thought I knew reasonably well, and I was astounded at how many things I had 'known' relied in part on my prior limited sight. Everything I wanted to undertake seemed to unveil new challenges for which I had insufficient solutions. Everything took longer, felt harder, and all too often produced raw emotions of inadequacy. Although I had tremendous support from my Mom and the many friends in my world, I lived alone in my home and commonly found points of frustration.

In one early experience I went into a walk-in storage closet in my basement to get supplies. As the rough-edged shelving might produce splinters, I could not simply trail my hand along the shelf. Unable to find the items I wanted by exploring shelf to shelf, I managed to get turned around. Since the open doorway was on an odd angle I failed to find it in my first few attempts to exit. I was frustrated and even briefly, in a panic. How could I possibly become lost in a simple closet?!

I knew that if I calmed myself and applied critical thinking, I could find a reasonable solution to this simple challenge. I also knew essential training, better suited for sightlessness, would be coming from the NH Association for the Blind in the near future. Nevertheless, feeling trapped I actually stopped, sat on the floor, and surrendered to sobs of sorrow, frustration, and perceived hopelessness. Ostend, of course, was right there in moments and his gentle muzzle nuzzle was soothing as well as the means to help guide me without harness from the closet and back to the stairs.

Ultimately though, it was my time walking with Ostend in harness in which I experienced the full measure of freedom I needed to suggest to me what my world would become with a little training. I trained with him to travel outside, following the rules of the road and sidewalk well enough we could do this much more comfortably, than the tasks which were so often thwarting me in my own home. It was counterintuitive to feel more confidence and comfort in leaving the confined and purportedly more known environment of my home for the vastly less predictable and uncertain streets of my neighborhood. The simple difference was that outside I would put Ostend into his harness, relying on him and on our training. These walks were comfortable routines with ever expanding territory, using his confidence and guidance to bolster my own as the bonds of trust and teamwork continued to strengthen. We spent that first fall of 2000 getting outside multiple times each day for longer and longer walks. I learned to understand the sounds and smells of my neighborhood rather than relying on the now-absent visual cues. The independence and freedom I felt while walking with Ostend is difficult to describe. Our partnership reached such a pinnacle of appreciation that my dependency on him did not feel at all like a dependency but rather a deepening of our teamwork. It was a symbiosis full of pride and accomplishment, without the feelings of being a burden which I often felt when needing the support of another person.

I received the help of many people during my earliest period of adaptation, my 71-year-old mother foremost of all. She would drive to visit me twice each week. All the challenges of mail, financial paperwork, medical forms and home chores were things we worked together. She probably did a little too much for me and for many years I did not have to tend to some of these common chores. She often said her reward in all of this was our shared time, time with Ostend and hours working together tending the landscaping of my yard, one of her favorite hobbies. My reward was getting essential life skills managed, steadily learning and growing comfortable with my total blindness and enhancing a priceless deepening of my relationship with my Mom.

During this time the NH Association for the Blind scheduled additional home visits to adapt my previous training to my now-total blindness. These provided some supplemental training and further home alterations to expand my independence. A dab of fabric paint on the thermostat providing tactile reference to a desired temperature, braille lessons and a braille labeler for home goods were early tools. They also provided a refresher to my cooking techniques for safety and success without my sight. Along with all of these came very productive mobility support for Ostend and I to learn the city bus routes. A dog guide does not, contrary to what some might believe, read the signs on the various poles. I could ask him to find a pole and he would do it, but whether it's a speed limit, no parking, or bus stop sign would remain a mystery. It was therefore helpful to teach Ostend and I the specific bus stops we were most likely to use. One of the strengths of a guide dog is their ability to remember any point we suggest to them is important. Praise them for a specific sign and they will tend to show it to you when you are near it in the future.

Thus, it was that Ostend and I began our independent travel to downtown Nashua multiple times each week. I was studying for my black belt and commonly made three weekly trips to the dojo. I'd enter the hallway and have Ostend find me the bench by the entrance into the formal dojo. He'd quickly tuck under the bench to be out of the way and watch as I trained. He was so well behaved, and beloved at the school, often taking the time to allow me to educate students young and old on the guidelines for interacting with a service animal. He built several friendships and I could often tell who had arrived at the Dojo by the fervor of his wag or for a very few especially loved friends, by the jingle of his collar telling me he'd actually gotten up from under the bench, without permission, to greet them.

Ostend had an infectious love of life, rejoicing in every moment spent with each and every one of our friends. His tail was nearly always held high and curled slightly back allowing his beautiful feathering to cascade down. His chest had a similar feathering which completed his majestic bearing. He was a golden child, and these quickly became our golden years.

Ostend accompanied me to every home Patriots game, although given the popular response he received, it might have been fairer to suggest I was his accompaniment. I wasn't certain how he would react to a stadium of 60,000 overly exuberant fans. I need not have been concerned as his wagging tail and alert ears made it clear he was attentive and enthusiastic, possibly believing they were all cheering for him. At times I think that may have been true. He was a frequent presence on the large screen "jumbotron" and the stadium speakers often played "Who Let the Dogs Out" by Baha Men as he proudly leaned over the rail from our field level front row seats after particularly exciting plays.

In fact, on our trip to New Orleans for the Super Bowl his status was made clear. We arrived at a Patriot Pep rally at a bar on of Bourbon Street to find an enormous crowd gathered. I thought it was simply too crowded for us to safely attend. But the owner and mass of fans wanted the Ostend present. They turned on his theme song while clearing a path to an alcove they reserved with a table turned into a pedestal to keep him safe, wagging and adored by the throng of fans who knew him as the Pats dog!

He and I made several trips around the country as I'd found a liberating confidence in our teamwork. Often Patriot away games were part of the purpose and ensured there were friends there to join us, but always they included adventures well beyond the games. Out in San Diego we body surfed in the exhilarating waves of the Pacific Ocean. I was amazed and delighted to learn Ostend not only loved the sport but excelled. He would ride each wave fully into the shore while I invariably tumbled out long before him. As I spluttered to my feet he would run back out to retrieve me and guide me to the next wave. Later that trip we shared an incredible afternoon and evening wandering the gas lamp district on our own. This was before the comfort of cell phones or an accessible GPS but I decided if my friends couldn't find the 6'4" blind guy with his dashing Golden Retriever guide dog, I'd simply take a cab back to our hotel.

So, it was that I strolled alone into a restaurant for dinner. Drawn by the pleasant music and scintillating aromas, I was seated by the hostess Ingrid, an older woman quite thoroughly charmed by Ostend and his skillful work at guiding me. We talked music, food, adventure and a love of life all through the night as she frequently returned from tending her duties as hostess. I was surprised but the company was pleasant, and I knew the allure of my Ostend-tacious pup. It had pleased me to learn I had found Croce's Restaurant and Jazz Bar. I appreciated Jim Croce's music and hadn't heard the story of his dream to open this restaurant and that it had been fulfilled just one week before the plane crash that took his life. When the night had run late I asked the waiter to call me a cab and bring me my bill but only received the cab. He informed me Mrs. Croce had taken care of my bill! Though I never encountered her again to thank her, it was just another tale in the saga of Ostend.

Pictured: Randy and Ostend outside the Whitehouse in 2002

During a trip to Miami we took an excursion into the everglades; first a stroll along their paths to hear the exotic sounds and smell the scent of the hot and humid tropics. We then decided to ride a hovercraft along the shorelines amidst the alligators. I relied on the descriptions of those with me, but Ostend's head would focus on the location of every alligator with an intensity which made it clear he was concerned! Soon we rode further out to the open, slowly flowing waters where I was invited to step out and wade the everglades. Ostend stayed in the boat with what I'm told was a look of deep concern for my well-being. We were, after all, partners who were intended to keep each other safe.

In terms of keeping me safe, no moment captures the incredible bravery and essential benefit of a guide dog more than my trip to New York City for our appearance on the Rosie O'Donnell show. I was travelling with Rick and Monique for the short walk from my hotel to the studio. We were walking along the sidewalk and paused for a four-lane road with a do not walk light. Two lanes came out of this street and two lanes turned into it, so we would need to cross quickly when we got our walk signal. My brother told me to go and we set out with him on my right across the first two lanes. Ostend on my left was passing the cars waiting to turn at their red light. Just as we passed the first two lanes I felt Oz turn in front of me and shove his shoulder into my legs. At that moment I simultaneously heard the squeal of tires and my brother's shout. A car travelling parallel to us at high speed had decided to blow through the red light and turned left into our road just as I was getting to his lane. Ostend had been shielded from seeing it partially by my brother's presence to that side and all of it happened so very fast we barely had any reaction time. Ostend's push moved me back just enough, but it also caused my torso to angle forward over his body. The driver's side mirror of the car struck my right hand as it sped past us and continued, the driver apparently undaunted by how close he had come to terrible tragedy. Ostend's quick action had probably saved me from severe injury or worse. He had turned his body into the front of a speeding car and trusted himself to push us both out of the way with mere inches to spare. My heart was pounding, my hand was throbbing, and I was terrified for him and for me. I was so angry at the driver of the car and yet had to get us out of the street quickly. I picked up the harness and Oz lifted his tail commencing with a proud walk-trot as if nothing unusual had taken place. It was his job to keep me safe which he had done with the same skill and grace as he did everything. Reaching the sidewalk, I had a small meltdown of anger and fear mitigated by a swell of pride, appreciation and love for my brave boy. He loved the fuss and attention of course, and when I was done he was ready to return to work as calmly as if it was just another day.

I attended a few concerts with Oz through the years. One concern was to ensure I never exposed him to unreasonable amounts of noise as his ears were so vastly more sensitive than my own. One venue we particularly enjoyed was the Great Woods Pavilion in Mansfield, Massachusetts. The parrot-head in both of us made many a sojourn to celebrate the joy of life at Jimmy Buffet shows. Touring the elaborate tailgate creations led to fun anytime and more so when you had the Prince of Charm with you. Finding the right ice-breaker to make social overtures is important in connecting with people. This is particularly true for those of us with an additional challenge which may create feelings of uncertainty or awkwardness for others. Many people simply get nervous when they realize I'm blind, and the most common response is to become silent which is the least helpful reaction.

I've often joked that nobody ever asks to pet my cane and that is to simply highlight the power of a guide dog as a force for social connection. With Ostend, it was easy to just relax, meet new friends and enjoy the experience before heading into the show. Great Woods offered Visually Impaired seating in the front and center stage area which meant we would not be in front of any tower speakers. The sound level was reasonable and though I could not see the quality of my seats it made it easy to get someone to join me. It also put Ostend front and center. I mention all of this to share a poignant moment with my pup as Jimmy sang "It's my job" – a song about simply loving what you do and trying to do it as well as you can. As he played he showcased a video of people doing all manner of jobs and of course people from the tailgate engaged in all sorts of celebratory shenanigans. Every time the chorus for "It's my Job" came on, there was a video of Ostend guiding me through the winding pathways of people and props with his head and tail high, so very proud of his work. He was the epitome of that song and they captured my celebrity guide wonderfully.

Another of the hobbies we shared involved my attendance at Pennsic. This massive event run by the Society for Creative Anachronism (SCA) brought 12,000 people to a campground in Western Pennsylvania for two weeks of camping, classes on music, arts and history, activities like archery, fencing and thrown weapons among many others. Merchants sold everything imaginable, and many campsites created enclaves for celebrations from cultures and times throughout history. The sheer acreage involved in this sprawling town which grew out of the campground was a challenge for the sighted newcomer. I had the chance to study some of the layout in advance, aided by a fabric paint tactile map created by my friend Leslie Birt. Making our initial travels with friends, Ostend and I quickly became comfortable, if not expert at finding our way throughout the broad expanse of the site. I did necessarily teach Ostend where the preferred points were for his relieving since grass plots were quite likely to be someone's home.

One evening late in the event we travelled with a large contingent from our camp to a Bardic circle for a night of singing and storytelling around a campfire. We had to leave a gate and enter an auxiliary area at one of the furthest points possible on the site. The well-attended gathering continued far beyond our normal waking hours. As each member of my own camp made their departures they politely inquired if I wanted to join them. But I was so confident in Ostend, and our teamwork I declined in favor of hearing more of the music I was enjoying so well. I stayed even when the final person from my camp made their second departure after having returned to see if I was absolutely certain I could find my way home alone.

Finally, after 3 a.m. the night was over, and our ever-gracious host made the offer to guide me, but I roused my sleeping Ostend and asked him if he knew the way 'home.' He quickly began to stride toward the gate and so I confirmed my confidence in him and bid my hosts farewell. He set a pace quicker than usual and began to steadily speed up from there. I felt the corner we rounded where the gate should have been, but nobody stopped us to check and I like to think we were a blur of motion too quick and sure to be halted. I smelled the stale area of the closed medieval food court as he turned correctly towards the plains. Our twists and turns all seemed accurate but the frenetic pace was a surprise to me even as we passed the distinctive sound of the pumps for the solar showers, telling me I would be stopping soon for the gate to our own campsite, yet no stop came. Ostend, instead, nearly sprinted the final fifty yards to the end of that dirt road to precisely the point I'd taught him was our relieve spot demonstrating to me that his night had been long and his urgency driven by need! Still in all that there was never a question in my mind that he knew the entire route of the make-shift town without hesitation and my freedom was complete.

We had one other camping trip which bears mention amidst the hundreds of worthy tales I could tell of our exploits together. There are many further tales of hiking to share but it was Ostend who guided my first sightless steps in the forest. A small group of friends coordinated an overnight camping trip into the Pemigewasset Wilderness. Before that trip we undertook a trial run on the much easier Lincoln Woods trail which is effectively an old railroad bed. That had been challenging only in the frequency with which Ostend had to pause for a still exposed railroad tie which might cause a stumble. After a few miles we detoured a very short distance of actual White Mountain trail to a natural water slide. Here Ostend's guiding needed to be very attentive and I had to use all the balance and awareness of my training to navigate it successfully. The trail was exhausting but short enough and well-travelled enough to be reasonable.

Thus, our overnight Pemigewasset trip was scheduled to hike towards 13 Falls campground. I slowed the group considerably, relying almost entirely on Oz except for a few scramble points. We hiked a long, challenging and rewarding day to a secluded spot where we made our own campsite. We didn't reach 13 Falls but we certainly reached a milestone in our journey. Our success on that trip was a foreshadowing of the prominent role hiking would eventually take in my life. What I knew in the moment was pride for Ostend's eager willingness to put his full focus into whatever task lay ahead. He was always enthusiastic for adventure and managed all his work with an enviable grace of motion and attitude. He guided me when my balance was still fully sound, and we knew few limits.

Our success in both achievement and attitude made the descent we experienced so much more difficult. In 2003, I suffered a head injury in my Houston hotel room while navigating without Ostend. At first, we didn't understand what that would portend. I found myself listing and struggling to find balance on our return home the next day, but that was only the beginning. This radical loss of equilibrium would take my hand off the harness with which Ostend had guided me so effectively and place it instead on the rim of a wheelchair where I would be trapped for nearly two years. Ostend's devotion to me never wavered in this time and he would constantly come to heel beside my chair, dip his nose under my wrist, lift my arm off the wheel and slide my hand across his head. With my hand on his head I could feel his face tipped towards me, eyes no doubt imploring me to rise from the chair and return to our joyous strides. I could not walk and could barely stand even for mere moments.

Instead I crawled to the floor to be with him. I crawled outside to relieve him multiple times each day until my knees were filling up with fluid. I had my knees drained every other week and I was forced to admit I needed help. We had lived alone for all our time together but now I brought in my friend Bren Campbell to live in our home and help me care for him while I struggled to take care of myself. He would rush to me immediately after every time out whether for walk or relieve and I clung to him in those darkening days. The doctors and I worked hard on the medical reality, but it was Ostend and I working on the challenge of my heart and spirit. Through the course of a year I brought in several different friends to help us at home. Ostend was my one constant until the spring of 2005.

Pictured: Oz rests in one of his favorite sleeping spots.

That spring he became sluggish at the end of his walks and we thought my emotional challenges were taking a similar toll on him. Perhaps absorbed in my plight, perhaps simply by not being able to take him out, I didn't fully understand the warning signs. He fell over one day, and we brought him to the vet who thought he was dehydrated, which seemed strange since he had access to plenty of water. The vet gave him a subcutaneous injection of fluids. This created a camel hump on his back which felt like half a cantaloupe and caused me to be concerned. They dismissed my concern and suggested he would be fine now that they had dealt with his dehydration. I felt judged by the veterinarian who didn't know Ostend or me but saw my disability and with a dismissive air suggested I did not give sufficient care for my dog.

A second collapse happened, but the veterinarian simply repeated the diagnosis of dehydration. Despite my frustration and belief this was wrong, I accepted this poor diagnosis, a choice I will always regret. A month later on May 23 Ostend collapsed for a third time and this time, I knew beyond any doubt it was something much worse. I was home alone with him, cradling his head on my lap. I could not rouse him and in a desperate panic I called our neighbor, Vanessa Benson and her son Tom, who immediately came to my aid. We somehow loaded Oz onto my lap, wheeled us out to the car and shifted us both onto the front seat and headed to the animal hospital. I felt so numb holding my barely breathing boy. He didn't squirm or shift, simply laid against me sighing heavily. Vanessa seemed calm as she spoke to reassure me things would be ok but I don't think I comprehended any of her words. All of my thoughts were on Ostend's plight and my considerable doubts for the veterinary care we would receive. This was an emergency and I thought returning to the vet I felt had failed Ostend was our only immediate option.

This time, the staff immediately recognized the gravity of the situation. After a few simple tests, an ultrasound showed that Ostend had a cancerous tumor growing on his heart. While it did not cause him pain it had grown large enough to split his heart…and my own heart split as well. His pericardial sack would fill with blood and prevent his heart from beating enough to get oxygen to his muscles. The vet could drain that fluid and it would revive him briefly for a few minutes but ultimately it was too late for any hope of saving my boy.

My throat constricts, and a deep ache fills my chest each time I recall our final moments. I held my beautiful boy entirely on my lap as I sat sprawled on the floor. He was resting quietly, breathing deeply and I was stroking his downy soft ears. He made a sudden lurching motion I feared was a seizure or pain and I was in a panic for my beloved boy who did not deserve one moment of suffering. All at once he stopped and my Mom, who had joined me understood and explained. He had gone through a Herculean effort to move his body just enough from me because he had to release his bladder and he refused to relieve on me. It was such a heart-rending amount of effort during his struggle. I shifted us further away and the tech cleaned up the room, so we could have a little more time for our final farewell.

A short time later I wrote words I often share on the anniversary of Ostend's passing, and I believe it appropriate to share them here as well.

When the Lilacs Bloom

Wednesday, May 25, 2005: Today there is the fragrant scent of lilacs on the air. Just over five years ago on April 19, 2000, I said farewell to my most loyal and loving Modi. On that day, my family through Rick and Monique gave to me a lilac bush to plant in Modi's honor. Modi had the chance to approve of the bush before it was planted since we had time to prepare for Modi's passing and this was time for the most loving farewell I could imagine. Each June near to my birthday, the lilac offers forth its fragrant bouquet in full view of my bay window into the back yard. Each time I detect the distinctive fragrance, I take time to warmly reflect upon the great companionship shared by Modi and myself. I consider it a delightful tribute to a greater experience than some may ever know. Such is the way of those magnificent bonds we forge in our lives. There is of course tremendous sadness with their passing even as there is a stronger and more marvelous connection which will outshine the bitter sharpness of pain and grief when first we lose beloved friends. So, on April 19, the leaves of the lilacs may begin the budding rebirth of spring time so that in Modi's passing anniversary, I may feel the continued yearly power of life and the continued potency of those many loving memories. Now we are in the season when the normal lilacs bloom and upon my table sits a vase full of them lovingly cut by my mother to ensure I could share in the delightful reminder. As my birthday remains a few weeks ahead, the bush from Modi is just starting to bud flowers. His is a Miss Kim Lilac which delays long enough to give me an annual birthday gift from my boy. Yet amidst the scents of the present lilacs and the recollections of Modi comes a sharing time.

Yesterday, May 24, 2005 at 5:54 PM, my magnificent Ostend had the last beat of his heart while cradled in my lap. I laid in exactly the same room as I had with Modi some five years earlier and all the pains were equally sharp. Perhaps more so in that Ostend was a sudden and unexpected parting. Ostend had a tumor inside of his heart and it was bleeding steadily into his system. He was valiant and stoic to the end much like his counterpart in my Modi. While I know a myriad of marvels with each of these boys and while Ostend and I have a legacy of adventure in which our unique travels shall always be remembered for our worlds, this is the time in which pain and sorrowful grief must powerfully overwhelm what will eventually become the same warm reflection I share with the memory of Modi. I know I must honor his life and our companionship with the strength to strive towards those times and so shall I manage. I already feel the hope of looking forward to that time even as I know it is far too recent a wound to my own heart for such to be readily reached. Still I take some small comfort in knowing such will come.

Modi left me in the early precursors to springtime, when April showers begin the return to the lilac's life. Ostend said farewell when that precursor of life has surged into the bountiful flowers. They each shared such a similar and pivotal part of my life and my love for each was never diminished by my love for the other. That is the marvelous gift of love that requires no rationing to share its splendor with all those whom are valued treasures in our world. I shall love them each continuously with the fervor which is our way together. When the lilacs bloom I shall be reminded of the love which never wavered from each of these companions. Though it is always with me and I will reflect often upon this love, I am simple enough to appreciate the value of symbols and the reminders of the world around me.

In respect and tribute to Ostend he shall have his own symbol. There is a place in front of my home which has called for a planting. To this location I shall build a small shrine with a marvelous plant as centerpiece. There is a blooming bush known as a "bleeding heart" which in my visual days was always a delight to me. In honor of his bleeding heart and the pain to my own heart, such shall be my tribute to Ostend as well. It blooms a bit later than the lilac and with this effort I will know that when my first boy Modi has sent the lilacs, they are a preparation as well for the bleeding-heart approach of Ostend. Equally poignant will be the reminder that in the bleeding heart is a beauty and delight which although symbolic in some ways of the pain is likewise symbolic of the beauty which was so great as to allow such pain. This hurt will go to splendor of recollection in which our beautiful sharing is recalled fondly and with warmth. Each year I shall look forward to the world reminding me of my boys When the Lilacs Bloom.

For all the bravery in those words, I was at the lowest point in my life. The worsening of my medical reality had brought me to total blindness, trapped in a wheelchair, and now my most loyal and loving companion was harshly and abruptly taken from me. How many times would I struggle to manage the challenges facing me, only to have a new challenge seemingly throw me deeper still? How many times could I get back up to my feet? I think of Nelson Mandela's quote and I'd rather not judge or be judged at all. I would rather understand the secret to getting up when it feels futile to do so.

The truth is that it took time and there are obviously days I still struggle, with even small frustrations getting the better of me. I just choose to not linger long in those moments of despondency. I choose to find ways of building positive momentum. I think of how much Ostend tried to guide me when I was in the wheelchair, ever hopeful and optimistic we would go forward and find another adventure. Maybe Yoda had it right "Do or do not. There is no try." I understand that if I let the challenge get the better of me nothing will happen. If I simply choose to take small steps towards a reachable positive I begin the journey in the right direction. It's easy to build momentum once you get started, and from those darkest days my desire to honor Ostend was my inspiration. All the adventures we had shared would not have been possible if I'd quit at blindness, I had every reason to believe a world of adventure awaited me if only I could choose to move forward.

I also know that in moving forward I would not be leaving Ostend behind. The potency of our shared experiences intertwined our lives. He would always be a part of me in those forward journeys. Similarly, he was vibrantly with me in the recollection of those difficult moments he guided me through, both literally and figuratively. During the harsh emptiness of his physical absence, I held the treasured memory of our incredible journeys and adventures close. I would use those memories to bolster my spirit for the difficult path ahead.

Full Tilt Full Time Fan of the Year

"There is an old saying about the strength of the wolf is the pack, and I think there is a lot of truth to that. On a football team, it's not the strength of the individual players, but it is the strength of the unit and how they all function together." Bill Belichick

I sat poised on the very edge of my seat on the first balcony of Section 215 in the Louisiana Superdome on February 3, 2002. There was an eerie silence as the entire stadium took an anticipatory breath waiting for the snap of the final play of Super Bowl 36. My dear friend Jose Acevedo huddled beside me, our arms interlocked with our hands on the other's opposite shoulder, partially to give me his precise location to tune my ear for any detail he might share, but also to prevent the potentially disastrous plummet that my exuberant reaction to a prior play had risked.

My focus shifted to the field where kicker Adam Vinatieri prepared to attempt a game-winning 48-yard field goal. My New England Patriots, lifelong laughing stocks of the, NFL were poised to defeat the St. Louis Rams, known as the "Greatest Show on Turf." There are moments in our lives which seem to stretch on endlessly and in which our mind can travel incredible journeys in the blink of an eye. This was such a moment for me, I had little difficulty recalling clearly how this incredible Super Bowl journey began:

The Patriots had announced me as their 2001 Fan of the Year with a trophy presentation at what was scheduled to be the final game ever to be held in Foxboro stadium. My all-time favorite Patriot player, Tedy Bruschi, had handed me the trophy before the game in a short ceremony in the end zone, directly in front of the seats from which I had watched more than 100 games as my sight slid slowly into darkness.

The stadium wasn't quite ready to admit defeat though, as they had to delay demolition since the Patriots earned a surprising home playoff game against the Oakland Raiders for the Divisional round, on January 19, 2002. Even that truly final night of the stadium was magical on so many levels, starting with the snowstorm which blanketed our tailgate, the game and ultimately the hopes of every Raider fan when Adam Vinatieri kicked a 45-yard field goal through a virtual white-out to send the game into overtime.

How many times have I relayed with humor the story of confusion in those snowy conditions as the kick sailed, nearly invisible to even the sighted around me. "It's low" woefully exclaimed one of the fans near me, followed by Jose's attempt to clarify: "No Good." My dismay was only brief as the throng of cheering fans led me to question Jose for the Abbott and Costello styled exploration of the differences between "No good." And "No, Good!"

The kick was good, and the Patriots would dramatically defeat the highly favored Raiders in overtime by a score of 16-13 on a game winning Adam Vinatieri field goal. The winter wonderland had cast a magical aura around the stadium and the kick heard around the world lifted the legend of Vinatieri and foreshadowed the Super Bowl ahead. That win set the stage for an AFC Championship game in Pittsburg against a Steelers team who few gave New England any chance of defeating. I was certainly one of those few and the excitement encouraged me to fill my home with friends to celebrate the event.

We crowded a patriotic 76 people into my home on January 27th, including several newspaper reporters and a film crew from New England Cable News who were broadcasting live from my home. When they showed up in their TV Crew shirts which were an unfortunate black and gold, Steelers colors, we quickly found Bruschi jerseys for all of them to wear.

Just before this game I received a call from the marketing firm representing the VISA NFL Hall of Fans. I had been named the Ultimate Patriot Fan and a plaque with my story and a photo of Ostend and I would be going into the Hall, which is a wing of the Pro Football Hall of Fame. This sounded so ludicrous to me that I was still dumbfounded when they dropped the even bigger news on me. Another Patriot victory would not only send my team to the Super Bowl, it would send me to the game, with an all-expense paid trip including hotel accommodations, air-fare, game tickets and the option to bring a friend of my choosing!

Things seemed to align as if written for a storybook and there were many times I wondered if I was not perhaps living in a dream. If so there was much more time left in my sweet slumber. Though Tom Brady's injury in the second quarter might have given us fears of the New England Nightmare returning, the team rallied around veteran Drew Bledsoe and held on for the win! Champagne corks popped in my home while Drew took a knee on the field with tears streaming down his face. There were more than a few tears at the Nashua Pats shrine as we celebrated well into the night and I received many congratulations for the trip of a lifetime ahead.

Early the next morning I had a car sent for me; a phrase that just never seems like it should belong in my world. The producers of the Rosie O'Donnell show wanted me flown to New York City on Monday to overnight before a Tuesday morning filming. I was struggling with the notion of a car being sent, but the greater reality of being a guest on a national television show hadn't had time to settle over me yet. Once I was checked into my hotel room, just a few blocks from the studio, the mounting excitement pushed thoughts of sleep from my mind. I sat with Ostend and listened to the city which never seems to slow or sleep, and finally determined I had to get some rest. Leaving a wakeup call, as accessibility of alarm clocks wasn't so easy in 2002, I did manage to sleep. Waking to the noises of morning and in a panic that I might be late for this incredible opportunity, I called the front desk only to learn it was just midnight. When you can't see light it's hard to discern day from night in New York City. We repeated this exercise a few times before they assured me my wakeup call would happen and I finally rested enough to rise and meet my Brother Rick and his wife Monique who had come into the city to join me for the show.

Everything happens fast at a film studio, make-up, green room, briefings and then out to the live audience with bright lights everywhere, rolling, swirling and moving cameras that often overwhelm their human guests…their sighted human guests. Ostend was magnificent; putting his focus on the work of guiding me and ignoring the many distractions, to the delight and amazement of the production team. They had never had a guide dog on the show and Ostend was proud to charm Rosie as we played the underdog card well enough that she went off script and made her pick for the Patriots. I met Kathy Lewis, the ultimate Rams fan, and we shared an appreciation for positivity and sportsmanship: all part of the friendly rivalry which I most appreciate. I was looking forward to my time with her as we both celebrated our incredible fortune in being nominated to the NFL Hall of Fans. The full measure of this honorific would have to wait as there was too much excitement for the impending game ahead. New York was a whirlwind trip as I had to return home and pack for my immediate flight with Jose to New Orleans.

Back in Superdome Seat 215, a clashing of helmets followed by the resounding thud! of Adam's foot striking the football abruptly recalled me from my reverie. Jose and I stood in unison, rising as the crescendo of the crowd's roar grew to a raucous peak. The staccato punctuation of Jose's voice overlaying the call from the Oakland game with "It's Gooooooood, good, good, good, good, good, good!"

Tears flowed down my face this time. I shouted in joy with my arms thrust upward in the victorious moment. I hugged Jose, strangers came down to hug us. "We Are the Champions" by Queen began to boom through the speakers and my dream seemed to last and last. "Beautiful Day" by U2 followed as red, white and blue confetti fell and Jose described the pandemonium on the field as players hugged each other in similar celebrations to our own. I had desired this moment intensely for such a very long time. My hope and belief had blended and battled against improbability and years of frustration, its final arrival left me in shock.

Pictured: Randy and Jose at the Louisiana Superdome for the Super Bowl, 2002

This victory was the reward for all my trials and tribulations as a Patriot fan. It all began in the fall of 1976 when we had just moved to Columbia, NH and I turned the TV to one of the two stations available in northern NH at that time. The New England Patriots were playing, and second year quarterback Steve Grogan was running and passing in a way which captivated me. I had never watched football until that moment and recall after the game going down to the river with my dad to fish. We had our first talk about the Patriots that day. He followed the Boston Bruins and Boston Red Sox but knew only a little about the Patriots. He told me they hadn't been very good, but he liked this Grogan kid. We talked about the good teams like the Steelers and the Cowboys but also how and why he always preferred the home team. I started watching occasionally and began to learn more about the game. That year was unusual for the Patriots as they earned their way to a rare winning record and a spot in the playoffs. Things fell apart in ways I didn't understand at the time but would come to expect as the follies and failings inherent in the franchise. Still, I had been charmed by a winner and my fandom was born.

As I was a skinny kid, my Mom opposed my playing football, which is part of why I knew so little about it. Colebrook was too small to have an organized football program but that didn't stop us from playing our own pick-up games. I started taking every opportunity to play and, conveniently, Nerf footballs were storming the country. I had all of the normal boyhood dreams of becoming a pro-player but mostly I just wanted to experience the game more and more. I was undersized and a little slow, but I was tenacious.

I still remember an illicit football game on the golf course where we often played our games. I was just 13, short and scrawny when I ran down a much larger, faster and stronger opponent, and performed what I now understand is a very dangerous horse-collar tackle. The tenacity of my tackle surprised me probably as much as all my friends on the field that day. It transformed how they treated me while my confidence surged as well. My limitations physically are part of what propelled me to respect a hard-working over-achiever ahead of a talented prima donna. It also is what began to help me appreciate the defensive side of the game and players such as Steve Nelson who once led the team in tackles while playing with casts on both hands!

My fan appreciation of the sport in those years was mitigated by my own desire to participate in any activity rather than watching whenever possible. Despite that, I still snuck in a fair bit of time through the years to watch my seemingly ever struggling Patriots.

While I was at the University of New Hampshire in 1985, my Patriots had a tremendous season. After barely making it into the playoffs as a wildcard team they became the first such team to ever win three road playoff games and make it to the Super Bowl on January 26, 1986. I gathered all of my very limited resources to reserve the basement of an iconic Durham restaurant, the Tin Palace. Exuberantly filling it with friends and residents of my dorm we thrilled to an early turnover and Patriots scoring first. Sadly, this was amongst the last bright spots of the day as the dominating Chicago Bears dismantled the Patriots in the worst defeat in Super Bowl history.

In subsequent seasons, off-field controversy rocked the team and we slowly and steadily slipped into the unenviable position of the worst team in the league. To my dismay we were the Patsies or the New England Over-Paid-triots when people talked with me about my team. But my loyalty and passion were undaunted, which is why graduation from UNH led to my decision to purchase season tickets in 1988, initially through a shared account with a long-time ticket holder who worked at Digital Equipment, and ultimately to my own seats in Section 116, row 2 seats 5 & 6.

These seats would see me endure seasons of 1 win and 15 losses where a near empty stadium was commonplace. Nonetheless I would stay and clap until the last player left the field and then depart as one of the final fans out of Foxboro. I remember many games where I didn't expect a win but hoped to find a few gems of quality play from the team or a particular player.

What made this experience worthwhile for me? What is it about the game which enticed my extreme fandom? Football combines a blend of different types of physical athletes and styles of athleticism into a complex team-based strategy. The pure size and strength competition on the line is infused with moments of technique and strategy to either create run/ pass lanes or seal them. Behind these lines a leaner and still powerful body type manages an intermediate strategic area by reading and reacting to the actions of the offense. Meanwhile on the outside and deeper areas smaller, quicker athletes commonly bring their styles to bear against similar opposition. Behind all of this the coaches utilize the game's many pauses to choose personnel groupings, positional formations and designated plays to attack and counter attack the opposition. It's a blend of the mental and physical which resonates with my own strategic interests. The pauses in action allow for spectators to discuss what transpired and to predict what may be next, and this social aspect is something I also deeply appreciate.

All of these things are also well suited for the descriptive prowess of a good play-by-play announcer. So, whether listening to the radio, one of my many friends, or both at once; I had a source of support for the sport during the time of my initial sight loss and through each subsequent slip towards total blindness. In fact, this support only served to bolster the social aspect of my interaction with football and enhance the experience further for me.

Each home game in Foxboro I would bring a different friend to the tailgate, and we designed ways to enhance the entire experience from the pre-game tailgate, to the in-stadium game time and post-game tailgate. It became a playful competition in which I rated each of them on the fun we had together, and they would choose next year's game attendance in the order of their finishing rank. Arriving at the lot as soon as it opened, I delighted in throwing a football and in those early years, still catching it. As my tunnel vision required me to focus on a smaller and smaller area it became easier for an errant throw to run me into things. One parking lot pass had me leap for a catch, and while in the air, hit a moving car which somersaulted me to the gravel ground. I held up the ball to show I'd held on before hobbling back to discuss the need for more careful throws and louder warnings. All too soon my days of catching were replaced by simply throwing or playing games where audio cues allowed me full interaction. The Sunday tailgate feasts and lawn chair relaxations were simply my seasonal routine. Autumn Sunday mornings and afternoons provided countless hours of quality moments with good friends talking about football and life, and in the process escaping from my challenges with steadily progressing blindness.

Ironically, it was an aspect of my blindness which intensified my fan experience significantly. In the summer of 1995 my friend and fellow Patriotic compatriot, Brian "Coach" Poor had motivated me to get online. I began to work with computer screen readers such as JAWS (Job Access With Speech) to explore whether or not I could create a website. For my practice I chose to create a Patriot page and due to my uncertainty about internet anonymity, I used an old college nickname in the creation of "Zip's Patriots Page." There was a lot of learning on my part but plenty of fun as my limited sight allowed me to supplement the screen reader with some vision. My page was a simple testament to my fandom and included a weekly preview and review of the games as well as "Modi's Doghouse" for players who did not perform so well.

During this time, the team had been undergoing significant transformations. An interim owner, James Orthwein, had hired a highly respected coach in Bill Parcells before delivering the team to the local ownership of Robert Kraft. They had used a first overall draft pick on promising quarterback Drew Bledsoe. Everything came together in 1996 and the team pounded out enough victories to take the second seed in the AFC playoff race.

As internet fan websites were rare in 1996, my site rose quickly in popularity and I had a significant community of fans following the team and my reflections on our rise towards the prize. As New England hosted their first playoff game of my time as a webmaster and even as a ticket-holder, I was caught up in the excitement. I put many happy hours into the preparation of the pages, answering questions and comments and in preparing for an elevated tailgate.

Game day arrived, and a fog-laden Foxboro had a surreal quality. NFL films had reached out to me through my website and planned to rendezvous with us in the tailgate lot before our showdown with the Pittsburgh Steelers! The film crew found Rob Webber and I and commenced capturing the celebrations of our entire tailgate crew. At one point, they even lowered their high-end video camera into our steaming pot of jambalaya. Wrapping up their piece, they asked me to call the first play of the game as I imagined it taking place. With a video camera in my face and boom microphone hovering over me, I unleashed my most enthusiastic announcer's voice: "Drew Bledsoe drops back to pass and fires a long arcing ball down the sideline to a speeding Terry Glenn who explodes past the Steeler cornerback with a burst of speed, leaping to haul in the touchdown and put New England up 7 right out of the gate!"

In the stadium the fog was so thick neither Rob nor I could clearly see the Patriots line up on the far side of the field for their first offensive snap. It was Rob who called out that he could see the ball piercing the fog towards our seats and suddenly there was Terry Glenn running out of the fog and underneath the ball for a huge gain. It wasn't the TD I had predicted but the moment of the pass coming through the fog and the excitement it built was incredible. It carried us and the team through a victory that day, and on to the AFC Championship game, also in Foxboro against the Jacksonville Jaguars, who had upset the top-seeded Denver Broncos.

Hosting that AFC Championship seemed unimaginable to me. Our tailgate swelled to a crowd of frenzied fans eager for the inevitable victory we all sensed. The long traditions of losing and being an embarrassment were finally past! Each moment of prior ineptitude and frustration would be the down payment for the sweet payoff of the reward for those of us who had endured them. Suddenly people cared about the team and even the anecdotes from years of tailgates and fandom. I shared these stories in celebratory delight leading into the game: a game which would produce its own stories such as the last gasp of the Foxboro curse trying to shadow the coming glory. The antiquated stadium and infrastructure succumbed to the demands of the prime-time spotlight. Foxboro Stadium lost power to the field lights in the middle of play and the game was forced into a delay while the problem was tediously

101

rectified, to the mockery of a National audience. Despite this setback the team persevered and held off a last pass rally at the goal-line to advance to Super Bowl 31. I watched my team earn their way to the Championship and felt nothing would stop us, things were different for the Foxboro faithful now!

All through this time Zip's Patriots Page was growing in popularity, thanks in large part to some tremendous help from my friend Melissa French. As part of the hype around the Super Bowl, the Boston Globe and Boston Herald each did a feature on my website and thousands began viewing it daily. I was enjoying the success of the website, of the team and of the perceived promise that things had changed for the New England Patriots.

This proved to be not quite the case, as a coach and owner dispute turned ugly at the worst time, in an echo of the situation which tainted the team's first home playoff game during my early fandom back in 1978. This time the coach was Bill Parcells and he was not only leaving New England but seemingly signing with the rival New York Jets unofficially before the Super Bowl was even played. The distractions filtered to the team and his coaching. Though we rallied to within a single score and captured the momentum, a historic kickoff return by the Packers turned the tide back to Green Bay and the Patriots were losers again. The coaching changes had a detrimental influence on our team. Eventually, Parcells lured away several players including one of our most talented. Despite a few years of promise the team spiraled downward yet again. I stayed loyal and hopeful, enjoying many more wonderful moments of celebration for the afternoons shared in friendship, tailgate and enthusiasm for a sport which held all the elements I loved. We didn't have to be winners for me to enjoy and find value in the experience. I did want to see players who would give their all and play with heart.

It is not surprising that in this time I would find my all-time favorite player in a linebacker named Tedy Bruschi. As a rookie in 1996 he caught my attention initially for sharing my birthday, and then notably for his having been tied for the all-time sack lead in college football. I had long appreciated Andre Tippett's contributions to our team in this role and wondered what this allegedly undersized player might provide. When an event on our birthday enabled me the chance to wish "Happy Birthday Rookie" to him, I thought little of it. He took note and we had a very brief talk as he thanked me and showcased some of his now legendary charisma.

I watched this rookie closely, finding inspiration in his relentless pursuit of every play. Friends and I made a home brew beer in his honor which we playfully dubbed "Bruschi Brew." The beer needed a slogan and being a fan of the playful double entendre, I decided to honor his efforts with the phrase "Full Tilt Full Time." We of course gifted a couple of bottles to Tedy along with a t-shirt bearing the slogan. He continued that admirable approach to his play throughout his entire Patriot Hall of Fame career. With a simple birthday wish a rare friendship between player and fan was born. It developed over the course of his 13 years with the team, deepening when our paths paralleled in an entirely unexpected manner. His 2005 stroke resulted in impairment to his walking ability and disruption of his right visual fields while I was totally blind and relegated to a wheelchair! His journey back to football and beyond is chronicled in his book "Never Give Up" in which he kindly thanks me for some inspirational support.

We both moved past those days and one of our crowning moments of connection was his induction into the New England Patriot Hall of Fame. As he walked down the red-carpet past where I was standing and cheering for him, he stepped off the carpet and wrapped me in an embrace of friendship I will forever treasure. On his day, he paused to tell me "We made it Zip, we did this together, you are a part of this." As just another example of my charmed life, a friend of mine captured the moment with a photo. At the precise moment of his photo a sun ray parted the clouds and illuminated the exact spot Tedy and I were standing!

Pictured: Randy and Tedy share a moment in the sun.
Photo credit: Rick Pereira

The proverbial sun also started to shine on my team in 2001. Second-year coach Bill Belichick put together a veteran defense even as he was forced by an injury to Drew Bledsoe to hand the quarterback responsibility to Tom Brady in only his second year. Tom's accuracy and poise as well as leadership altered the team, who began to pile up hard-fought victories. Their steady, if unspectacular rise was built on fostering a team-first mentality. They were the hard-working over-achievers I delight in supporting and they began to capture the region, especially in a year when patriotism was emphasized around the nation. The fall of the twin towers in New York City inspired a patriotic focus across the United States and by virtue of their name, the New England Patriots experienced a surge of support.

By December the Patriots were making a legitimate playoff run and I received the phone call informing me I'd been selected as the New England Patriots Fan of the Year. I hadn't even heard of the award as it was relatively new, and the Mastrangelo family for which it was named chose the award based on the nominations for a person who epitomized everything a fan of the team should represent. They told me they had received more nominations for me than they had ever received before. It took very little work to discover that unbeknownst to me, my friend Melissa French had reached out to my website community and asked anyone who felt I was a worthy candidate to write a letter on my behalf. The result was something beyond what I could have ever imagined. Far beyond the raucous enthusiasm of a fan reaching the pinnacle of fandom, this award initiated an avalanche of experience and opportunity which has enhanced my life to this very day.

"The avalanche has already started, it is too late for the pebbles to vote!" according to the character Kosh from TV's Babylon 5. This quote comes often to my mind in reflection of being swept up by events: Being Patriots Fan of the Year for was a tremendous honor. Having it happen in the year of the team's historic rise to their first Super Bowl Championship was simply unimaginable. Being reasonably articulate, having a devastatingly handsome Golden Retriever for a guide dog in a time of countrywide unity and patriotism led to a series of fantastic opportunities. There were countless newspaper, magazine, radio and television interviews throughout the journey to the championship. There was an invitation to the White house courtesy of NH Senator John Sununu, to ensure I was with my team for their congratulations in the Rose Garden. There was an induction and plaque of Ostend and I at the Pro-Football Hall of Fame in Canton Ohio. In 2007 as the Patriots were amidst an undefeated season, HBO Inside the NFL filmed an 11-minute video of my fandom and approach to life which was nominated for a Sports Emmy award! I've experienced my team winning multiple championships and, in some ways, have become a part of the team history with thirty years of tailgates and even more of gathering friends and fans into my home.

Football has provided many things for me through the years. It was an idle boyhood dream, entertaining diversion from the hard edge of sight loss, a passionate pastime of community building, and the platform for early public speaking which would help me further my foundation. Ultimately, my signature Patriots moment centers on the emotional surge of appreciation for that very first Super Bowl victory. I still feel the heart-swelling surge of pride, awe, and belonging at the booming words of the pre-game introduction "Choosing to be introduced as a team, the 2001 New England Patriots."

I realize nothing is assured and that I am fortunate beyond all reasonable expectations with the depth and breadth of my rewarding experiences centering around the New England Patriots. I frequently choose to invest fully into the moments and opportunities of my life, and this is part of why so often they result in rewards beyond the normal expectation. There's no guarantee of this reward of course, but there is so much benefit from simply being invested in those moments. When things do go awry or I'm struggling with a little failure I sometimes take a step back, listen to "A Beautiful Day" and hear the clash of those helmets, the thud of Adam's foot and the staccato "good-good-good-good" of my cherished friend Jose.

Wheelchair, Momentum and a Hiking Stick

"The miracle is not to walk on water. The miracle is to walk on the green earth, dwelling deeply in the present moment and feeling truly alive." Thich Nhat Hanh

I stepped into the hotel room, easing the harness off of Ostend with a finishing kiss on the top of his head. It was so easy to admire his tremendous work ethic and so fun to reward him at end of day with a round of play. Rambunctiously I told him ok and was immediately rewarded with the sound of his prancing paws challenging me to race into the room and wrestle him.
I strode confidently towards the main area, arm naturally reaching to trail the day bed Jose had been using. I had only the merest thought of something odd, before the unexpected jolt of a far- too-solid wall in place of the day bed, stood me upright briefly before my legs crumpled beneath me. I wavered on the edge of consciousness, but Ostend was nudging me, and the disorientation eased slowly but steadily.

I was in Houston Texas on November 23, 2003 having returned from celebrating a thrilling overtime victory by my New England Patriots. Unbeknownst to me the hotel staff had removed the daybed because Jose had departed. I struck my head solidly against the wall which was a concrete support pillar and thus entirely unforgiving. I arose annoyed at my careless confidence and the painful reminder of my error.

I experience such moments more often than advisable. Whether due to my blindness, my confidence, or my lack of complete and thorough attention to the cautionary practices necessary, accidents happen. These impacts do take a toll on me. Usually it's a bump or bruise which needs time to heal and I presumed that this head trauma would be no different.

But the next morning I woke, and my thought process felt slow and foggy. I had some difficulty with my balance and walking. I tended Ostend's breakfast and relieving needs as normal and then met with my friend Monty Rodrigues for our return flight back to New Hampshire. Monty also noticed my slurred speech and off-kilter walk. After discussing the accident, we felt that I probably had concussed myself. He gave me a little more verbal support than normal, and Ostend also showed signs of concern by setting a slower, more cautious pace and shifting quickly into a heel to inquisitively nudge me at every pause.

Despite this additional caution, as soon as I lifted the harness handle he was eager as always for our adventure ahead. Between the guidance of those two friends things went smoothly for the first leg of our journey, although our flight was late arriving to Baltimore. We learned that our connecting flight was all the way across the expansive airport, and the airline personnel encouraged us to make the best time we could.

We set out very quickly with a rolling carryon wheeling behind me. Ostend and I were already moving fast, and when Monty took the moving sidewalk, not a safe option for guide dogs, Ostend and I just picked up the pace on the concourse beside him. As Monty started to jog on the moving sidewalk we sped up to match. A dizzy blind man virtually running through an airport with a carry-on behind him – clearly, I was not in the right mindset to make the wisest of decisions! Little did I know, this would be my last opportunity to run for many years.

Arriving home, I went to bed exhausted, waking only to find my condition had worsened dramatically. I was severely nauseated, vomiting violently over and over again. I arranged a trip to the emergency room where a CT-scan ensured there was no brain hemorrhaging, but the doctor confirmed a concussion. The vomiting eased to sporadic daily outbursts, but overall, things did not get much easier. Days became weeks and steadily the staggers and sways in my steps grew more pronounced.

It was a challenge to go anywhere, knowing I had a significant chance of needing to vomit and also that I would struggle with the simple act of walking. The vertigo caused me to lose track of where I was even on a simple walk in my neighborhood, and attempting areas with moving vehicles, heavier traffic or uncertain routes was simply impossible.

My final excursion was an attempt to walk to the bus-stop to attend an event in Nashua downtown. The swirling sensation of vertigo made almost every step feel like I was turning corners left and right even though Ostend was walking me straight along the side of the road. I could hear the sounds of traffic in the distance which normally provided a natural background landmark of direction, and yet now seemed to be swirling in chaotic patterns around me. I was wandering lost in streets I knew like the back of my hand and could not find enough steady, stable focus to reach the bus stop or even return to my home.

I stopped in frustration. Anger roiled as I stomped my foot, desperate for any outlet to my fear and confusion, yet only filling myself with shame for the irrational response. What was happening to me? Why was it happening to me? Standing with legs spread to better balance myself, I swayed from the roaming bouts of vertigo and bitterly held back from a silent surrender. I struggled to pull myself together, feeling lost and isolated in a world suddenly grown larger and more frightful. I was interrupted by a patient nudge to my leg. A body sway told me Ostend's tail was giving a slight wag of encouragement and I was ashamed again for leaving him to worry for me. Ostend's gentle touch brought me back to our partnership, and I resolved myself to attempt to reassure his concern and confusion. In so doing I eased some of my own emotional burden, but all of the physical difficulties remained.

After more than an hour of unsuccessful wandering, I was mentally weary, exasperation growing once again. Desperate, I chose to have Ostend take me to the nearest house. Knocking on an unknown door I humbly explained that I had become lost and asked for their help. Friendly strangers told me where I was, only two streets away from my house. It took another two stops at random homes for assistance before I finally successfully reached my own home. I sat on the floor and began to gently pet Ostend's back in appreciation for his patient support, relief at being home safe and as a weak distraction from the terrible reality closing in. My orientation skills were severely deteriorating, and I was not safe to travel outside alone. It was that stark and simple, and the knowledge filled me with dread.

I ceased going to Karate and virtually all trips, even assisted, outside of my home. Then the falls began. At first, I only fell occasionally but soon it was daily. By mid-January, more than 50 days since the first signs of trouble, the vomiting had not ceased, and I had lost nearly 20 pounds. My diagnosis was changed to post-concussion syndrome and the doctor was uncertain how long it might take me to recover. A first positive sign came on January 18 as I did not vomit for the entire day. It was easy to take this as a sign I was getting better, and either way it provided a tremendous relief for my physically ravaged body.

Unfortunately, the intensity of my balance loss and resulting frequency of falling continued to increase. It felt as though my once very stable perception of "downward" shifted erratically, causing me to pitch dramatically in various directions. From there of course, actual gravity would take over and finish my plummet to the ground. I was clearly getting worse. The complexity of a brain injury complicates diagnosis, exploration and treatment tremendously. As an additional concern, my lack of sight increased the risk factors, so these tumbles sometimes caused me to strike my head on the edge of a counter or similar object. It was entirely possible I would further the head trauma and accelerate the downward spiral of my health.

To make matters still worse, I was sleeping poorly; vertigo remained even though my stomach had seemingly found sufficient fortitude to withstand the nausea. Prolonged sleep deprivation began to wear on me mentally, physically and emotionally during an already incredibly difficult time. I was getting worse and my frustrations began to grow tremendously. I was advised primarily to rest, wait and observe. Neurology appointments are often difficult to schedule with any time urgency, so I went months between tests, results and conclusions. The initial focus was entirely on treating symptoms and with my generally low sleep a primary focus, the real issues seemed to be unchecked.

At one point the neurologist entertained a diagnosis of depression, on the basis that I reported the situation was having a deleterious impact on my life, and my sleep continued to be exceedingly infrequent. I was angered by what I considered to be a bogus diagnosis. In fact, my deep frustration and resentment towards the doctor caused an internal struggle for me as I attempted to cope with the considerable strain of the situation. Most of my concern was with my neurologist's overall treatment. He seemed focused on the post-concussion diagnosis and my insomnia treatment, neglecting all other possibilities. I desperately needed him to address the vertigo and my failing ability to safely walk!

Compounding my stress was a new symptom, one of the strangest and most alarming experiences of my life. I had routinely created vivid mental images of the environment around me which I used to help me interact with the world. Occasionally I would learn about the presence of something new and my mind would seamlessly insert it into the mental image. During this time, I began to lose control of these images in strange and macabre ways. I was hallucinating in garish and distracting detail. My hallucinations usually had a loose correlation to what I was doing or where I was located, but they went well beyond the bounds of my usual mental map of objects. For example, walking with friends in Boston in the early evening, my mind began inserting imagined scenes from a post-apocalyptic world all around me. The footsteps of actual people walking past us became leering characters. Due to the swirling feelings of my vertigo, people and objects would shift erratically in front of me. Although I felt no physical sensation of collision I felt a mental jolt instead, as if I'd walked into a ghost!

This caused a great deal of panic and I feared that I might be losing my sanity. I apprehensively confided about my hallucinations and fears to my primary care physician. He didn't have any comforting answers but was willing to do a little research. He found there is a phenomenon, Charles Bonnet Syndrome, which can in some cases of blindness cause just such hallucinatory effects. Understanding the likely cause of these hallucinations brought me tremendous comfort but did nothing for the overall deterioration of my health.

My June 2004 neurology appointment brought the reality of my decline into sharper focus. While navigating the narrow hall of the office, I used the doorway for support during a wave of dizziness.

Stepping forward and facing a second wave I attempted to anchor on the divider they use as a wall, but it could not support my weight. I toppled the structure, tumbling forcefully and sprawling awkwardly in a heap on the floor. The staff rushed to help disentangle me and ensure I was not injured beyond the desperation of my steady descent towards helplessness. My neurologist decided it was time to take more drastic action. Although I had little confidence in his ability to manage my overall medical situation, with tremendous anguish, fear and regret I supported his decision to restrict me to a wheelchair for my safety. I think it would be difficult for anyone to forget the day such news arrived and certainly I will never forget 'wheelchair day': June 8, 2004, one day before my 38th birthday.

My walk into the doctor's office using every wall for support was nerve-wracking. My fall was embarrassing and scary for me, my mom, and what felt like the entire doctor's office. Leaving the office in a wheelchair uncertain if I'd ever walk again was devastating. Mom had given me the ride to the doctor's office as she had done for so many things. I was, however, too big and heavy for her to push in the wheelchair. The immediate and obvious problem we faced was finding a way for me to steer the wheelchair without sight. A few difficult attempts met with failure and frustration for both Mom and me. I finally discovered a method, however inadequate, to transition away from failure and frustration. I could use my legs to walk while seated as my leg strength was not affected. I would probe out with my foot and then dig in my heel and pull with my legs so the chair rolled forward. It was slow and very limited with no steering option. I could use my arms on the wheels to steer and to roll it, using my hearing to track her voice in front of me, but navigating anything narrow was tedious.

We made it out to the car where I leaned against the back to collapse the chair, awkwardly lifting to stow it in her trunk while barely keeping myself upright. I had leaned against the vehicle but without holding on my stability was still in question. I paused, holding tightly in realization that this was something I could repeat only at significant risk. Closing the trunk, I used the side of the car to support myself as I slid/walked my way to the passenger seat. Easing myself into the seat I was quite simply too overwhelmed to fully grasp the magnitude of this life changing moment.

I sat silently, so many thoughts running through my mind about how I'd get into the house, how I'd handle the stairs in my house, would the chair fit through the inner doors, and many other questions. Suddenly I realized the car wasn't moving or even started yet. There was an awkward silence looming between mom and me. She broke down crying in the car while I reached out and gently took her hand. I felt the full measure of her incredible love for me. Slowly she shared with me the terrible sadness tearing at her heart. She too realized this represented a challenge on levels we had not fully begun to comprehend. She didn't doubt that I would rise to the challenge and really wanted me to know how much she believed in me, but she was completely distraught at her feeling of being powerless to help me. It pained her to watch me struggling, feeling unable to provide more direct help either by pushing the chair or even supporting me to keep me from falling.

She had always been there for me through my sight challenges, but this was different, she didn't have the physical strength to provide what she thought I would need for help and it was emotionally devastating to her. I just listened and stroked her hand hoping to soothe some of the pain. Putting my focus on her instantly distracted me and provided a fair bit of the clarity I needed. My first thought was of how much she was hurting for me and how fortunate I was to have such tremendous love and support from her. I knew I had to help her realize she would be part of the assistance I still needed. I also knew we needed more help than what we had because this new challenge was simply too much for both of us.

I promised her I would make some changes to the medical team so we could get things under control. I shared my appreciation and need for the love and care she always gave to me and assured her she would always be needed to help me get through these challenges. We would just have to find different solutions. Her crying eased, and I wish I could have seen the resolve I knew must be on her face. I've often told people I'm the diluted form of my Mom's determination and even as I was trying to reassure her, I wanted to feel reassurance from her in return. My promises were strong words which I fully meant, even though I knew I would need support if I were to achieve them.

I spent my first weekend in the wheelchair with friends, who gave me exactly the support I needed. A group of my SCA friends, known as Clann O'Choda, were celebrating a weekend event at a

Yale University Camp in East Lyme, Connecticut. I planned to cancel given my new situation, and knowledge the site wasn't wheelchair accessible. They wouldn't hear of my missing the event and their determination helped me to start my newest journey with resiliency instead of excuses. Even more important was the uplifting warmth I took from their kindness and caring.

Bob Dunn, Leslie Birt and Jeff Collins in particular deserve my deepest appreciation. Many times, that weekend I was between two of them, held by shoulder support to walk, and nearly toppling all three of us when a burst of vertigo caused me to lurch awkwardly in unpredictable directions. They helped me tend and care for Ostend and worked to give me as much dignity as possible at a time when I felt so very far from grace and comfort. Unable to see or walk I felt the most disabled of my life. Fortunately, I felt my many friends understood both the gravity of the challenge, and my frayed yet determined resolve to not allow this to define me. The weekend had much music, laughter, feasting and friendship which prepared me for the arduous climb ahead.

On that Sunday morning I rolled my wheelchair out onto the deck overlooking the campsite's small pond. Few people were up but breakfast was cooking, and I wanted a moment of solitude to reflect. I had Ostend's leash while rolling out there carefully to ensure his paws were safe from the wheels, a continuous daunting concern since I couldn't see him and was working so hard to manage my own navigation. Wisely, he'd started leash leading forward to give me a little direction and help me choose a path around the haphazardly laid out chairs. When I felt the warmth of the sun hit my face I stopped, locked the wheels, and called Ostend beside me. Our bond was so close that solitude for me included his presence beside me. I took a moment to listen to the birds, feel the light breeze, the morning sun, and smell eggs, bacon and blessed coffee! My head was swirling but there was a calmness to the moment which belied my vertigo. It was the moment I needed to catch my breath in the midst of my struggles. I wanted more of these moments surrounded by such cherished friends and a world with so many marvels. It's so easy to forget these things while we are struggling and yet they are precisely what we need to better face our challenges. I knew this morning and this magical weekend would do much to brace me for my next steps.

I knew our medical approach needed to change because I was still getting worse. I also believed this must be somehow connected to my previous neurological disorder in some fashion. My present neurologist didn't seem to be addressing any possible connection, nor taking any actual steps towards halting the serious deterioration I was experiencing. I reached out to my primary care physician, Sean Fitzpatrick, and shared my concerns. He had joined me during the very last stages of my sight loss and understood some of the treatment process. He connected me to the most well-recommended neurologist he could determine for my situation, Dr. James Russell at the Lahey Clinic in Burlington Massachusetts.

One of Dr. Russell's first actions was to put me back on the Solu-medrol dosages which were thought to have previously halted the deterioration of my optic nerves. Within a few weeks the worsening of my balance seemed to halt, followed by a very slight improvement. We didn't expect nerves which had died to rejuvenate but those that were damaged may have recovered to allow for the slight improvement. I was still severely vertiginous and restricted to the wheelchair, but it was a real positive step.

When I was losing vision, it was easy to discern if my nerves were experiencing deterioration, as the inflammation to the optic nerve was visible by looking through the pupil with magnification. This is a simple, non-invasive examination in the doctor's office. We now had reason to suspect my condition could attack other nerves within my body and it would be much more difficult to locate those or determine if they were actively declining.

Some initial reports from MRI studies of my brain suggested there may have been damage to my cerebellum, a balance center, which could explain my most recent challenge. Ultimately my overall condition eluded any specific diagnosis. It seemed similar to Multiple Sclerosis, although as the results were explained to me, my brain scan showed just a few bright spots of high impact, whereas an MS patient would have thousands. As all tests for MS were negative, Dr. Russell provided a diagnosis of mitochondrial disease. He told me frankly this was not conclusive, but rather the most likely scenario by process of elimination of other relevant maladies. Dr. Russell shared that this diagnosis presently offered no possible treatments. Although I had harbored some hopes for a treatment, this news was unsurprising, but the news which staggered me was his pronouncement that I would likely spend the rest of my life in a wheelchair.

Despite the uncertainty I was prepared to start moving forward, but I had a heart wrenching task ahead. I have long held tremendous appreciation and admiration for the puppy raisers who provide the love, support and training for the first 16 months of a guide dog's life. I join with the many who doubt they have would have strength to give up a puppy they've raised even knowing the tremendous work ahead for their dog. Now I felt faced with the need to make a similar choice. Ostend and I had just celebrated our fourth anniversary together but I was no longer working him and it seemed likely this would be my future.

I needed to call his school and tell them, so that someone else who might need his incredible ability to work could have him. The problem was I wanted him beside me as much as I've wanted anything in my life. I kept reminding myself his puppy raiser, Doreen, had made this sacrifice for me and I did not want to disrespect her kindness, generosity and selflessness. I picked up the phone every day for a week without being able to fully dial the number. Our bond had grown so close with all the wonders we experienced and all the challenges we endured, how could I possibly send him away?

I reminded myself constantly that Doreen had found this strength without even knowing who would receive the gift of her beloved Ostend. I had to find the wherewithal to honor her gift and his work. On my fifth day of trying my resolve finally held long enough to connect to the Guide School and tell them what was happening. I almost hung up as they transferred me. Ostend waited with me, head upon my lap, clearly aware of the grief painfully surging within me. I explained I was calling because I did not want to be selfish keeping Ostend when I could not use his guide work while someone else could. My exclamations of joy, "Yes, I will! Yes, I will!" and litany of "thank you, thank you, thank you!" could not be over quickly enough for me to hang up, drop to the floor and just hold my boy as I told him the good news. Ostend was 6 years old and considered too old for a retrain. If he could not work for me, he would retire, and I would have the first option to keep him if I wanted. Every single time I thank a puppy raiser for their choice I remind myself of how difficult it was for me to make that call and I celebrate the hero I consider them.

Buoyed by this great news, I set about trying to solve a host of new challenges in my life. My skill at everyday activities was insufficient for the combined challenge of blindness and my mobility impairment. Making matters worse, my home was not wheelchair accessible. Literally forced to my knees to accomplish the simplest of tasks, I finally realized I needed to swallow my pride and seek the help necessary to truly move forward. This is when my friend Bren moved into my house to help with Ostend's care and support some of the immediate challenges as I began to problem solve.

Bren had the summer fully free to help before she returned to school and this provided the start I needed. I had lived alone for quite a few years and all of the time since becoming totally blind. This was a loss of independence, but it was also the addition of a great friendship during a very challenging time. She immediately formed a bond with Ostend and I took great comfort in knowing he was getting some of the additional exercise which I hadn't been able to provide. With her support and encouragement, I put my energy into three primary pursuits; I tried to find ways to live life as typically as I had before the wheelchair, I attempted to resolve all the challenges I was experiencing with the chair, and I began to explore solutions for getting back on my feet somehow.

My pursuit of a typical life might have seemed unrealistic were it not for my incredible community of friends. There were certainly some who did not visit or engage as much during this time, but the vast majority found ways to help me wrestle my chair to all the experiences we envisioned. Bren was foremost in those despite having returned for her Master's program on Long Island, New York. She made frequent weekend trips to NH as we began to see each other romantically. In her absence from the home, two friends moved in to help support daily routines which were still difficult with my wheelchair. Jennifer Kett and Brent Walton each took a guest room and split fewer tasks, ensuring that I felt a continuation of my growing return to independence.

Many different friends ensured that I still attended every Patriot game. We did switch to the wheelchair section for the most part but there were times my incredible friends had to push me through snowbanks to reach the stadium and through areas not designed for, or respectful of, wheelchair travel. I attended a Jimmy Buffett concert at Fenway Park where a broken subway lift system followed by three cab refusals resulted in my friends recruiting strangers to help carry me and my chair down several flights of stairs to get home.

Pictured: Randy at a tailgate for a Patriots game against the 49ers

I often had to wrestle with my own humiliation as well as anger at the injustice of my situation. What made it easier was my overwhelming appreciation for the eager, caring so prevalent amongst my friends. Even the times I had to calm them from angry responses to some likely unintended impropriety by a stranger, it was clear to me I was fortunate to have people who value our friendship so deeply. It was, however, astounding to discover how many places had doorways too narrow for my chair, no bathroom accessibility or an entrance process which was at best humiliating, such as the ride in the trash elevator for one restaurant. Strangely, people presumed exceedingly negative things of my abilities, often choosing to talk to those with me about me rather than engage me, even once I demonstrated I could talk for myself quite normally.

This certainly took a toll on me, but I heard how much more strongly it affected my friends. The salient part of this time of my life involved the vast majority of my friends continuing to invite me and help me integrate despite it being harder for them. While it was limiting at times, for all of us and often frustrating, as we encountered accessibility blocks beyond what my blindness had ever provided me. Every trip in or out of the house was a crawling challenge with a wheelchair carry until Habitat for Humanity spent an afternoon building a wheelchair ramp for my home. I was touched by the kindness and generosity of the volunteers and organization. I was elated for the freedom the ramp would provide in allowing me to leave my home under my own power. I was, however, deeply disturbed by the permanence the ramp symbolized. I was determined to work through the most awkward parts while developing better solutions to hopefully feel like less of a burden.

Each trip out was necessarily without Ostend as he was no longer my Service Animal. Many people leave their dogs as part of the natural course of their life activities but my bond with Ostend was based on being together every moment of every day. He didn't like being apart from me and I felt less complete without my guide partner. In working towards independent travel with the wheelchair, I continued to find using my legs from the seated position allowed a slow rolling walk. I could hold a cane in my hand and sweep for objects with a modified approach and some mitigated success. This led me to wonder "Would it be possible with a dog guide?" Ostend certainly wanted to be in a heel position and to leash lead me if I gave him even a bit of allowance, but I had to be worried for his paw safety.

Michelle Pouliot at Guide Dogs for the Blind was developing just such a program, and we spoke a few times about the process. Encouraged by her words, I began to slowly expand some of the work Ostend and I did just around my home, yard and on bicycle paths with the accompaniment of friends. We had a few months of incredibly exciting work together and the momentum was the most uplifting progress of my time trapped in the wheelchair. Encouraged by the growing positive experience, I ordered a new harness as I'd sent his official guide harness back to the school. Tragically, I was never fully able to explore the possibilities of this approach with him. My loss of Ostend intervened, as I've painfully shared already.

That setback almost broke my determination. When the harness arrived a few weeks after his death it taunted me more cruelly still. Yet the memory of Ostend's eager enthusiasm to encourage me to move ever onward with our wheelchair work was ultimately one of my biggest motivations. I simply refused to dishonor his love and determination for us to stride forward by quitting on him or myself.

I began to use my cane in conjunction with a variety of solutions such as an electronic proximity detector which sounded an alert when I approached obstacles in the chair. The hardest part was that with any rolling I could easily become disoriented, and the significant remaining vertigo only exacerbated my confusion. I also struggled to use my legs to pull myself up any incline and needed to turn backwards to push up these, which made it impractical to get the cane ahead of me. It was slow and limiting and with inherent risks as well. The possibility of using a power wheelchair was met with significant safety and liability concerns from the manufacturers. In short, my progress, after a hopeful start, was not particularly promising.

Fortunately, I was reaching out online for ways to get out of the wheelchair. My doctors were similarly exploring every opportunity for me, and we eventually connected with Dr. Peter Catalano, an Otolaryngologist based out of the Lahey Clinic in Burlington, MA. He was working on an experimental treatment process for balance challenges called transtympanic injections. Effectively boosting the balance signal to my brain through a steroidal dose to the inner ear. We find our balance from three different and significant methods. First, the visual horizon which for me was not available, second, proprioception which is our connection to the ground and third, vestibular as provided by our inner ear via the semi-circular canals. I was admitted to this program, which involved six separate transtympanic procedures, three for each ear. There were six weeks of intense physical therapy between each procedure and I was connected with Joann Moriarty-Baron, an innovative therapist with an expertise in neurological balance issues.

The results were incredible. By the second procedure I was frequently using Lofstrand crutches for a limited walk. Basically, these extend forward and provide two additional supports, almost replicating a four-legged walk. My balance was improving but not enough to stand safely. Practice makes progress though, and the more I could expose my brain to simulations closer to my goal the more I would likely learn. Short steps became longer steps and I pushed myself every day. By the third procedure I could use the Lofstrand crutch in a sweeping gesture much like a blind cane, allowing me to expand my walking range. With practice and eventual doctor's approval I was able to use my "four legged" Lofstrand approach to walk down my wheelchair ramp, down the driveway to the mailbox and back. It was exhausting, mostly mentally, but accomplishing such a simple task as getting my mail on my own filled me to bursting with pride and hope.

My next significant step was to a three-legged approach and Joann experimented with quad-canes and an assortment of options before her creativity and willingness to think outside the box changed my life. She suggested we try a hiking pole! It was sturdy enough to handle my leaning weight, light-weight enough for easy manipulation and designed with the possibility of a healthier, longer stride which was our goal for me. It was not a smooth transition but as the transtympanic procedures were completed and my vertigo reduced significantly, I began to have enough equilibrium to work with the hiking stick to keep or catch my balance. I still spent most of my time in the wheelchair but as often as I could manage I would practice walking drills to improve my strength, stamina and balance with this new technique. As February 2006 provided roads clear of snow and ice, I set to walking up and down my street with the hiking stick in my right hand and my blind cane in my left hand. It didn't matter to me that February was the shortest month of the year, I set my sights on being free of the wheelchair before the month was over. It was my goal, my mountain, my mission to complete a journey which every reasonable expectation suggested would not be possible.

On February 28, one year, eight months and twenty-one days after first being relegated to it, I rose for the last time from the wheelchair! I walked out my front door and circumnavigated a full block of my neighborhood. I returned home and sat on the couch, weary and proud. I celebrated for sure, but already there was a new goal in my mind. If I could walk, albeit with a hiking stick, would it be possible for me to get a dog guide again?

A Colebrook Boy at Heart

"The Child is father of the Man" William Wordsworth

Sprawling on the early spring grass of my backyard for the first time in a long time, I marveled at the feel of the sun on my face. I breathed in deeply, savoring the earthy soil aroma surrounding me as I listened to the birds chastising me for intruding on their lawn. Undaunted by their determined chatter, I stretched and luxuriated in my yard. They could take refuge in the two trees which arched over me because I was reclaiming the lawn as my own. It had been too rare a treat for me to work my way back here when I was bound to the wheelchair and I was reveling in my return to this place of serene reflection.

There was a soothing comfort in the cool rigid metal resting in my hands. I ever so gently held my hiking stick across my lap, allowing my fingers to trace its outline, the connection points, the rigid grip and the rubber-capped tip which could bite into the ground for a more solid connection to the earth. I used my hands to see for me, my mind building an image of this wonderful tool which had

121

been the final piece in stepping away from the wheelchair. A hiking stick. What a strange hiker I made with my still vertiginously awkward gait. I thought back through my hiking history from the woods behind my childhood home in Nashua, to the very real mountains explored in Colebrook.

Although I didn't use a hiking stick back in my youth I certainly enjoyed many a grand hiking adventure as a young boy in our town nestled at the base of the lesser known and yet quite majestic Monadnock. I recall how drastically different a world it seemed to me as we moved from the civilization of Nashua to the seeming edge-of-the-map wilderness which Colebrook represented to my ten-year-old imagination. "Beyond here there be Sea Monsters" is scribed to mark the edge of old maps. "Beyond here there be Mountains" is how I thought of everything north of the towering cliffs of Franconia notch. It was wilderness and woods at a different level. My drive to explore and adventure in them did nothing to reduce my deep awe and wonder.

It was 1976 when we moved into a small house in a collection of four homes just south of Colebrook in the village of Columbia, NH. Columbia was too small for a school or post office, so we travelled the six miles into Colebrook for all our needs. Living in such a rural environment, Mom, Dad, Rick and I came together by need. Everything was new and different including all of the people. We had our first woodstove and learned all the responsibilities and family chores which come from supplemental wood heat. I had my own bedroom for the first time, and yet we gathered together for Mom's cherished family time more frequently as there were fewer outside distractions.

The nearby families had children younger than I, though near enough to my age. I was accustomed to older companions and though my new neighbors became my friends Rick transcended our age difference becoming my best friend of all. When he wasn't studiously attending his homework or music lessons we'd explore the nearby fields, a pair of abandoned foundations and beyond. I was required to stay with him for any deeper exploration out of line of sight of our home, which was a change from the rules I'd known in Nashua. Instead of feeling restricted by this, I reveled in the company and imagination of my brother and our explorations. The woods began immediately behind our home and no trails seemed to break their wildness. If we travelled deeply enough into them, the

Connecticut River made a boundary, but one with more warnings of peril than my prior, friendlier, woods.

It was a boundary I explored many an evening as my Dad and I took the opportunity to bond over one of his primary passions: fishing. As many evenings as possible we would rush through chores and an early dinner to take our gear and hike down the embankment, through the woods and ultimately to varying resting places along the banks of this isolated river. We'd sit for hours trout fishing as the sun set and sometimes even later by the light of a Coleman lantern. I loved these moments not because of the fishing, though I was as excited as most ten-year-old boys I suppose. It was this new treat of extended time with my Dad. He'd tell stories or share his ideas for innovation and invention. He had a bit of the strategic mind and while it was usually pitted, often in defeat, against the mighty river trout; frequently it inspired the problem solver also budding within me. We wanted to catch the low feeding Brown Trout but not the bottom feeding suckers. We developed innovative fishing gear from corks and other items to lift our bait out of the muck. We made many experiments with different materials and approaches and I loved the time.

Pictured: Randy proudly displays fish he caught in Colebrook, 1978.

We also began our first quality sports talk. Sometimes we'd listen to the Red Sox together, but he also humored my newfound interest in football and the New England Patriots. One of the wisdoms he shared was especially true in our two-television-station reality of northern NH but had wider ramifications He said, "I choose the hometown team partly because it is who I'm going to be able to see on TV and hear on the radio so much more often than any other team. I also do it because loyalty has its own rewards in knowing all of the fun history because you are a part of it." How true those words would prove in my life!

Late night fishing sometimes made for difficult school mornings. There was one school bus for all the grade levels and so Rick and I rode the bus together every day. I marvel to think how my Junior in High School brother could be so patient with fifth grade me, but Rick was incredible during these times. I felt like he always wanted to sit with me and talk about the wide assortment of interests my overly enthusiastic and flighty immaturity encouraged. I never felt like a burden and my admiration for him grew steadily during these years. He was unquestionably my very first role model and my hero.

While I didn't want to do the amount of homework Rick did on his way to being Salutatorian, nor did I want to emulate the rigor and intensity he brought to his flute playing, I did want to emulate my big brother for being smart, funny, quick witted and mature. Perhaps I didn't understand the word mature but he did things adults did and so I wanted to understand and try them, hopefully skipping the boring parts, though if he liked them maybe they there was a secret to make them less boring. In that regard, because of his creative imagination, time with him was never boring, just all too short for me.

At school I had found a couple of significant advantages which would make a marked difference in my being accepted into Colebrook. At fifth grade we had the start of music training and I was ahead of the curve because I had been taking drum lessons for a couple of years in Nashua. This let me take an early lead in the percussion section. A similar benefit came from Nashua providing several earlier years of organized basketball league, so as Colebrook began their program I was again quick to take a leadership role. This helped me receive acceptance although not without some conflict as the new kid in town. There were many cultural shortcomings which alienated me: many times, social rank at fifth grade was established by quick fist fights. More often than not it was the posturing and threat of these, but it took a bloody nose or two along the way with a pretty even split between who had their nose realigned, me or my classmate. As fifth grade wound to a close I had been reasonably accepted and it felt like home for me.

The transition had been particularly difficult for my parents. Finding work was always a challenge and opportunities were more likely to go to locally known connections first. Our moderate finances were depleting and in April my Mom convinced my Dad to take us on our first epic family vacation. She feared, accurately, that it might never be possible again and wanted something rewarding to counteract the struggle of our first hard winter in the north. We went to the Magic Kingdom, Disney World. As a family who spent every Sunday evening watching "The Wonderful World of Disney" together, this was an idyllic vacation. Space Mountain opened that year and I remember riding in my Dad's arms with my brother ahead of us as the rumble of the car shook us through blast off and into a solar system which thrilled and terrified me.

Rick and I received permission to go to the park together as long as I never left his side, and I remember stepping up to the elevator with him, getting on and pushing the button to start our journey. He jumped out at the last-minute calling "Ha!" and I could not stop the door from closing. I had a moment of panic as I'd now broken my parents' rules even though it wasn't my fault. When the door opened Rick wasn't there of course, so I pushed back for our starting floor and to my disappointment he wasn't where I'd left him either. Head bowed I stepped out and did the slow walk of fear back to our hotel room. This was precisely one of those instances where Rick's cherubic reputation and my less than stellar track record would result in my being grounded.

I knocked on the door and tried to explain, but my parents confirmed my expectations of punishment even before Rick arrived. Having desperately tried to reach me by stairs and failing twice, he opted to blame it on me. I could only hold the grudge for 40 years or so, but it was vastly mitigated as he also lobbied to get me out of trouble and spent the rest of our week doing things to make it extra fun for me such as riding the Haunted Mansion and Pirates of the Caribbean as many times as I wanted. The overall trip was a grand adventure though I had designs to trade Space Mountain in for another mountain which had captured my imagination for almost a year.

On a warm June morning in 1977 the not-so-intrepid Pierce family set forth to climb Mt. Monadnock in Lemington, VT. This name likely comes from the Abenaki tribe and their word, menadenak, meaning isolated mountain. Mt. Monadnock looms over Colebrook from the west. It was our first summer in our new northern home and whether in part due to my beleaguered parents surrendering to my incessant encouragement or my Mother's hope for an epic family outing; we set forth with the barest of preparations.

The frequent drive from our home in Columbia into the town of Colebrook was entirely in view of this majestically isolated mountain. An old fire tower was often visible from a distance and teased an additional reward for those able to summit the 3,148-foot peak. Though it had dominated our horizon, overshadowing the town, we had not learned very much about the mountain or the hiking trail we would need. We heard that a tricky point was to cross the stream and follow the trail on the other side.

Barely a two-minute drive from the center of Colebrook, we parked our Ford Bronco and started up the obvious dirt path. Almost immediately it reached a tiny stream which I leapt with the boundless energy of my first real mountain hike. Mom was barely able to call me back from race desire to race ahead and leap up every rock step. Begrudgingly I kept within the sound of her voice and found the balance between the wild freedom of exploring eagerly and the recalcitrant heeding of each reminder that I'd overstepped my boundaries. I did surge back to my family to share discoveries; news of an exciting rock formation just ahead, or a deep gorge with a new and more serious sounding stream. Ultimately, after a couple of hours we came to a series of flat rocks by the stream which was perfect for having our lunch together. We failed to realize this was actually the important and tricky stream crossing.

With lunch complete and many stories half fabricated of the brave adventure, we set out along the seeming trail on this side of the stream. Before too long I was still ahead but struggling to discern trail, game track or bushwhack. It is here where my Dad's experience as a hunter took over and we followed the ridge lines of the mountain while casting towards the lost trail occasionally. We knew we had lost our way, but Dad was confident he could navigate to the summit and find the fire tower. Being smallest I scurried through the brush and branches but closer than before until another hiker joined us, also having lost the trail at the crossing but confirming that was where we all likely went wrong. He was hiking faster than our group and I was trying to hold the lead and, in my exuberance, I managed to outdistance the calls of my family and was soon lost to them. Fortunately, our new friend realized my blunder and helped me circle back to reconnect and mitigate the understandably fearful and angry initial reaction of my parents.

It had been several hours since we first lost the trail, but finally we were close enough to the summit that the trees had become mostly softwood. Dad and I climbed trees high enough to look over the tops of the other trees, find the fire tower and work our way steadily towards it. As we came to an old rotting and decrepit ranger cabin, I was astounded by the sudden feeling of ancient forest. It felt as if man had tried to come here and been turned back violently by the forces of nature. Weary from the climb, unnerved from having lost my parents and finding this different scene was shocking to me. We had our trail though and took it to the tower where I became fully fearful. Many of the steps of the tower were missing and the metal frame while solid enough, seemed to make many strange noises in the strong summer breeze. I made it up a few landings but as I cleared the height of the trees I could not muster the courage to climb higher. Rick and Dad, to my shame, went all the way up to the top shouting down in appreciation of the amazing views. Even my Mom went up to the top, but I had met my match and wanted no part of climbing any higher on that tower...on that day. We gathered again at the base of the tower and took the much easier trail back down to our missed stream crossing. Boyhood jubilation returned to my step along the way even as physical weariness began to get the better of me. I let go of the fright which had limited me atop the mountain and appreciated that my family had come together and reached a peak. Soon I would learn of another sort of mountain facing my family which would intrude on all of our lives.

I heard the fragments of a dark and secret series of conversations which began with a phone call one fateful evening that same summer. My parents tried to keep most of their difficulties from us, but this was something different. Rick and I conspired to try and understand what was happening but it wasn't until they sat us down to awkwardly explain that I learned the words I wouldn't really understand for several years. My 21-year-old brother Dan was gay and apparently for my parents, members of a much older generation, this was a very bad thing. Compounding this news was the manner in which my parents learned of it. Our neighbor's children, my friends, found their father in bed with my brother. Their mother made the emotional call informing my parents and seeking a resolution which, ultimately, was not found. I understood the extreme emotions but not the meaning behind much of this revelation. Suffice it to say a world of misconceptions and a generally uninformed era left my parents feeling they had failed a second consecutive child, while infusing me with some of their strong beliefs about the causes and propriety of homosexuality. I would take many years to achieve healthier perspectives on all forms of diversity. Due to the shame they felt my parents attempted to hide the news from everyone.

I was confused and disheartened observing the intensity of the rare but awkward interactions between Dan and my parents. Even their discussions about Dan unpleasantly dominated mom and dad's conversations. All of this was another burden on my parents and the proverbial straws were mounting upon the camel's back.

Pictured: A visit with Dan, 1978
L-R Bud, Dan, Randy, Rick

128

The next winter brought the infamous blizzard of 1978. It was a difficult year for my parents though I continued to thrive in school. Rick graduated second in his class and was heading to college in the fall, the first of our family to do so. Employment challenges encouraged my parents to make the second move of my life. We moved into a home near the center of Colebrook to allow our single car family easier travel to work opportunities. The old Colonial was older, cheaper, and also purportedly haunted by a prior owner. It had a finished main floor, but the upper floor and attic were entirely gutted and made many noises to augment the rumors of a haunting. I had a small room apart from the rest of the family and so by necessity set to work on my fear of the dark! I did so with curiosity and the occasional foray upstairs to find the source of a noise despite a pounding heart.

Rick had a larger room with enough space for an old second-hand upright piano which would bring us even closer that summer. Nearly every evening he played, and I sang from songbook after songbook. He would patiently guide me as he worked on his own performance and I simply adored time with my soon to be departing older brother. He even composed a few of his own songs with lyrics written by my cousin Scott. Several of those I can still sing today.

When Rick was at work or busy with his own social life I began enjoying the freedom of living in town, closer to more of the many friends I made in the few years in Colebrook. We took bicycle trips to the beautiful Beaver Brook Waterfall for picnic lunches. To my delight I could walk from our home to Mt. Monadnock in less than five minutes. I climbed the mountain dozens of times, including the tower which had bested me on my first attempt. On my second attempt of the tower my legs were shaking as by sheer force of will, I forced myself to take each of those early steps. I found the fear was greater in my memory than in the actual moment. Still, I was nervous, and my friends were watching. So, in one of my earliest memories of overcoming obstacles, I climbed above tree-line hesitant to allow my friends to see my fear. As the beautiful mountain view unfurled I was invigorated to rush the rest of the way to the top celebrating my success.

One particularly grand adventure involved a determined search for the rumored lost gold mine of Mt. Monadnock. My friend, Lee Brooks and I spent several weeks in which we climbed the mountain nearly every day after having found a hidden trail behind a meadow.

We suspected it must be there for a reason and when the trail petered out into game trails we started hiking ever growing concentric circles. It was a jubilant moment to find a boulder, broken on the back side and scarred by the signs of many long-ago campfires. We knew we were close. Looking up the steep slope behind the long-forgotten campsite we noticed a narrow scree filled crevice which seemed like the only possible way to continue from this point. With a bit of difficulty, we scrambled our way up roughly 50' to a small ledge, finally finding the old mine tunnel confirming our place as explorers, at least in our own minds. The gold turned out to be iron pyrite, fool's gold, but we hauled out our treasure as rich as kings in our victory.

Living in town it was now easier for me to be involved in more activities, and I was soon exploring scouts and drama as well as the sports and music which had been a part of my regular activities. My friendships deepened more than ever before. Perhaps with Rick gone I needed to reach out and perhaps living in town made it easier, but I had a core group and several close friends including Dana Nugent and his family. Although he was a couple of years younger than me, he was very athletic and equally adventurous. His family could not have been more kind to me almost making me feel like an adopted son. We spent many adventures at their camp on Diamond Pond or various country trips, but I especially recall how often, kindly and thoroughly they welcomed me at meal times. I had quite a reputation at their home for being able to eat any and all leftovers! Sadly, part of the reason for this is that while I was thriving in many ways, my parents now struggled more than ever.

Money was extremely tight, and meals became leaner than we ever chose to tell anyone outside of our home. The Fuel Assistance program enabled us to have assurance of some heat but there were many evenings with little or no heat and desperation grew enough my parents could not shelter me from it. I had a job working to clean the church and mow the cemetery but most of what I earned went to help with our meals. This was hardest on my mom and her health suffered from the cold coupled with the heartache of our destitute life. To make matters worse, our beloved family pet, Puppy, was aging poorly and had to be euthanized. She was always my Mom's dog though she had been a part of the family for my entire life. I was not there when the veterinarian came to our home, in part for lack of full appreciation of the finality and in part for my selfish desires to be out with friends. Puppy was not my dog, but she had watched over me from the cradle through my teens. The loss of Puppy saddened me but when I came home and saw how it had devastated my Mom, I understood a little more of the poor choice I had made.

Overwhelmed and seeking answers, our family left the Catholic church which was a lifelong source of comfort and generations of family tradition for my mom. Introduced to the radically different approach of the evangelical faith by her sister Rachel and brother Larry, my Mom found hope in a new approach. It was hope for change in our financial downward spiral, her feelings of isolation and with many aspects of my brother Dan's tumultuous life. We joined the Assembly of God church and found a small, close knit, highly supportive community.

The abundance of change and uncertainty occurred at a tremendously influential age for me. Emotionally, it was a time of high confusion spawned as much by my hormones as the overwhelming challenges my family was facing. Although I was an altar boy before, our new faith advocated a more outspoken approach to religion. With considerable good intent but insufficient judgement or social grace I tried to "spread the word". Following the guidance of our new church emphatically was to my social detriment. This approach marked my first real taste of ridicule and persecution. As a result, several of my friendships were tested and my eighth grade seemed more challenging than any year prior for me. Despite the fellowship's comfort and encouragement as well as my successful completion of Junior High School, my parents made a difficult decision. Without enough work to sustain us in Colebrook we sold the house and moved back to Nashua even though it meant we would no longer be home owners, for the first time in my life we would rent an apartment.

The summer of 1980 began very hot and humid. The shabby apartment on Gilman Street exacerbated the oppressive conditions. Our morale was low, and bickering was commonplace. This deepened the divide in my parents' marriage. Their relation did not last the summer and my dad returned to Colebrook on his own. Mom and I had the apartment and no car, but she had a factory job which she used in part to pay my tuition at Bishop Guertin High School in Nashua. As a college preparatory school, she hoped it would help propel me to a better future but the overall challenge in our lives was excessive for such a goal. I did well, having excellent grades and adhering to the elevated behavior borne of our evangelical faith until one of the most influential moments of my young life arrived.

We made weekly visits to my Aunt Rachel's home in Nashua where I played basketball out back with cousin George. Mom visited with her siblings Larry and Rachel. They discussed the many difficult aspects of life for all of them with the backdrop of their newfound evangelical fervor. The problem on this early October evening was that money was missing from my Aunt's home and they had found marijuana hidden in their house. My Aunt and Uncle had prayed for guidance and believed they received God's message that I was the culprit. Faced with this information my Mom prayed similarly and came away with the same belief. They confronted me with the accusation in their living room and my world fell out from beneath me.

I knew I hadn't done anything of the sort although I did know that George was smoking pot. What I realized is that these three people who were previously so influential in my spiritual guidance were now telling me they had been directed by God that I was guilty. Something was clearly very wrong with their guidance. A more mature and rational version of myself might have managed this conversation very differently. I was confused, angry and fourteen years old. After a harsh shouting match, I walked out with no idea where to go or what to do with myself. I crossed Nashua as the darkness descended.

Near the highway I decided to call my Dad with the idea that while Mom had always been nurturing and compassionate, she was no longer being fair or reasonable and Dad seemed likely to be fairer to me. I stepped up to the first public place which was, as I learned, a bar. A caring patron saw the tears and asked what I needed as I approached the door hoping to make a phone call. A handful of donated coins later and I was talking from a payphone with my Father who made me promise to return home to my mother that night. He in return committed to come down that weekend to sort things out between mom and I, and if necessary to move me north.

That week with my mother was one of the worst of my life. She launched a barrage of escalating accusations against me every single day. My frustrated denials grew ever angrier and she used this behavior as proof of my guilt. I said my own cruel and inappropriate things in response which worsened the rift between us. She struggled the most with my rebellion against her faith. This entire ordeal shattered my trust in the delivery of God's message. This issue was too significant for any immediate resolution - it caused ripples of influence forever forward in my life. It took me years to cultivate a higher comfort with my spirituality which became a deeply personal pursuit with extreme mistrust of others' intrusion on that journey. As a result, Mom would always be most sad that we did not share the same expression of faith. In the more immediate moment it took forever for the weekend and dad to finally arrive.

Dad was as reasonable and fair as I hoped. The family talk clearly showed him that the situation was untenable. He kept his word and on that weekend, I moved out of Nashua and back to Colebrook. Technically I moved back to Columbia as we stayed at the farm owned by Jackie Cass out in the very remote Bungy Mountain region. It was on a dirt road with only a shared party phone line possible. It was also a tremendous inconvenience for both Jackie and Dad to bring me into her home and yet my Dad made the choice seemingly without hesitation. This was an abrupt change to an entirely different and more rustic way of life. I came to really appreciate the remote location. There was so much new and exciting land and a barn to explore. Our kitchen table overlooked a meadow often graced with morning deer and always highlighted by a range of beautiful mountains. Jackie worked as a cook, so meals were plentiful which suited my eager appetite.

I thrived on the chores, especially splitting and stacking wood. My daily duties were a vital part of the functioning of our home, leading to a shift in responsibility which helped me feel more mature. This was mitigated by the boyish joy I had from the litter of puppies which our dog Tippy provided. These mongrel Beagle pups were largely my responsibility and a marvelous outlet for fun. They followed me everywhere and one of the purest moments of joyous delight came from the sledding hill beside our home. I would hike up the hill with my sled, lay on my stomach as the line of pups all climbed atop me for the ride down the hill. At every bump or turn another pup would slip off and tumble into yapping pursuit as we sped away. The same two clever pups, Regal and Jake would always bite onto my collar and make it to the bottom. In so doing they earned their way into my top choices to stay as the others each slowly found other homes.

I also welcomed the reunion with my school friends lost for all of a summer and part of our freshman year. I was back into basketball and determined to increase my ability there tremendously. My prior year had ended with a broken ankle and a sportsmanship award at which our coach, praised my talents as the essential point guard and ball handler for the team while inadvertently raising my awareness to the fact I was the slowest member of the team. I had not realized I was so very slow until he called me out with well-intentioned words: "For the slowest guy on the team, it was incredible how much we struggled to get the ball up the court without him." From the time the cast had been removed I'd begun to study running and pushed myself to be quicker and faster. Since I previously allowed my basketball skills to carry me and not pushed my speed I arrived on the junior varsity team determined to focus on speed and skills steadily. I found quick success and was invited to join the varsity team as a freshman though my father determined that would not be allowed due to the heavier pressure on my schedule. He was probably correct though I didn't want to admit it.

Where I was not challenging myself particularly hard was at academics, I was cruising with as little work as possible, so I could just enjoy myself. I had rebelled from the good behavior of my prior few years and made some reckless choices of which I am not proud. One particularly painful example involved my secret fortress. I scouted half a mile into the deep woods and found a grove of pine trees just below a small ridge line. I carried scrap wood from the barn and built a treehouse in a trio of these trees. During the construction I managed to be sufficiently sloppy as to fall from a board I had not yet finished nailing. I recalled hoping for moments I might hit a branch until I hit that first branch and then desperately hoping the ground would be next. It was incredibly lucky that soft needles and dirt, as well as, that one painful branch broke my fall enough to leave me without serious injury. It was a slow humble hobble home that evening. There were worse decisions for certain, though none of them did me permanent harm academically or physically.

There was procrastination and an attitude of nonchalance in my letter writing to my Mother. Perhaps as a result of some of my choices or just from the difficulty of the situation overall, my Mother wrote me one of the toughest letters I ever received during this time period. She told me it was too hard having me remote from her and that each letter hurt tremendously and so she needed to cut off all contact with me. She was moving and would not tell me her new address and did not want me to try and find her. I was devastated. I felt the weight of responsibility for some part of this awful situation. I didn't like the part of growing up which meant understanding the consequences of my actions, especially when their seemed to be no right choice.

I took a lot of introspective time in the peaceful solitude of the woods which surrounded me out on the Cass farm. I'd learned a bit of rugged independence out there and Mom's decision put that to the test. Several months later she recanted but through the process I had grown more willfully independent. I eagerly welcomed the return of contact with her even though a part of "her boy" had matured in a way from which I could not return. We had a few years separated while Dad and I lived on the farm. During this time, I learned to use a chain saw, drive a car, make maple syrup, ride motorcycles, and handle a snow machine while often working on the Harold Perry farm.

To my discredit I created a mostly unintentional wedge between my Dad and Jackie. To resolve the tensions, he moved us out of the farm and into a place in downtown Colebrook. We were not there long when my mom noticed the opportunity this presented. My Mom's desire to be with me was so great she chose another tremendous sacrifice and my parents reunited with her moving back to Colebrook. Finances were still very tight, and we soon moved to a smaller and cheaper place in Columbia, barely large enough for our belongings. We made it until just after Christmas when my parents, both without work, moved back to Nashua. This time to help me keep some stability, they arranged for me to stay with the Nugents to finish out my Junior year at Colebrook. It was a strange experience to live without both of my parents and I returned to my most exemplary behavior in large part to appreciate the kindness and generosity of Gail and Peter Nugent. My presence was a significant change in the lifestyle of the three sons, Dana, Marc and Scott but they never once made me feel anything other than a welcomed member of the family.

I had come to appreciate my teachers so much more during my high school years. I had previously appreciated David Killiam, our elementary and Jr. High Music teacher who brought so much more thoughtful consideration beyond the music. I remember his mock trial in which I had been selected to be a defense lawyer and encouraged to advance my debating approach. While many people over the years may regret his encouragement, I appreciate the early guidance tremendously.

Richard Bond had been a social studies teacher who held me accountable for an early lie which I sustained for several weeks regarding my part of our class project due to my sheer procrastination. His efforts helped build a better integrity against both the dishonesty and delaying tactics which did me such a disservice. Mrs. Maxwell gave me my first superlative for most emotional delivery ever for my recitation of the Gettysburg Address.

It was, however, high school English and the incredible William Schaumberg who ignited my passion for meaningful reading, philosophy, critical thinking and independent mindfulness. Whatever zany antics he needed to reach his students were common practice in his class and if I didn't know better I'd have surmised Robin Williams used him as the model for many of his roles, most notably as John Keating in Dead Poet's Society. Talking to his tie when intelligent life in the room went vapid or climbing on his desk to shout his barbaric yop were some of his eccentricities to reach us. Thanks to his style, I can still recite several Shakespearean soliloquies, Aristotle's definition of tragedy and William Cullen Bryant's Thanatopsis "To him who in the love of nature holds communion with her visible forms, she speaks a various language." I too speak a more varied language for the powerful and positive influence of Colebrook Academy on my education and life.

Yearbooks released and the class of 1983, filled with many of my cherished friends, was graduating and departing. All those signatures of farewell and goodbye would ultimately apply to me as well. For me, the school year's sullen surrender to summer brought my move back again to Nashua with the vague hope I might return in September to finish my senior year. It was not to be, despite an incredibly earnest effort by my parents and me. We sought out every possibility to avoid my transferring for my final year including a potential stay at a boarding home, the Colebrook House. This final chance ended when a car accident in August depleted my summer savings too much to afford a return to Colebrook on my own.

My Colebrook days had officially ended, though with a remarkably positive influence on my life. In small towns it is possible to be involved in so many activities and I had rounded my skills tremendously. I was graced with some of the finest teachers who challenged me not just to learn but to think with equal fervor. I learned to meet new people and develop friendships multiple times through our numerous moves. An aspect of adaptability became essential in those moves as well as appreciation for the diversity I encountered. I touched an older way of life, a simpler and quieter life while having opportunities to build my independence. I was not quite an adult, but my boyhood was past. It was a story-laden past for certain in the many tales shared here and not, it is clear to me that I will always be a Colebrook boy at heart.

Pictured: Randy playing basketball in 1978

Coming of Age

"It's a tough world to find yourself in, but an even tougher one to be yourself in." Chris Colfer

The summer of 1983 involved the hardest physical work of my young life. My dad found a job for the two of us cutting trees, splitting and delivering cord wood all over southern NH. We were in the woods for first light and home after the sun set most days, but the money was good, and we spent most of the time together. I was living with my mom and dad in a small apartment on Fletcher Street in Nashua in the hope that my earnings might enable me to return to Colebrook for my final year of high school. The independence I'd gained from living without them made some of our interactions difficult, but the long hours and exhausting work generally smoothed over the rougher edges. So, did morning coffee with dad.

We owned one thermos and he liked his coffee black with extra sugar, so I learned to drink coffee and to drink it the way he liked it. We'd pass the tiny thermos lid cup back and forth waiting for the sun to rise and planning out the day, the week and sometimes a little further into both of our lives. There was warmth in the cup and warmth in our words. It was a time to share our loves, hopes and yes, grievances we each felt with our world and occasionally each other. Fortunately, it was also an opportunity to commiserate on the injustices we both felt and this brought us closer together. I saw how very unhappy he was with his life. He loved living in Colebrook, did not appreciate Nashua, and with little surprise, his relationship with my Mom continuously challenged both of them. There was a sort of pride for me in feeling like an adult with him for the first time, but I could not shake the sadness I felt for him. I understood his feeling that he was caught in a cage after having felt freedom, and every single day broke his spirit a little more.

Part way through the summer, I experienced a literal unlucky break of my own. I was standing on a steep hill cutting a felled tree into logs for splitting, when the soft ground slid out from under me. As the ground gave way, I took a step for balance with the running chainsaw in my hand and stepped directly on one of the cut round logs which immediately rolled out from under me, sending me up into the air. I landed on my back in the middle of the log with the chainsaw grinding to a stop in the dirt beside my left shoulder. There was a sharp pain in my back and my legs went numb and limp. My dad heard my saw go silent and then my frantic calls for help. He came quickly to find me panicked, still unable to move my legs. We were in the woods of Mason, NH with nobody else expected on the site. He stayed with me, unsuccessfully attempting to calm me. All I could think was that I was paralyzed and everything I dreamed was over. He remained steadfast, planning how to get me help without moving me or leaving me. Suddenly, I felt the slightest tingle. Slowly more tingling, feeling, and finally movement returned to my legs. Dad drove me to the hospital and the medical team determined damage to my Lumbar L5 was serious enough to end my physical activity for the summer but would not require any surgery. A fortunate outcome perhaps, but there's little fortune felt in an immobilizing back brace certain to ruin the summer of an active 17-year-old.

Informed by the doctors that I would be laid up for several weeks, I purchased my very first computer, a TRS 80 Model III microcomputer. I had marveled at Lee Brooks' explorations on his Texas Instruments, TI 99 computer back in Colebrook and thought to learn how to program while confined to bed rest. I discovered a natural aptitude at programming. It was enjoyable, and I soon had designed my own version of the Tron Light Cycles game for play on my computer. I called my game "Sir Round" as the simple smiling face graphics would move towards each other and build the maze patterns designed to trap the opponent with a little strategy and quick reflexes. Time with my computer represented the simple birth of my engineering vision from the inauspicious start of a small landslide, a misstep and a revving chainsaw!

As my back healed, I went to work at Delta Education, a company producing and distributing science and math kits for schools. Both my mother and brother worked there, and at varying times I had done simple labor jobs for them. They gave me the opportunity to work in their shipping department, and in part due to my newfound computer competence I occasionally was called upon to provide simple technical support. I built a positive rapport with all the various departments of the company. This gave me many much-appreciated hours of overtime to support each department, as they requested me through to the end of the summer.

That summer included another major responsibility, as my first nephew, Chris, was born in August. Rick and Monique were living in Nashua and I spent as much of my free time as possible making visits to them. I delightedly, albeit awkwardly, learned the nuances of life with a newborn baby in our family. I held my brother in high regard, noting with some wonder that Rick had finished college, married, become a father and then bought a new home not far from where we lived. He remained my role model and I still loved our chances to talk, though private conversations were rare. More often I happily settled for of us playing board games or making short trips together with friends and family.

My summer of celebration had a sudden and somber ending. Driving home from Rick's I was in a car accident, although nobody was hurt there was significant damage to both cars. Since it was Dan's car on loan to my mom, virtually all of my savings went to repair my brother's car, abruptly ending the final possibility of returning to Colebrook. The way things conspired to keep me in Nashua felt tremendously unjust; nobody would ever want to transfer their senior year! However, with this final development, my parents ran out of reasonable options.

A solid surge of culture shock started my senior year of high school. Just a few days before the start of classes we made the final decision that I would transfer to Nashua High School. I went from a class of roughly 60 students to a class of more than 1100 students in the blink of an eye. I also encountered a bit of bureaucracy for the first time I could recall, as matching the requirements from my college preparatory program at Colebrook Academy with the similar requirements of Nashua, dealing with already filled classes, and the semantics of prerequisites proved to be adversarial. It was almost comical that for some time my graduation was deemed impossible due to my lack of credits in physical education. Colebrook did not have a gymnasium and so this state requirement had been waived, but Nashua would require me to have four full years of credits despite my having several varsity letters in sports. We finally did reach a compromise that allowed me to enjoy two consecutive periods of gym every morning for the year.

I strode into the halls of Nashua High school disappointed that I wasn't returning to the comfort of my friends and determined to prove the quality of my Colebrook education despite any rural, "country yokel", stereotyping. It was a daunting notion to once again try and build an entirely new social circle. To my dismay it soon became clear that by senior year most of my peers had established their friendships and were not entirely open to welcoming new friends into the mix. My one saving grace was the discovery many of the ladies in my classes tended to be more welcoming. Whether innocent flirtations or simple acquaintances they provided the foundation for the many more friendships I developed with women throughout my life.

The administration's hesitation in allowing me to take the top-level classes resulted in an easier course load and exceptionally high grades with minimal effort on my part. This had several immediate benefits. The marked improvement in my grades for my final year provided an excellent resume for my college applications, resulting in significant freedom of choice in my university and curriculum. More immediately my teachers and classmates acquired the perception that I was intelligent, and through their interactions my own confidence and capabilities increased. I was proud of my grades and found a renewed enthusiasm for my school curriculum. I made more of an effort to ensure I followed through to comprehend the small things which had eluded me along the way, becoming more fully invested in learning.

I also had the time to continue my job at Delta Education. As I demonstrated my competence in managing my schoolwork, I increased my hours and was given a promotion to work for the owner's son in the Information Technology department for part of my shift, and to handle a software division with high independence for the rest of my shift. I was feeling very confident and comfortable with life.

I tried out for the Varsity basketball team, understanding the competition would be far more intense. Confident in my abilities and work ethic I put forth my best effort and performed sufficiently well to expect I would make the team. On the day of the final cuts coach Noucas called me into his office to share news I had a hard time handling. He thought I had played well enough to earn a spot on the team, however there was a "but" attached to those words. A state guideline prevented a varsity athlete from transferring inter-state and playing in the same sport for a certain amount of time and I had transferred late, meaning I would miss the very first part of the season. Worse, given the fact I had not played with the rest of the team before, and as a senior represented no possible future development, he was begrudgingly choosing to cut me. I respected how he told me and I understood what he shared but it didn't help me feel any better. I lost most of my barely developed school spirit with the news. There was a frustrated edge I allowed to linger for some time afterwards.

At home my parents were no longer facing financial struggles, but they had traded one woe for another as disagreements had become commonplace once again. The frustration my dad had shown in the summer continued at home and one autumn evening over dinner my parents' argument escalated. Perhaps as part of my own frustrations, or possibly in recollection of some of the harsher prior confrontations between my parents; I chose to assertively intervene on my mom's behalf. My poor efforts intensified the hostility until my father and I stood toe to toe. I'm not sure if I previously realized I was now physically larger. I did realize I had escalated the conflict further than I hoped or planned.

We fought, with my dad swinging fast and furious. I blocked his punches but found I could not find it in me to return the blows. Instead, I chose to wrestle hoping to use my larger size to subdue him. Ultimately, I pinned him. We had reached an impasse: I had put him in a terrible spot with my challenge and there seemed no easy way out. I was afraid and felt trapped by circumstances which had spiraled so swiftly out of control. I understood that my dad felt similarly even as he refused to calm while I held him pinned to the floor. We had grown so close that summer, I was surprised by the force of his attack, but this moment was the breaking point for all his frustrations.

My mom frantically called my brother Rick who hastily came to calm things enough that we could disentangle physically, although our emotional separation proved to be much more drastic. I moved in with Rick and Monique for the rest of my senior year. While I was not entirely at fault in what transpired, I do own much responsibility due to my immaturity and frustration levels at the time. My mom worked steadily to reconcile my dad and me. It took many months of short conversations and slow reason to repair enough damage that we could jointly attend family events. The good news is the episode seemed to alleviate the strain on my parents' relationship, at least for that year.

Pictured: Randy models his cap and gown
from his Nashua H.S. graduation. 1984

My year at Nashua High School allowed me to build many friendships, advance my independence and have a very active social life. Rick and Monique's kindness and tolerance proved beyond measure. In sad truth it exceeded my own respect for their generosity at times as my rebellious tendencies led to some poor choices. Fortunately, I made enough good choices that my grades remained top notch and earned my acceptance into the University of New Hampshire Electrical Engineering program.

I found an immediate and glorious opportunity in my college career. For years every move had left me trying to work my way into pre-existing social groups. For the first time I arrived along with a host of other freshman, all on level social ground and as a result the skills I'd learned enabled me to flourish. My roommate, Chris Boilard, was a familiar face from the basketball courts of Nashua and as we shared a major there would be plenty of opportunity for our friendship in the years ahead. All around me was a ready and eager source of people for virtually any experience I might want to undertake. It was an incredibly social time and I was fortunate the first semester involved a condensed review of the foundations I had learned in high school. My grades were good since less initial effort was required to offset the highly playful approach I was enjoying.

I found an early morning job learning to cook breakfast at the college Memorial Union Building (MUB) alongside Mark Schrader. As an upper classman he gave me a lot of insight into University life. I used the MUB as a center for a variety of Work Study jobs. I was a doorman for the nightclub, which helped my finances while mitigating some of the weekend reveling as I worked virtually every weekend night. I had the chance to meet and work with a variety of different bands and headliners and eventually was invited to work additional hours for MUSO, the organization responsible for hosting the various acts brought into the MUB Pub.

During my extra time spent at the MUB, I often engaged in conversation with the culturally diverse students who used it as a base of operations. This exposure to a wide array of philosophies and people was tremendously invigorating to my curious mind. I came to appreciate "coffee" philosophy as well as the challenges to my ingrained core beliefs. I took a special appreciation for learning to be more kind to others and caring to our environment. Dabbling at homework and welcoming the distraction of some new friend's cause or campaign of the day was commonplace. My education outside of the text books brought me tremendous gratification.

Despite the initial ease of the material in my classes, I had a full load of courses and spent much of my time with the same core group of engineering friends. One of these, Melody Pauling, I met at orientation, and she provided help in the scheduling process. Because of this, all of our classes were together, and she eventually became my first serious romantic relationship. Melody was a sweet woman who made the fall of 1984 more magical for me. She

Pictured: Randy (right) poses with Mark and
two other fraternity brothers in 1987.

charmed my family with her intelligence, kindness and maturity. There was instant hope by my family that her school discipline and good behavior might help to settle my more rambunctious side. While she did teach me to use a calendar planner to manage the more complex schedule of college life, it was, ironically, her encouragement which directed me to explore the Greek system in my second semester. Mark Schrader's guidance brought me to a new fraternity on campus, Phi Kappa Theta.

I was initially derisive of fraternities but in the interest of being open minded had rushed several. I found to my surprise most had quality people. While the collective aspect did too often result in the stereotypical animal house for some, there were enticing qualities for others. In Phi Kappa Theta I found an unusual collection of individuals with a fun-loving attitude centered on quality values. There was an attitude of acceptance, kindness and good-natured fun at the heart of all their events. My fellow pledge class was diverse which suited my own unusual blend of attributes. A college version of the jack of all trades, I held some of the jock persona in my love of sports. Philosophical conversations in the MUB had awakened an 'earthy-crunchy granola' side, the electrical engineering 'geek' was vibrant through the excellence of UNH's engineering program, and the roots of an outspoken leader had begun to emerge within me. As part of only the fifth pledge class I appreciated the ability to have a significant role in shaping the organization from a foundation I already respected. Our class made up nearly half of our total active members, furthering our influence. So, although the guidance of those ahead of us was strong there were opportunities and I felt part of a healthy and large team.

As my engineering classes became more challenging and I sought to reduce my working hours in the years ahead, I applied to become a Resident Assistant (RA) which would provide me with room and board. The application process provided energized training sessions for leadership, responsibility and awareness while simultaneously connecting us to other like-minded, motivated candidates. Investing eagerly in all facets of the process, from the interviews to the interactive activities provided me more growth and development. Being selected to serve as an RA boosted my confidence heading into the summer of 1985.

I returned to live with my parents for the summer, a little concerned about how my dad and I would get along. Time away, my maturing, and the foundation we'd built during our coffee sharing mornings allowed us both to put the awkwardness behind us for good. Things went smoothly at home, and also at work as I returned to Delta Education full time for the summer, working in the IT department. One of my assignments required me to write a series of procedural manuals for the programs used by each of the departments in the company. After the normal work day, I volunteered for all the overtime shifts possible in the various packaging departments where I had worked in the past. This allowed me to build up my college savings, even with some reasonable summer social life.

I was all too eager to get back to school although it brought with it the dismaying discovery that my financial aid package had been reduced by exactly the amount of my room and board, since my RA commitment provided for this. Unfortunately, this meant my savings were tapped and I would have to continue working excessive hours to account for the lost funds. I made many strong connections with the residents on my floor although learning to manage the responsibilities for them had some stumbling blocks. For example, I made the choice to 'write-up' an alcohol violation for a beer sitting out on a shelf of a fellow engineering student's room. He called me into his room to ask me for help on a problem and I made a disappointing decision. Rather than overlook it or managing it in a variety of gentler ways I took the textbook approach and created a tenuous relationship for the rest of the term.

The position caused some isolation, particularly on weekends, as RAs often had a policing role in the eyes of our fellow residents. Walking rounds of all the floors every few hours, it was common to hear the revelry ahead of us change as open doors were slammed until we had passed to ensure we didn't witness any outright violations of Hall policy. Most people treated us normally outside of these times, and certainly I had close friends throughout the building with many positive interactions, but the echo of the slamming doors would linger in lonely reflections.

Fortunately, my fraternity brothers made for plenty of breaks from the long hours of work on my steadily harder engineering courses. They provided social times for the weekends when I wasn't working at the MUB pub, and friendships for visits, dinners and a host of intramural sports and activities crammed unrealistically into my busy schedule. This did not stop me from accepting the position of Housing Chairman when the position was offered to me that year. Our fraternity owned land in the town of Durham but did not have an actual house. It had been a goal from the first to find the means to build a brand-new structure on our land which would become a quality lodging for brothers and a central gathering point for all future activities.

The executive officers were talented and determined and much of the early planning had been developed, but I was definitely being entrusted with a fair bit more responsibility than ever before. I met regularly with the architect, the alumni foundation from a previous chapter of our fraternity at UNH, and eventually the builder. The planning, organization, communication, presentations and decisions would be crucial to our eventual success. I received more credit than deserved because our entire team did so much to make it all happen. Ground was broken in the spring of 1986. We didn't have a home ready for occupancy in the fall and scrambled to secure housing for everyone disappointed by that sad setback. But in January of 1987 we proudly moved into our brand-new fraternity house and the first major project of my life was a surprising success.

Meanwhile, the summer of 1986 provided another fantastic opportunity for my career development. A resident of my hall and new member of my fraternity connected me with his father, who had a summer job opportunity at Digital Equipment Corporation. I applied and interestingly they needed somebody with an engineering background and ideally the ability to write some supportive documentation for them. I provided copies of the manuals I'd written the previous summer and found myself hired immediately. This was my first professional job and for a premier company in the field of electrical engineering. I used the job and my parents' support to apply for my first car loan and bought a Ford Tempo to get to my new job.

Sitting in a cubicle reading company information on my first day, I was dismayed to learn my manager was not going to be present and they were not entirely certain how to handle me that day. A friendly voice inviting me to coffee changed the course of the day. Keith Niskala was a talented technician working on an important problem and we spent the morning talking through the situation as he studied test results and patiently explained as much as possible to me. I asked for some clarifications and through his explanations Keith found new inspiration on this old problem. Throughout the course of the morning he made some extremely important discoveries which led to a major breakthrough and at his insistence I was brought along for the entire process. Although I deserved none of the credit, the attention brought by Keith's solution changed Digital's plans for me and I became a network testing technician for the entire summer. This let me work in the area of network communications and allowed for tremendous amounts of overtime, as they often needed someone to come into the building after hours to record the data and switch the testing configurations. The confidence shown in me included allowing me to take some introductory courses with the new hire engineers to the company. This provided me friendships even as I was learning significantly from their experiences. My managers made an offer for me to become a full-time employee while they paid for my degree program part time but I was determined to finish my four year degree program at UNH.

The fall of my junior year saw me living off campus for the first time. I chose to relinquish my position as an RA, anticipating my financial aid would return the funds equivalent to my room and board. I was mistaken in this assumption, which caused a strain on my finances yet again. I continued my work in the MUB and supplemented it with hours at the Kingsbury Hall engineering library. Classes were very demanding, and I experienced my first real academic struggles, wondering at times if I might fall on the wrong side of the statistics suggesting that only 1 of 3 engineers graduated in the program.

I had taken another ambitious role in the fraternity as Pledge Educator, which was incredibly rewarding for the bonds of friendship forged but unkind to my limited time. I continued to participate in intramural sports, but more than most years dedicated myself to improving my grades. When our fraternity house opened for the second semester I reduced my Phi Kappa Theta responsibilities, choosing in part to rest on the previous semesters of hard work while appreciating the friendships and social outlet my fraternity provided. The enticement of the job at Digital motivated me in a year of work hard and play hard realities. That spring at the job fair and interview process for seniors, Digital had their representative reach out to treat me to lunch and a confirmation of my plans to work for them again in the summer. With his approval, I brought along one of my best friends, Rob Webber, who would be interviewing with them later that day. Lunch and conversation proceeded very well and unsurprisingly Rob soon had an offer to work for the Network and Communication group where I would summer hire.

It would be nearly impossible to overstate my joy in the summer of 1987. My friends at DEC (Digital Equipment Corporation) welcomed me back with enthusiasm. I quickly fell into the comfortable routines of the network testing process, with the additional benefit of having Rob working with us. My managers invited me to learn continuously more about network communication engineering, providing me with ample hours to prepare me for the finances of my final year of college and an atmosphere of social camaraderie sufficient to ensure I felt I could happily work there after college. To that end they made me a generous offer for full time work upon my graduation, and I returned for my senior year with the security of an offer in hand.

The idyllic summer fell into a fantastic fall. As a senior I felt on top of the world and though illusory in some ways, there was some well-earned truth to the confidence and comfort earned. I was now manager of the MUB Pub and needed to work fewer hours. My schoolwork, while still difficult, was eased somewhat by the absence of job competition stress felt by many of my peers. . The fraternity continued to be a positive outlet which did not unduly demand time or effort from me. There was a touch of nostalgia for the graduated friends lost each year and for the inevitable changes which come to organizations who require so much transition.

Still, I was content with so much of my life. I had dated a few ladies through the years and while no relationship lingered particularly long, I felt fortunate for the friendships and the insights each provided me on my journey of discovery. I very much wanted to find the perfect person to be my wife, have a family and celebrate long happy years together. While my dream didn't have a white picket fence, the more clear complexities of relationships were part of my ongoing education. There was one last relationship from my college years. I hoped my journey to coming of age had brought that life partner but, the next year was telling.

In May of 1988 I graduated with my Bachelor of Science in Electrical Engineering from the University of New Hampshire. I started working at Digital immediately, eager for the paycheck and the atmosphere of friendship. Rob Webber and Paul Albino invited me to rent a room from them at their condominium in Merrimack, NH. We dubbed it 'the Mansion' as we three friends spent the summer playing every sport imaginable. We had softball leagues, basketball leagues, dart leagues, an active social calendar with our girlfriends and at home with Bino's vast collection of arcade games and the 'keg fridge' which suited the lifestyle we lived at the time. I fulfilled a dream by becoming a New England Patriot season ticket holder almost immediately as my newfound freedom of finances and time had me exploring every hobby I needed to delay during my college years.

I used the DEC electronic bulletin boards to create a gaming group for the Dungeons and Dragons hobby of my high school years, and soon had another diverse group of friends. Sean Griffin was one of those gamers and we became fast friends, playing darts, softball and eventually undertaking those ever so significant fencing lessons. It was a year of jubilant celebration as everything in my world seemed to go positively my way. I was even able to help my Mom purchase her own car, as I traded my Tempo into a vehicle I could finance entirely on my own. I was so proud to purchase my Honda Accord LX with the custom installation of the rare car CD player!

Little did I know I would only have a few months to drive my new car before things would change dramatically. So many times, I heard my blindness was such a tragedy, such an awful thing in my life; perhaps the worst thing to happen in my life. Having experienced so much personal growth and enhanced vision from the loss of my sight, I'm fairly convinced it is closer to the exact opposite. It may have been one of the best experiences as the adversity would become the catalyst motivating me to achieve more for myself. Certainly, I was happy and successful as I left the University of NH and began my career at Digital Equipment and perhaps I might have continued on a journey of success. I am doubtful the same tremendous catharsis would have propelled me through the many incredibly rewarding experiences which followed my adapting to my blindness and even after getting back on my feet after the wheelchair!

The Mighty Quinn

"Walk with the dreamers, the believers, the courageous, the cheerful, the planners, the doers, the successful people with their heads in the clouds and their feet on the ground. Let their spirit ignite a fire within you to leave this world better than you found it." Wilfred A. Peterson

I delighted in the sheer joy of walking once again even though it still took a fair bit of concentration and effort. My world was expanding, as each day I could take further steps of independence with my hiking stick for support and blind cane for navigation. It was slow progress except in comparison to my solo efforts while in the wheelchair. I dreamed of improving enough to be approved for a guide dog again, but not just for the benefit of travel. I keep a plaque in my home which accurately states: "No home is complete without the pitter patter of dog feet." This was the longest period of my life without a dog since Modi and I had formed our bond. I was missing my dogs so much more than my guides.

In February of 2006 I called Guide Dogs for the Blind to share my progress. To my surprise they instantly included me in plans for

152

already-scheduled home visits for March in New Hampshire. My excitement was strongly mixed with apprehension because my walking was still awkward and slow despite my significant improvement. I feared they would reject me and it would take longer to convince them to visit again when I'd had more time to practice and progress.

The trainer arrived on a particularly warm March day and after asking me a host of questions about my prior guide, my medical challenges and current ability, we took a walk together. Nervous beads of sweat instantly soaked my forehead as I strode slowly forward with the blind cane tapping and sweeping in coordinated rhythm with the hiking stick in my right hand. It was complicated, akin to tapping your head while rubbing your belly. At times I leaned more heavily on the trekking pole and other times I was more stable, but it was never smooth or comfortable. We went to the first street crossing as the trainer observed my ability to be aware of the crossing and manage it correctly. After a few further strides he stopped me. I was dejected at having failed so fast until I heard the enthusiasm in his voice: "Randy, I believe a guiding harness in your hand instead of a blind cane is really going to be a gift! It will improve your balance by adding stability and speed." He was so right! We each held an adapted harness for the trainer to simulate the work of a guide dog and instantly I had an extra balance point for stability as well as the more definitive direction the harness provides me.

I had practiced this "Juno training" before Ostend, but the benefit this time for my balance condition was beyond my expectations! We moved together with a far more natural gait for me and while I did have to catch my balance on the hiking stick a couple of times it was the smoothest walk I'd experienced in my short time out of the wheelchair! My smile was apparently out of control and this poor, kind trainer took me for the longest walk he could manage, given the hot weather, to let me fully appreciate and celebrate the feeling of freedom. Arriving home, it was his turn to give me the smile, at least in his voice, as he told me I was a priority candidate to get a dog immediately.

Just two months later, I flew back to the Oregon campus of Guide Dogs for the Blind, nervous and still awkward in my solo walking. I met with the class trainers and my concerns escalated. They were unaware of my need for the hiking stick, and these were the people who trained and selected the dog match for me. We discussed the situation and forged ahead, matching me with a Labrador Retriever named Cosgrove. He was a fine pup but he viewed the hiking stick in my right hand as an obstacle. Every time I planted it forward to take a step, he would shift a little left, seemingly to help me avoid bumping into it. Additionally, if there was a left turn available he'd start to subtly take the turn. Given the storm of vertigo still roiling within my mind, I would often miss these shifts and thus our navigation was simply not working. The instructors and supervisors met with me to discuss the options. They could invest a little extra time in Cosgrove and me to work through the challenge and convince him to ignore the hiking stick. It would mean more work for both of us and it would detract a little bit from the others in our class. They suggested I return home while they began specially training another dog who was nearly ready for class. I could return for the next session and have a dog which had been exposed to a hiking stick and was ready to fit my need perfectly. I agreed to this option and went home, while noting through an email list that Cosgrove had been matched to someone else later as a successful guide. Our three days together had teased me quite a bit but I wanted to make the right choice.

Unfortunately, Guide Dogs for the Blind was having some internal difficulties at this time. Whatever administrative miscommunications occurred were a significant factor in the failure of my attempt to receive a guide dog. Behind the scenes at higher levels this became enough of a concern that I was put on hold until they could resolve it to their satisfaction. But they didn't communicate any of this to me and weeks of silence resulted in my pushing back. I was assigned tasks, effectively delaying tactics, to get recertified with my mobility instructors. Glenn Gunn at the NH Association for the Blind responded within the week to test me and confirm I was more than sufficiently skilled. They provided this information to Guide Dogs for the Blind and yet I experienced more silent waiting, which led me to push back again. This time I was asked to confirm with my physical therapist that the hiking stick was the appropriate device. Once again, this was confirmed, and the paperwork faxed to them within a week, followed by still more silent weeks of delay. Frustrated and confused, I chose to apply to several other guide schools. I had several successful home interviews lead to offers to attend class and receive a guide dog. I selected the

October class at Guiding Eyes for the Blind and prepared to launch a new chapter of my life.

As part of the preparation we held a "Bardic" sendoff. Through the years I've often delighted in song and verse, usually with a mildly medieval theme. The notion of the bard as a storyteller bringing community together resonates strongly with me. I frequently host gatherings of friends encouraged to express themselves or simply support others who choose to share a poignant, humorous or favorite poem or performance. Saturday, October 14, 2006 filled my home with friends to share just such a Bardic themed event. A stronger theme was the strengthening support of my friends, who were aware of May's failure with Cosgrove. Whether the riotous table pounding merriment of a group chorus on "The Old Dunn Cow" or a touching finale of "Health to the Company", I end the evenings with elevated appreciation for friendship, renewed spirit and only a hint of sad nostalgia for the belief that as the final song's verse says, "we may or might never all meet here again". On this occasion, all had agreed in the confident hope our company would, in fact, grow by one member more; a new dog in my life.

Bren had joined the festivities, staying for the weekend as our long-distance relationship often encouraged. As a gift she had developed "Zip dog blog" for me. It was an automated update site, so I could simply send email entries to chronicle the entire guide dog training adventure ahead. We made an initial anticipatory entry, thus beginning to build a community through comments and responses. This heralded an entirely new phase of my online interactions in conjunction with my popular Zip's Patriots Page.

After the Bardic, Bren and I set off from Nashua. She dropped me at my brother Rick's home in Trumbull CT on Sunday, before heading to her own home on Long Island. I waited only one day more for the short commute to Yorktown Heights and the Guiding Eyes for the Blind campus on October 17. My nephew Chris provided excellent company and considerable distraction for the ride, which was just under one hour from his Connecticut home. I arrived early to the campus with some trepidation. Despite the resurgent confidence in so many aspects of my life, I could not escape the doubts developed from the failure I'd experienced half a year earlier. I was doing my best to mask those insecurities as we arrived and were warmly greeted by the staff. One of the trainers, Chrissie Vetrano, showed us my room and gave a quick orientation before I said my farewell to Chris. He gave me a long and strong hug and well-wish full of the confidence with which he seemingly always believed in me. I hoped to prove worthy of that confidence and realized it was my shortcoming to not be open to sharing more with him about my true feelings as he'd become a young man, far more of an adult friend than the young nephew I too often considered him.

It was time, however, to turn my full focus to guide school, and Chrissie gave me an instant confidence boost. The trainers were fully aware of the hiking stick and had prepared several adaptations in commands for me, since unlike most handlers, I would not have one hand as readily available. She also showed me my room was adjacent to the instructors' which led me to wonder if they anticipated mischief from me! I had a double room but would be the sole occupant of the room, at least until the hopeful arrival of the new guide dog in just a few short days. This suited me, as for all my outward signs of confidence and comfort, I still very much appreciated and perhaps needed my times of solitude. This was especially true given my doubts that my balance and vertigo would enable me to manage the physical training properly.

I'd want the solitude to reflect and to help hide any disappointment if necessary. I also knew that emotionally I was still struggling with the loss of Ostend even though it had been nearly a year and a half since his death. Rather than dwell on those thoughts too much, I used my early arrival to try and learn the layout of the campus which was, as I learned, under construction. I hoped this would be one of the last times I would navigate with the slow pace of a blind cane tapping out my search for obstacles while the right hand used my hiking stick for the necessary balance and support.

We took two days to learn the foundation of tools and techniques necessary before dog day arrived for my classmates and me. I took the optional evening class to discuss the transition from a prior guide to a new guide. This class helped me realize that whether we are retiring a pup or have lost them as I had with Ostend, the change is worthy of some forethought. We need to be open minded to the gifts our new guide will bring in personality, work and play. The instructor taught us it is common to have poor habits and expectations, both needing release, if we want to ensure the most reward from our new match. It's also important to understand the intensity of our prior bond often causes feelings of guilt in the forming of a new bond. While it is reasonable to experience these feelings, they are unnecessary, and we should not allow them to limit us if we want the next match to be successful. Sharing the thoughts and emotions with others who experienced transition previously or were in the midst of it helped me find some level of peace with my reflections of Ostend and my impending new guide.

The bond between guide and handler is essential. Significant preparation through the program and by the trainers is made to ensure the moment of first meeting is an exceptionally positive experience. Chrissie introduced me to Quinn, a 67-pound yellow Labrador Retriever as I waited eagerly in my room. She released him to me for that initial connection which was decidedly lukewarm. He was pleasant enough with a wagging tail and body wriggle but as quickly as he reached me he turned to stare at the door, clearly wishing for Chrissie. I tried a little of the tactics which Ostend had appreciated, such as a playful hand swipe to the shoulder and Quinn gave an interested response showcasing some playfulness but not full enthusiasm. I made several attempts when suddenly my observant new friend noticed a nyla-bone and dove for it with an eager passion for play which began our connection. Ostend had barely ever noticed his toys, preferring direct play with me. Quinn's competitive toy drive was incredible and for the rest of our time we played until he was a panting pile of puppy, ready to let me pet him only after I put the toy away.

I quickly learned that his work focus was as intense as his play drive during our very first dinner. This involved most handlers establishing the rules for settling their new guides while the presence of all the other dogs quickly led to distraction and misbehavior. Not for Quinn! He settled under my chair and ignored all distractions including the highly touted teasing of his trainer, Chrissie, though she told me he watched her every step with the laser intensity of those intelligent eyes. From the first he showed off a mastery of all the obedience commands and a willingness to demonstrate them in all environments as I simply had to give the voice command or hand gesture and he would respond. He ignored food distractions, though food was never his primary focus. A well-timed squeaky toy would turn his head for a moment if I didn't prepare him with advance encouragement, but his behavior was simply better than I had ever experienced.

When I let him "off-duty" by removing the harness, all that focus would unfurl into bounding episodes of what we lovingly called his puppy spaz, a barely controlled run around confined spaces at full speed with all his paws flailing into each and every turn. These were of course offset with tenacious bouts of tug of war, fetch or chasing his nyla-bone around me as I used my hands to keep it away from him. His deft mouth-eye coordination was incredible, catching everything I threw and always evading or soft mouthing when encountering my hands. These play sessions were as therapeutic for me as they were good for our bonding, and every return trip to our room ensured some fun for us.

After breakfast one morning we snuck in a quick round of keep away with his nyla-bone. His paws sliding on the tile made it difficult for him and for the first time one of his sharper young teeth caught me on the first knuckle of a finger. His contrite response highlighted his awareness and concern and my gentle reassuring stroke across his head and ears showed me by the position of those ears how much he regretted the accident. I gave him a quick ok to resume play and we plunged back into the fray as joyously as ever. Rushing out to meet our class rendezvous the gasp of my instructor alerted me to something amiss. Shouts of concern and alarm took a little time to sort as they realized neither Quinn nor I were actually harmed though apparently were both quite bloody. We both looked the worse for wear, and a trip to my room revealed a crime scene simulation as my small cut had been a 'bleeder' and had managed to place splatter patterns on virtually everything, including the two of us, before we ended our play. This involved a lot of clean up but Quinn was appropriately not charged with any wrongdoing. It was, however, suggested we might tone down our play sessions a bit in the future.

Perhaps the crime reference is appropriate for Quinn as I was informed he was from a program called Puppies Behind Bars. The most common practice for raising guide dog puppies is to utilize volunteer puppy raisers who take responsibility for the youngsters starting as early as 8-12 weeks old, depending on the puppies' demonstrated maturity. These incredibly kind and generous volunteers socialize the dogs, teach them most obedience commands and expose them to the many environments they are likely to encounter in their eventual careers as a dog guide. At roughly 16 months of age the dog is returned to guide school for the formal final training and testing. This simplistic overview does not remotely attempt to explain the amazing amount of work and care provided by the puppy raiser. In the Puppies Behind Bars program, prisoners demonstrating extended good behavior and responsibility could earn the privilege to raise a puppy in similar fashion within the prison. The puppy received weekend furloughs with other volunteers to ensure exposure to environments not available within the prison. Quinn had received an exceptional amount of quality one to one time with two different prisoners during his early years and their steadfast work with him certainly showed in the high focus he displayed in all our training work.

This is not to suggest he didn't manage things with a certain flair of his own. The morning after an intense October wind and rain storm had kept us inside, Quinn and I were selected for the first route of shoreline work. This requirement to walk close to the side of a road without sidewalks is fairly simple and just as in regular walking, guide teams are expected to walk facing oncoming traffic. As we set out for our walk, Quinn stopped me and refused my 'hup-up" command to continue forward. I probed with my foot and found a fairly large branch across our path, clearly blown down from the night's wind storm. I was unsure how far out into the road it went, how high its attached branches might be, and as a result what would be the official method of handling it. I paused to consider and resolved to ask my instructor when her laugh, quickly but poorly smothered by her hand, cut me off. I then heard scraping sounds and confusion clarified as the leash surged in rhythmic tugs. Quinn understood my dilemma, providing a solution by using his mighty jaws to lift a branch which outweighed him. Surging his body in a worm-like motion he slowly tug-slid it off the road, to the mirth and incredulity of my instructor.

The branch was our final obstacle to graduation as the marvelous Mighty Quinn charged through every challenge. Downtown Manhattan on a work day and even Grand Central Station were part of our final proving grounds demonstrating that our teamwork and bond had steadily grown to readiness. Each day I made the dog blog entry, most of them under the anthropomorphic premise of his writing them. People commented often at each post, showing a preference for Quinn's perspective which helped grow my own daily insight into my new boy's thoughts and mannerisms. He was occasionally a little grumbly when other dogs invaded his space and that gave me initial pause for concern. My trainers reassured me his reactions were normal and appropriate in response to the other dogs' inappropriate behavior. My relationships with our classmates were very good and I was appreciative of the compliment when they asked me to speak on their behalf at graduation. We were all eager to take our new guides home fulfilling the promise of our progress.

Typically, the trainers suggest minimal variance in routine for the first few days or even weeks at home. It was, however, football season and there was a Patriots home game the very next day after graduation. I agreed Quinn and I would not attend if they thought it the wrong choice, because my first goal was building the best teamwork for us long term. But the instructors were so confident in our work they encouraged me to make the attempt. As a little practice and celebration, I decided to take Quinn for an early morning walk around my neighborhood before we left for Foxboro. I chose the absolute easiest of routes for us and set out with Bren beside us to watch our great teamwork in action. It was an unmitigated disaster. Quinn was hesitant, pulling to the side, stopping every few steps for no apparent reason, and even drifting out at an intersection rather than rounding as appropriate. Where had our confident, capable and unflappable teamwork gone? How could I ever consider going anywhere with Quinn right now, never mind to Foxboro Stadium. I was stunned and frustrated, while Bren's concern and desire to help seemed to only increase our team uncertainty. In my growing exasperation I had a flashback to frustrations felt during my descent into the wheelchair. I determined to quell these feelings and identify and resolve the problem. With an embarrassed apology to Bren I asked her to meet us back at the house, so Quinn and I could work through it together without any outside distraction for either of us. I gave him a couple of shoulder rubs and then ran the routine of what I like to call the obedience aerobics. Each and every day we work the basic obedience commands together to build focus and intensify the bond and working relationship. I praised each easy success to bolster our confidence with positive reinforcement. Sit, Down, Sit, Stay, Heel and repeat! Relaxed, reassured and ready it was time to try again. Lifting the harness, I gave the forward command and concentrated hard to keep my steps as steady as I could manage, with frequent praise for his work and a quick "hup-up" to encourage him if he started to slow. There were many possible reasons for why things had started rough: the neighborhood was new to him, he'd slept in a new place for the first time in months and someone new had joined us for the walk, distracting me as well. Now each confident step-built momentum for the next and by the time we completed the block both of us had our confidence restored from the morning's momentary lapse.

We chose to continue our plan to attend the game on a beautiful November 4, 2006, with a contingency for stepping away if it proved difficult at any stage. Quinn was flawless at the tailgate and at the game, navigating the thousands of people on the journey into and out of the stadium with incredible skill. He mostly slept during the game, entirely unfazed by the excitement around him. This was the immediate standard for our adventures everywhere as he would creatively solve problems while never allowing any of our obstacles to challenge either of us individually or as a team. I quickly learned to trust him implicitly, such that on a gusty fall day taking our normal walk, I was surprised when he paused briefly then abruptly dashed in front of me, turned the opposite way and pulled forward to literally rotate me 180 degrees and stop. I understood almost immediately as a wall of wind, loaded with leaves, twigs and dirt, struck our backs. He'd noticed the wall of blown debris bearing down on us and realized it was going to run us over. Amazingly, he had the sense to get our backs to it and brace us with the stop!

Every day we walked together as I celebrated the gift of my return to walking. I loved even more the freedom and independence with which Quinn enhanced this gift. My gait improved as well, since at slower speeds my balance had more challenge. I liken it to riding a bicycle, if you ride too slowly it's harder to maintain balance. Add a little speed and the momentum provides some stability. Quinn provided the means for enough speed to enhance my stability. The practice helped my progress even though winter added the additional risks of snow and ice. I embraced the winter, these times and especially Quinn. Every work excursion I wanted to provide a special reward for his efforts, a payment of sorts. For him there was no finer payment than play and so we adopted the "playment plan" for each harness outing. Upon arriving home, I hung the harness on the door and dug out a toy immediately, to Quinn's great delight. This built up an expectation in Quinn so as soon as any trip turned back towards home he would realize play was in his future and quicken his step. He never went faster than I could handle, but he kept me on the edge of my limits, always testing me and as my skills grew he increased the pace a little more.

Pictured: Randy and Quinn enjoy some freedom in an early morning run at Hampton Beach, NH 2009

As spring arrived we broadened our range to include trips into downtown Nashua, scouting out territory new to him and a few years outdated for me. When an April phone call alerted me that my Dad had experienced a severe stroke it was with full confidence I used Quinn to travel an entirely unknown route and reach St. Joseph's Hospital in Nashua. Despite the stress on me and the uncertainty of my route, Quinn confidently managed his responsibilities, patiently waiting while I assessed the navigational clues to ensure we reached the hospital. I knew there were some early versions of accessible GPS systems and these trips increased my determination to explore them in the future. Finding the hospital was only the first part of Quinn's work on that day, though. He helped calm me as I faced my Dad in a coma and needed the support of the bond we forged to help me during those early hours. On our second trip the next day Quinn showed how well he learned routes with just a single trip and upon arriving to the hospital room, I let down the harness and put my hand to Dad's shoulder. Encouraged by the nurses, I talked to Dad hoping my voice might reach him. It was during a rest period for me that Quinn's gentle muzzle nuzzling of my Dad's hand suddenly caused my Dad to sit upright and look down at Quinn with what I'm told was a tremendous smile!

It was days before he could even rudimentarily begin to speak, and many weeks of recovery overall. Quinn and I travelled together daily to the hospital where Quinn's enthusiastic greetings were a salve for my Dad as much as, if not more than my own visits. While Dad would never be fully restored he made great strides. By May he was back to the assisted living facility and we received permission to sneak him out for a special treat. We brought Dad to Littleton MA for a Tedy Bruschi book signing. "Never Give Up" recounts Tedy's stroke recovery and at the signing Tedy took some personal time to show his empathy and encourage my Dad to never give up. My Dad never did give up and carried his autographed copy with him everywhere he went as one of the most meaningful gifts he would ever receive.

A major step for Quinn and I was heralded by a phone call from Bill Leblanc, the NH regional coordinator for puppy raisers of Guiding Eyes for the Blind. Bill had met one of my friends while working his puppy in training and wanted to reach out to talk with me about my work with Quinn. We met and became fast friends, only partially due to my appreciation for the great work done by the puppy raisers. Bill asked if I'd be willing to join him for a school visit to talk with the young students at the Memorial school in Bedford, NH on June 14, 2007. I had occasionally spoken to students and at schools and it seemed a great opportunity. We met outside the school on a warm and beautiful day to be greeted with many enthusiastic questions about what a blind person can do, and what a guide dog does. Ultimately, we created a makeshift obstacle course out of students, my blind cane and the playground. Quinn navigated it all wonderfully, showing off his awareness of height obstacles, ground obstacles and even moving students! The teacher, Cheryl Mousseau, invited us to return the next year and provided a couple of new toys to thank Quinn for his work.

That summer's celebrations had many highlights, including a return to the Pennsic wars with my friends in Clann O'Choda. They were glad to welcome Quinn to camp and his penchant for play quickly made him a camp favorite. He learned the layout of the massive campground turned town and I found almost the same independence with Quinn I had known with Ostend. My balance issues made things more difficult, but Quinn's steady work ensured

I was safe at all times. In the few years since I had been there with Ostend I was surprised to observe how many more service animals had become part of the event and doubly proud of Quinn for his focus in tending his work despite any distractions. I had to remind myself this was only our first year together many times because of the excellence of his work. This in turn provided me the confidence I needed to practice and progress on my own walking challenges.

Over the summer my walking improved so much that I found myself using the hiking stick less and less frequently. I decided to try carrying it ready to use but not actually planting it on the ground for support. Steadily the number of times I needed to touch it down became fewer. Some days I would be more tired, and it would seem like a setback but overall my progress was noteworthy, so that by August I didn't use it in the house at all, and began to take a few short trips around the neighborhood without it. It was clear the day was coming I would put it up for good and that day was October 1, 2007. As much as I had loved the hiking stick for getting me out of the wheelchair, setting it aside was a tremendous step forward in my quest for stability.

Life was on a tremendous upswing. I decided it was time to return to a passion which had helped me immensely and so I asked Quinn to bring me downtown for a visit with my Martial Arts instructor, Grandmaster Robert LaMattina at Tokyo Joe's Studio of Self Defense. We had a long conversation about the still-challenged state of my balance and he was, as always, incredibly encouraging, supportive and determined to teach me as long as I was willing and eager to work. I began with him in 1989 during the earliest years of my sight loss. Our initial goal had been to enhance my focus and orientation which it did fantastically. I also came to love the instruction, the workouts, the drive to learn and improve, as well as the community at the heart of the dojo. Their patient approach to my sight restriction and through every stage of sight loss enabled me to competently rise through the ranks and earn my black belt in Shaolin Kempo Karate even after total blindness. We knew I had much to relearn after my time in the wheelchair, and that now with my balance severely affected it would be even more challenging.

Quinn, like Ostend before him, learned the routine of my Dojo trips and workouts quickly, building his own friendships within the Dojo. Everyone who knew Ostend suggested he had some big paws to fill yet he was undaunted in taking on that challenge, quickly winning them over. As my work was more difficult this time around, I increased my time and dedication to match the need. Progress was slow but steady and so very encouraging for the upward climb.

It was quite the fall all in all, Quinn and I made visits to several more schools as many people wanted to learn more about our work as a team. Another team of mine, the New England Patriots, were undefeated and I was contacted to be filmed for HBO's Inside the NFL, on my approach to football, fandom and life. The HBO team joined us for a packed tailgate at my home while the Patriots were in Buffalo: yet another win on the journey to an undefeated regular season. The piece released to an immediate and incredibly positive national reaction and Quinn-boy was prominently featured. While the Patriots faltered in the Super Bowl against the New York Giants, the video, "Full Tilt Full Time Fan: Randy Zip Pierce", was nominated for a Sports Emmy Award. Quinn and I were treated to a New York City overnight to discover we, like the Patriots, were runners-up as well.

Our travels were successful enough that I decided to take another exciting opportunity and accepted a project for the Library of Congress. The talking book program annually invited a select group of clients and librarians to join them in Washington to review their processes and provide recommendations. On our own, Quinn and I travelled down to Foggy Bottom, an area entirely unfamiliar to both of us. I had recently acquired a Nokia N-82 cell phone with a talking software package included. I'd added the Wayfinder GPS application and believed Washington DC would be an excellent testing ground for the system.

The first day it was the four-pawed navigational system who showed his prowess. We were signed in and guided by the staff through the elaborate and labyrinthine structure of their building. They advised me that dog relief times would likely need a human escort as no guide dog had managed it on their first try before. Quinn eradicated all doubts with his unhesitating first attempt and I swelled with pride for my boy. That evening a group of us chose to go out to dinner together. Unfortunately, we learned the restaurant around the block from our hotel had a long line waiting outside. Using my new phone navigation system, I suggested several other restaurants, and our group decided on a destination a few blocks away. Since nobody knew the way, I navigated using the GPS and Quinn's guidance, leading four fully sighted librarians and seven other visually impaired clients. Arriving directly to the door I marveled at the advancement of our world and we celebrated. On the return trip home, the sighted amongst us opted to lead. At one juncture they had crossed a street and Quinn refused to follow. After two attempts to encourage him I called out to them with concern and they shouted back in appreciative realization that once again my furry organic navigation system was superior: they had missed the turn and Quinn was looking down the correct street to return to our hotel! For all the wonders of technology I will always marvel at both the dedication and ability of my guide dogs!

I learned much about technology for the visually impaired from the NH Association for the Blind, as well as my own internet research. An employee, Kim Stumph, assisted and inspired me with those early explorations. Through a strange coincidence, we had another connection. She, as part of her mobility instructor training, had been invited to Guiding Eyes for a seminar and worked with Quinn only a month prior to my arrival to meet him. Quinn was often a connector and Kim and I were certainly closer for the unique experience. Kim and many of the helpful staff at NHAB had warmly encouraged me to return to their annual Walk for Sight now that Quinn had me walking freely once again. I enthusiastically agreed, beginning a deeper connection with the organization.

My life would lose a little stability over the summer as Bren and I slowly eased out of the longest relationship of my life so far. Quinn did double duty support for both of us, and as is often the way of dogs, facilitated the introduction of a very important new friend. I made plans to head down to Pennsic once again. My friend Jeff Collins and Teresa Roberts encouraged me to join their friend Tracy for the ride to Pennsic. Tracy drove a mini-cooper, which seemed a tight fit for a tall man, a sturdy Labrador Retriever and two weeks of camping supplies for an 11-hour drive. We fit well in the car and in our conversations as we commiserated on the hurt of failed relationships. We also found much shared enthusiasm for life and adventure in our newfound friendship. In the SCA she counted herself as a fencer foremost. Tracy also told me about her print business back in her home state of Rhode Island. Business calls during the ride showcased a knowledge, experience and confidence which I admired. She was also a dog lover and Quinn was easy for her to appreciate. He worked his charms on her steadily throughout our occasional encounters at the rainy Pennsic retreat. It would be several weeks after Pennsic before we reconnected and began dating. The wait was worthwhile!

Long distance relationships are difficult, particularly when one of those involved doesn't drive. Her home situation was particularly challenging and so we expedited our plans more than we might otherwise have preferred, and she moved to Nashua in December to live with us. It was either going to be a misstep for our relationship or the chance it needed to flourish. But we flourished as a trio in oh so many ways. Tracy joined us as part of the Patriot Tailgate community, the Bardic gatherings, and the Karate family. We each had independent roles in all of these, although Quinn's stalwart guidance and relentless competitive playfulness certainly earned him a special place as the heart of our young family.

People regularly told me Quinn had the heart of a lion and that was perhaps appropriate for another journey we began together. Bill LeBlanc invited me to speak to his Nottingham West Lions Club in Hudson NH. Ostensibly he wanted me to demonstrate new technology, including the KNFB reader which allowed me to use the camera on my phone to scan any printed material and have it read aloud. Bill is a clever man and I fell for his ruse! Absolutely he wanted to show the technology to his local Lions club, but he also wanted me to meet the people and mission of Lions Clubs, the world's largest service organization. Thanks to the incredible vision of Hellen Keller, the Lions have been dedicated to supporting causes related to sight loss since 1925. It wasn't long before I was a member of the club with Quinn as an honorary member, proudly joining them in service in March of 2009.

During this time, I was still relentlessly trying to improve some of my persistent difficulties with balance. It wasn't often that I'd fall, but I could disorient myself with a quick turn of my head. If I wasn't careful and attentive I still had more staggers in my slower steps than I preferred. Standing still was possible but without something to stabilize myself I wobbled with some risk of falling. Dr. Catalano from the Lahey Clinic informed me of another opportunity. I eagerly embarked on a course of intense physical therapy using a device called the "BrainPort Balance Plus" by a company called Wicab. The concept was simple. A gyroscope was encapsulated into an electrical device which was placed on my tongue as I did a series of balance exercises. If my head remained level then I would receive no stimulus but if I tipped my head, the device sent an electrical signal onto my tongue indicating the direction of the tilt. The more severe the tilt the stronger the electrical stimulus. In this fashion I could learn to hold my head level and my body could learn to evaluate proprioceptive information from my head downward. As proprioception is one of the three methods of balance any improvement here would likely translate to greater stability for me.

I trained for several weeks at their Burlington MA location in exhausting, day long, multiple session events. The benefit was

Pictured: Randy and Quinn pose in Mine Falls Park, Nashua 2009

notable, as therapists measured how long I could hold my balance on various difficult surfaces while using the device. I was sufficiently successful to be granted permission to take a device home for several months of extensive therapy. They suggested I attempt at least three sessions of the balance exercise each day but allowed I could do more if I wished. My typical day involved seven sessions and my exhausted brain demanded more hours of sleep than I had experienced in years. By the end of the sessions I had not eliminated the vertigo as a daily challenge, but I had found countermeasures allowing me to mostly overcome its influence. This was as significant a shift as the trans-tympanic injections that allowed me out of the wheelchair, encouraging me to take my active lifestyle to the next level.

Quinn loved all of our walks but was happiest when they brought us into the woods. Initially this simply involved appreciating the shorter, simple trails of Mine Falls Park here in Nashua. Encouraged by my balance and reminded of my hiking stick, I decided we might try a small mountain trail together. In August Tracy and I took the lad to Pack Monadnock in Wilton, NH. We set out on the Wapack trail with my hiking pole once again in my right hand to reinforce balance on the far more difficult terrain we expected. Quinn guided me around the boulders along the wider trail near the base of the mountain, wagging enthusiastically for the new adventure. It wasn't long before there was no evading the obstacles and he used the intelligent disobedience of his training to stop, thereby alerting me to a danger. Tapping with the hiking stick I identified the roughly three-foot step up we needed to make in order to continue, I encouraged him to do just that with the command "hup-up" which translates to "go if you can." Quinn was prepared for this and backed up a step, the guide dog response of "No way, this is a very bad idea." I understood I might have to guide him a little through the pioneering a new solution to blind mountain climbing. So, although I had never climbed a mountain blind and he had trained his entire life for guiding a blind person, I foolishly took the lead. I quickly scanned high with my hand for head clearance as well as tapping the rock for stable footing. Then, ignoring his advice, I lunged up the tall step and promptly cracked my head on the thigh-thick branch which had been just out of the reach of my scan. Quinn was wriggling with an "I told you, I told you" exasperation to his demeanor. My clever boy had done the math, realizing I would hit my head, but I had failed to trust the process. If I was determined to ignore his advice, effectively challenging the process, I should have been far more thorough in my exploration. I paid the price with a solid knock to my noggin and a lesson for the future.

Putting my trust in Quinn is all the more impressive when considering the magnitude of his job. Imagine if you will, hiking a moderately challenging trail. Now imagine that someone roughly three times your weight and a bit more than three times your height is lumbering next to you with feet the size of a table. They are blind, have a balance disorder, you can't speak and oh – by the way – you are responsible for their safe passage. This is effectively Quinn's challenge. Quinn needs to plan our route along the winding, rocky, rooty trails, allowing the best footing for my steps while avoiding being stepped on and absolutely not have either of us plummet from any edge!

They don't really train guide dogs to haul us up mountain paths which are this challenging. I learned his signals such as subtle leans, body twists and redirections as well as warnings for a step, a sharp stick, a boulder, the path turning or even the occasional "No way is this a safe move ahead." The latter happened about four times in the course of the entire hike. Each time, I probed with my stick to understand exactly why Quinn had communicated with a pause, refusal and caring whine, that he could not lead me down the immediate trail ahead. Every time he was perfectly correct in his assessment. For him to have done less would have endangered one or both of us. I traversed these sections by removing his harness and proceeding on my own with a climbing crawl or other two-hand scramble. A call to Quinn brought him eagerly to my side in his full wagging pride and devotion to retake the guide role. He was amazing, constantly watching my progress. He studied my head, cane, feet and all the astounding challenges with a mind-consuming passionate devotion which made both Tracy and I in marvel at his magnificence.

Though Tracy was leading and chose her best route along the path, Quinn did not follow blindly but made judgements based on our needs, frequently diverting slightly from the route she chose. He made his choices efficiently and I quickly realized he had completely grasped the true nature of my needs and physiology such that he maximized our performance and minimized our risks. This was not just following Tracy but challenging the mountain course and ensuring we learned to communicate and manage the route. I'm sure there were several times he might have wished I would just understand and respond better to his excellent work, but he always patiently attended me. We soon developed a rhythm of confident work together to tackle and overcome the challenges of the mountain.

Every time my foot hits the ground on these walks there's a host of points which occupy my mind as I try to determine if it's settled safely, for not only that point but for both my prior step and next step. I frequently made several adjustments, often with Quinn's nudging. He never once failed to show me a step that required more of my attention and focus. Imagine your foot is on reasonably stable ground but there's a rock poised to gash your shin or knee if you don't lift the leg properly past it. In each such case, Quinn refused to move forward for me until I noticed. It wasn't enough to heel-toe walk here; you had to maneuver the whole leg in intricate ways during the hike. Now my hiking stick was a fantastically valuable tool in this process and Quinn quickly re-integrated it into his work. This meant ensuring there is more room on the right side, including room to swing the stick forward and evaluate my potential next step. It was a complex array of factors he managed – more than I would expect of a human but I'm not sure a human could have readily held his devoted single-mindedness.

Have you ever been so focused on some mental task, be it a book, a puzzle or whatever, such that your mind fails to properly recognize some interruption? You reach the point of breaking out of the task but only have a partial realization of the interruption. So demanding was my mental task that I often had to ask Tracy to repeat whatever she had said from her position several yards ahead of us on the route. It really required so much of my attention that by the bottom of the mountain I was exhausted. Quinn had to be even more insistent to all the real dangers yet his mind didn't ever slip. I could tell he was mentally tired because he slowed and was more cautious, but the trip was an entire, complete and amazing success. A friend attending the NHAB Walk for Sight with me had marveled over Quinn's attention to the details of our sidewalk travel. That was learning your letters and this was a Pulitzer Prize -winning novel.

I thought this hiking had the potential to become something more significant for us. Striving to achieve summits had an obvious analogy to the notion of Ability Awareness I had come to celebrate in my journey with blindness. I thought perhaps I might use the climbing of the NH mountains to raise awareness for the organizations I wanted to support. I learned there were 48 peaks which rise to over 4000 feet in NH, and it is often a hiker's mark of achievement to reach the summit of all of them. In order to give that goal true consideration I felt we needed another test hike, and we began to evaluate our options. Many people suggested Mt. Pierce in Crawford Notch because of the name connection, and also because the trail is well trodden. Others suggested Mt. Osceola because it had gentler elevation work and many felt it would be easier footing overall. On September 6, 2009 we set out for the summit of Mt. Osceola. Tracy, Quinn and I were joined by a group of friend for our very first of the 4000 foot peaks. Various challenges caused our companions to be considerably later than expected, but it was a beautiful day and so we set off confident and comfortable.

Unexpectedly, the trail was rife with rock fall, many small soccer-ball-sized rocks along the path made the footing extremely challenging for Quinn and I, more so than we had experienced in our prior work and so our pace was necessarily slow. My foot had to ease its way between rounded boulders to the narrow patches of safe footing. This was relatively easy for the sighted, but challenging for our style of work since Quinn could not walk beside me to show me the best foot placement. Often I had to step on rounded rocks which required finding the right balance point, this was difficult and resulted all too commonly in rolled ankles. A couple of arduous hours into the hike we realized what is easy for some is not necessarily easy for my challenge, and this would be a much longer hike than any of us anticipated. Our food and water supplies would be insufficient. This was exacerbated by the exciting news two of our companions were pregnant and hadn't realized the toll this hike would take. We passed on several opportunities to cut the hike short keeping the risk more reasonable, and instead unreasonably made our way to the summit at 4,340 feet. During our descent daylight was fading and we were unprepared for darkness. We were slower going down than up as I had to probe for footing even more carefully on the descent.

At about the half way point in our descent our fellow hikers, in consideration of the pregnant ladies, needed to forge ahead more quickly for their safety. This left Tracy, Quinn and me alone, exhausted, out of food and water, and regrettably working our way out of the poor decisions we all had made. Shortly afterwards, I misjudged a step down, sliding out into a sit-fall causing Quinn to leap up and lick my face. This was a rare choice for him and a clear sign of his concern. Bolstering my resolve, we continued with more caution until a bit further along I made another lapse and poorly managed the warning Quinn provided so that I fell painfully again. Tracy and I talked, knowing we had to get off the mountain but unsure what our best options were to proceed. She could see well enough to continue, but only barely and Quinn refused to guide me when I lifted the harness. He was clearly concerned that I was not being safe enough with his warnings and he didn't want to see me hurt. I gave him the good boy praise of reinforcement he deserved since I understood his decision. Using my hiking stick and Tracy's voice guidance I very slowly descended for nearly 100 yards before asking Quinn to give me one more chance and promising to give him my full focus. I'm sure he couldn't understand all my words, but he seemed to understand the need. He guided me ever so cautiously through the most difficult final stretches and eventually out of our 9.5-hour hike. Lessons learned and happy to have no serious repercussions, it was time for us to settle into more thoughtful problem solving before our hiking expeditions could blossom into some of the most epic accomplishments of my life!

On May 1, 2010 Quinn had his most important hike. We took the trails on the Welch-Dickie loop in Thornton, NH. It was Tracy's favorite mountain and we had a purpose. The first stretch of the trail let us test a rock-strewn but dry stream bed crossing before easing up a steady climb to the most beautiful ledges in the area. A cool breeze felt fantastic, but the next half mile was alleged to have a host of particularly tricky albeit rewarding sections of trail. This was a special hike because an engagement ring for Tracy was hidden in my backpack and I charged Quinn with getting us both there for the proposal. There were steep and slippery slabs, intricate twisting steps and switchback ledges, a rock canyon and even a leaping Quinn scramble from which his moniker "Adventure Dawg" was born. He fulfilled his charge as always, and we arrived on the sunny warm summit for the astounding 360-degree panorama which made it much harder for Tracy to say no. We took her yes to the top of Mt Washington on Independence Day that year, and again more legally on the Mt. Washington cruise ship on October 10, 2010 with Quinn in his tuxedo beside me, surrounded by many friends and family. I knew guide dogs could help find all sorts of things but "Quinn find a wife" was likely his greatest performance!

By 2011 we were climbing 4000-foot peaks with regularity and enjoying the obligatory tug of war atop each mountain. In our downtime, literally, we were making regular visits to schools to talk with students about reaching their peak potential. Quinn certainly was performing above and beyond the call of duty as a guide dog. Tracy found his puppy raiser's journal which had been kindly gifted to me by his sponsors from Puppies Behind Bars. A subtle but significant detail had eluded our notice previously. On the back cover was a photo of a young Quinn puppy sitting atop a flight of cement stairs. A note added by his raiser says: "Stairs...I want to climb mountains!"

He was certainly doing so and yet there was another pioneer project ahead for him. In order to improve my fitness for hiking I was taking longer and longer walks with him. At each point in our walk where we turned around and headed towards home, Quinn would pick up the pace because he knew the playment plan assured he would get his reward as soon as we arrived home. I found myself holding him back as we were already fast walking and guide schools strongly discourage running with your guides. This changed a little during our annual visit with the trainers from Guiding Eyes to ensure we were a healthy and happy team. Noting that I was holding him back but that he was performing all the guide warnings perfectly, I was given permission to let him pick up the pace. Given the quality work we were doing as a team, in controlled situations I was granted some judgment to stretch our legs.

Quinn's excellent judgement was confirmed as we reached a sidewalk and he immediately slowed to an appropriate pace. This enabled me to start jogging with him. I still recall the first time I realized I was truly running as we shore-lined a 1.5-mile loop near our home on a brisk morning. Hearing the footfalls of someone ahead of me I gave a greeting to announce that we were approaching. As we passed him an odd laugh enticed me to ask if we'd done something wrong, only to hear with some amusement: "I'm going to have a hard time telling my wife I was passed by a blind guy and his guide dog while running this morning!" Were we really running? How much more running might we do?

I decided to test it and add some safety by having friends run ahead of us. This way I could see how Quinn responded to the increase in speed and also expand our route selections. We used bike paths and Mine Falls Park to open up our running, and before long had enough confidence in his incredible work to enter a race together. The best part of all of this was the sheer joy for Quinn in each opportunity. He was eager to run and seemed determined to run down anyone ahead of us and refuse to allow anyone to pass us if he could pick up the pace. I'm not ashamed to admit I often held back his pace in our work together. He always watched for the right opportunities of spacing for us to pass safely and loped along joyfully at a comfortable pace once we'd settled into our routine. In the dozens of races, we ran together the advocacy work with race directors and the inspired reaction of our fellow runners paled beside the incredible independence and freedom we shared.

Stairs....I want to climb Mountains...

Pictured: The image from Quinn's puppy book

On his birthday in 2012 we ran a trail race at Beaver Brook trails with the encouragement of Bob Hayes, and it was perhaps one of Quinn's most masterful performances. Running down a gentle rocky slope, he helped me weave around the people we passed sighting in on Bob just ahead of us. As the trail came to a small stream crossing with a plank bridge we'd practiced the day before, Quinn noticed the backlog of people waiting to cross, including Bob, and turned slightly right aiming towards the stream. He slowed as Bob's surprised warning reached me, paused at the edge and dropped into the hiking-leaping crouch I'd learned so well. I gave him the "Jump" command and we leaped, clearing, ok mostly clearing, the stream together and continued racing down the trail. At the bottom we rounded the corner with Bob having caught up and raced back up the gentle slope towards the finish. His four-paw drive might have lent me a little power as we surged up the hill to complete the 5K course in an average of 7:20 minutes per mile...on trail...with a double stream crossing! We made it home in time to watch a Patriots away game together with all his friends and handfuls of well-earned Charlee Bear treats for the heroic birthday boy.

We signed up to run the Boston Athletic Association 5K road race held on April 14, 2013. It was the day before the Boston Marathon and shared the same finish line. A now-famous race day photo shows us crossing with Quinn's tongue hanging out and a look of joy on his face and only one paw barely touching the ground.

Pictured: Randy and Quinn 2013 BAA 5k

I on the other hand, have the look of a tired person trying to keep pace with my guide! Unfortunately, that joyful image would be replaced by a horrific tragedy on the very next day. The Boston Marathon bombing exploded the finish line changing the course of innumerable lives, including mine. Safely at home but worried for our friends in the area, I thought how terrible it is when people do not learn how to communicate and resolve differences in healthy ways. I cheered thankfully for the incredible heroes who responded to save lives and support the many in urgent need even as I thought more seriously about my running future. I knew I wanted to be part of a positive response to the horrors of the day and I made a promise to run the 2014 Boston Marathon. I didn't plan to run it with Quinn, but I expected he would help me train.

First though, there was a little hiking work to finish. We completed the 48 during our historic winter climbing of 2011-2012. The movie Four More Feet captured Quinn's glory well, but the summer hiking quest was the harder work and a few peaks remained. Willem Lange and the Windows to the Wild show wanted to take a hike with us before we completed our 48 and they managed by the barest of margins on a casual hike of Mt. Willard. I had become so confident in Quinn's abilities I didn't invite any support hikers with me, just the film crew and their celebrity host would be enough for us to share the magic on the trail together.

Quinn, once again, was spectacular and at the Crawford Notch depot after the hike I gave him the bonus tug of war we hadn't enjoyed on the overlook ledge which had too many people for his normal reward. Overly enthusiastic, Quinn broke the tug toy which had served us from the first hike back on Pack Monadnock four years earlier. This was a bad portent as we had two hikes remaining for the official accomplishment, Mt. Isolation and Mt. Flume. He would of course make those hikes but before the episode of our show, "Hiking in the Dark" could air on NH Public Television, Quinn would begin showing signs of sickness. A strange lump appeared on his head and progressed as we endured weeks of testing. A hopeful initial diagnosis of poly-myositis gave way to the more devastating reality: Quinn had Osteosarcoma, bone cancer. Worse, this typically large-limb cancer is often treatable by removal of the leg but in Quinn's case it was on his skull and it was undoubtedly terminal. Tracy and I were frantic for a solution, there had to be a way to save our brave boy. How could my second dog guide, my best friend to follow my best friend, also be dying from this unfair, awful and deadly disease. Ostend had broken my heart and Quinn healed it only to suffer a similar fate.

Tracy and I were hurt to our core, the sickening grief which makes every breath physically painful until you force yourself away from the ugly reality facing you. We searched thoroughly for every possible treatment which would give him a chance at quality life, and after exhausting all options we resigned ourselves to the only reasonable alternative. We would do everything which brought him comfort and joy. His days would hold all the play, love, care, friendships and joy his condition would allow until that was no longer possible. Then we would find the strength to end his pain before it was too great.

He could not open his mouth very much and so we bought the flattest toys we could find so that our play driven boy could still play. We fed him soft food by hand to ensure he had the means to get nutrition. When his strength was there we played, and when it ebbed or showed the distress of discomfort we simply loved him, stroking his golden fur and wished futilely he didn't know we were so terribly sad. Every week a new envelope arrived, full of well-wishing cards from the roughly thirty thousand students who had their lives touched by the Mighty Quinn during our school presentations. My email overflowed with messages of support, and all of those helped ease the boundless hurt which was building. Dr. Jody Sandler and Dr. Richard Kaas were extraordinary, capable and caring vets and people.

On January 20, 2014 my dear friend Bob Dunn arrived all the way from Australia to bid farewell to his friend Quinn and lend some crucial support to Tracy and me. It was time to make the most dreadful decision I think any of us may ever make. For all we may know that the end of suffering is so necessary and so much a kindness; it still feels like the worst of betrayals. Quinn had short moments of lesser pain and his drive, determination and devotion were unrivaled in the world. He insisted on wearing his harness and guiding me into Mercy Animal Hospital much as I insisted in cradling my beloved boy in my arms as I listened in distress for his final breath. Still I held my boy and whispered all my love and devotion back to him as they gently told me he was gone. I knew this was both true and false for my Quinn could never truly be gone from me or even from this world where he had forged such a remarkable legacy.

The next day WMUR-TV carried the news of his passing. It was front page news on the Nashua telegraph and several other papers in NH ran feature stories on his life. His friends at Eastern Mountain Sports provided an incredibly touching tribute in which they shared a powerful and accurate epitaph: "To call the Mighty Quinn a Service Dog is akin to calling a hike of Mt. Washington a stroll in the park!" Windows to the Wild released their episode shortly after his passing and it won a New England Emmy Award for their quality work. I'll always remember their touching tribute to the legacy of a one-of-a-kind dog who took me to impossible heights. What I'll remember most though, is Quinn's relentless dedication and devotion to every task we chose together and to me personally. We were friends and I will treasure my great fortune in having been touched by one of the greatest spirits I have ever known. Bob Dylan had it right: "You've not seen nuthin' like the Mighty Quinn."

Hooray Tracy

The best and most beautiful things in the world cannot be seen or even touched. They must be felt with the heart." Hellen Keller &
Anne Sullivan

Quinn's death devastated me despite my determined efforts to apply all the experiences and beliefs I had developed in order to cope. At times of loss or grief, I wish people all the courage, strength and support they need. I had that support in spades, most notably from my similarly grief-stricken wife Tracy. As Quinn departed our lives, we leaned on each other: Her teary eyes made her sight little better than my own. Sobbing gasps made it hard to talk and so we simply held each other in silent support and understanding of the loss we shared.

There was not always such a strong connection between Tracy and Quinn. Her first meeting with him in February of 2008 at an O'Choda Gathering was rather anticlimactic. I was tending a camp chore and opted to leave Quinn outside of the kitchen to ease any concerns regarding service animals and sanitation. I tied Quinn to a table and put him in a "down stay", which was virtually unnecessary, as his laser focus would allow nothing to interrupt his steadfast watch over the door that my friend guided me beyond to start my chores. Unbeknownst to me, Tracy came upon the handsome hero dog and thought to get some quality puppy time. All her dog-toned imploring fell upon ears tuned only to the sounds of my voice and eventual return. Each pat she gave to his soft fur met with determination to let nothing distract him from the desired return of his "Dad". "Boring Dog" Tracy concluded, and the rest might have been history if not for Jeff Collins' and Teresa Roberts' meddling! Perhaps innocently, they had invited Tracy to the event and encouraged her to attend many of the activities throughout the weekend. It just so happened I was hosting a Scotch tasting as one of those opportunities. I liked to give a historical reflection on the origins of the elixir, conduct a structured taste testing and generally enjoy the company of my friends and their expanded circle of friends at this well attended event. Tracy participated, sharing her enthusiasm and general appreciation, although we had few interactions beyond the passing introduction and mutual enjoyment of single malt scotch.

This was enough of a connection for Teresa to invite Tracy to join us for the NH Association for the Blind's annual Walk for Sight in June of 2008, still on the mostly innocuous side. Better still, we were sufficiently simpatico for her to accept. She lived so much further south it made sense for her to stay overnight at our home in Nashua. This provided an excellent opportunity for deeper insights into each other, and quality time with my friend Teresa as well. I enjoy meeting new people and Tracy and I had a lot in common. I learned we shared an appreciation for martial arts - she had a black belt of her own in American Kenpo Karate. We both enjoyed the aforementioned Scotch, philanthropy as evidenced by her supporting our charity walk, the Society for Creative Anachronism, SCA and of course dogs, as Quinn's more playful off-duty mode started to win her over.

Later that summer of 2008, Teresa and Jeff further influenced the situation by encouraging us to travel together for the long drive to the Pennsic War event in western Pennsylvania. I suspect they were hopeful Tracy and I might develop a relationship, yet they kept this aspiration secret from both of us, knowing we each had ended our prior relationships with some difficulty. Whether anything connected for us, the support and conversation was likely to be therapeutic and that is exactly how the trip transpired.

The simple physics of our journey were interesting. Somehow, we had two weeks of camping supplies, two people and one guide dog all nestled into Tracy's Mini-Cooper for an 11-hour drive! Tracy will tell you that she is 5 feet tall and I would be wise to just nod and agree but that's still a lot of cargo for a small vehicle, and we definitely received some interesting looks as we climbed out at various points along our journey. The real interest for me was inside the vehicle as I experienced Tracy managing her family printing business remotely with a calm efficient competence. I was inspired by her leadership and professionalism, as well as the casual switch to comfortable and personable interactions when off the work calls. I hoped to emulate her professionalism for my new role with the Board of Directors at NH Association for the Blind. I was fascinated with Tracy's confident demeanor, and her depth of diverse knowledge. I very much enjoyed our many commonalities as well. We had a kindred problem-solving attitude and 11 hours of travel passed all too quickly with the luxury of our exclusive conversations.

Pictured: Randy and Tracy at an event early in their relationship

Even with the early flirtation stage just underway, I felt the excited interest of new relationship energy. Those miles of

Pennsylvania Turnpike reminded me of a song as many experiences often do. "You're My Home" by Billy Joel says, 'home can be the Pennsylvania turnpike' and 'wherever we're together that's my home.' We went our divergent ways for Pennsic but she remained on my mind throughout.

After the deep connection of our travel time, home for two weeks was separate campsites at the event, only occasionally crossing paths. She departed the event early and we returned to our geographically separate homes, but our conversations resumed immediately through our computers. Music is very important in my life and we shared favorite songs along with our life interests. While we have different musical styles, it was an entertaining exploration. One bit of the entertainment arose from my sending her a link to a song I liked only to receive a surprising response. "The song is ok, but I really like the dancing." What dancing was she talking about? Apparently, the music resource I'd been using for some time, unbeknownst to me, was a full-blown video site! The interesting secrets hidden from my sightless and apparently only partially attentive website searching, gave us instant amusement and a reminder of the different ways we interact with the world. I had never realized YouTube was a video service.

We both wanted to move from light flirtations to actual dating, but this was challenging given my inability to drive. Tracy made the trek from Rhode Island to New Hampshire a couple of times before we made the truly big plunge. I'm not talking about the incredibly magical weekend retreat to Ogunquit, Maine with Jeff, Teresa and several friends but rather the end of that weekend when I brought her to a Patriots tailgate and game at Foxboro! I was introducing her to an entirely different community of my friends, eager to show them this fun new person and hopeful for further compatibility. The Patriots were decimated by the Miami Dolphins and many friends, playfully invoking our mock football superstition, advised I end this young relationship immediately. I pointed out that Quinn had also lost "his" first game and we worked out marvelously. After all our superstitions are not serious and my interest in Tracy was absolutely real.

We communicated with each other every day by computer or phone. I relished each call from her and with a little crafty deception managed a recording of her shouting "Hooray" which I converted to my ringtone for her. This brought me much mirth, but I was going to need to advance beyond phone calls and computer contact for us to stay in touch in early October. My impending vacation to Disneyworld was going to make this challenging. Plato suggested that necessity is the mother of invention and the necessity of keeping in contact drove me to learn to send and receive text messages. How else could Tracy learn the epic tale of Quinn's first encounter with the evil villain Cruella deVille?

In October at Disneyworld the villains come out at night. Cruella approached us with her trademark cry of "Puppies, you brought me puppies!" She paused and whispered a request "Can I say hello to your service animal?" I put Quinn off duty and told her yes and the two immediately began to have a playful greeting. The problem for the actress playing Cruella is that Quinn was on long leash and as he wriggled his way around her he was apparently tying her up with his leash resulting in her very real call for help as she began to topple. Struggling in her restrictive costume, she was barely caught by her accompanying staffers. We all had a good laugh at the hero-dog once again emerging victorious over the villains of the world. My eagerness to share this and many other tales with Tracy made it clear to me how much I was treasuring her place in my world.

On my return home, Tracy and I took our first official public date to Ye Olde Commons where she had first met Quinn and where I was to marry two of my friends. This was my first wedding as officiant, and while generally comfortable with public speaking, I found myself surprisingly nervous. Their ceremony was such an important and significant event, I wanted to help ensure it was as close to perfect as possible. Surrounding all of this was a first opportunity for me to introduce Tracy to many of my friends. I appreciated how well she helped ease the introductions, as well as provide me a blend of encouragement and distance to address both my nervousness and my responsibilities. It was uncanny how well she read and naturally reacted to what I most needed in so many situations, blending independence and companionship with an easy, fun-loving grace.

Speaking of responsibilities, it was time for Tracy to meet my parents. Dad had moved to Nashua and into an assisted living facility as his health deteriorated. His spirit was strong and his infectious smile on display as he enthusiastically met the lady who I had told him was enhancing my life. Tracy easily charmed him and keenly saw through the challenge of his condition to the underlying qualities of the father I appreciated even more in his later years. My Mom was more demanding in her desire to ensure anyone in my life was going to give the love and care she wanted for me. But Tracy won mom's heart as well and quickly became a part of the family despite the weekend-only nature of our visits.

We decided to take a risk in our young relationship after only a few months. With only one of us commuting there was a significant burden on Tracy and she wanted to relocate to Nashua to allow us to be closer. She found a decent job opportunity though she was departing a very comfortable job she had developed for over 19 years. We chose to live together, accepting the risks for the benefit of not straining our time or finances by the need for a separate home. A massive ice storm heralded her arrival in December of 2008 and as power outages struck the area, my home filled with friends taking shelter as we have gas heat, hot water and little need for lights when I'm around to find things. This provided the full celebration her arrival warranted, and our house transformed into a home much as Billy Joel had predicted. It was a home full of laughter, working together and stepping slowly towards adventures.

My literal steps became steadily smoother and easier as with Tracy's help I completed the Medical "Brain Port" training. This was an experimental rehabilitation tool using a gyroscope integrated with a medical device during physical therapy exercises. The process was helping my brain to enhance my proprioception, which improved my balance significantly. This in conjunction with my multiple long days of karate training had me making steady progress with my balance and orientation.

Tracy took up studying karate with me at Tokyo Joes Studio of Self Defense and we occasionally had the opportunity to work together as she learned an entirely new system of martial arts. The dojo represented another community of friends we now shared along with the Patriot tailgate friends. We both appreciate the benefits of community and with her help I was soon exploring the social media networks of Twitter and Facebook to help support the blog I was writing about Quinn. These also helped me transition away from the work I'd done to run Zip's Patriots Page for over a decade. I still loved the Patriots but my life was following different paths which didn't allow time for the website work.

One of these paths was enabled by my balance progress. Between Quinn's passion for guiding me and our discovery of how much he particularly loved walking in the woods, we were starting a new journey. Maybe I should say restarting in Tracy's case, as she had prior experience hiking in the White Mountains. Although I had put down my hiking stick as a regular aid for walking, with her encouragement, we thought about my picking it back up to hike a little in the woods with Quinn guiding me. It was an oh-so-significant step for the three of us to visit Pack Monadnock in Wilton NH on August 15, 2009. We had been overcoming figurative mountains, but this was a chance for us to climb our first actual mountain together!

When I am learning a new set of skills, challenging myself mentally and physically to an extreme; I am unfortunately not always an easy-going, comforting communicator. Tracy patiently allowed me the freedom to make mistakes while always being vigilant for opportunities to help Quinn and I learn and grow as a team. I relish our ability to discuss plans and strategies in advance, reflect and revise afterwards while balancing the enjoyment and endurance of the experiences in between.

Pack Monadnock was hard work. The trail took 4.5 hours of grueling effort for the upward climb alone. Quinn and I worked to understand how to communicate through the harness while integrating the hiking stick back into our work in such difficult environs. Tracy and I similarly sought balance in how much talk was supportive, what information was distracting, and the ever-important separation of the strained tones of difficulty or frustration from any intent of personal slight. Amidst all the work, Tracy pulled me aside at several moments along the route and at the summit to appreciate the scenes nature provided which even sighted eyes might miss if they didn't choose to be aware, to step back from the toils of the trail and look around at the beauty of the world surrounding us. We shared these gifts and the realization Quinn was guiding us to something incredibly special with the work we were doing together on these mountain trails.

We began to form a vision of many mountain hikes and how it might help raise awareness to support a few of the causes we cared about. Tracy's experience running a company provided much of the foundation for the work on, 2020 Vision Quest. Even as we laid the groundwork, Tracy's community building and social media experience connected us to another instrumental opportunity. The Teva Life Agent competition was seeking an outdoor adventurer with a project they found significant and worthy of attention. They held online voting for video submissions and ultimately used the popularity of the video to choose their ambassador. On the merits of Tracy's marketing, persuasion and determination we were thrilled to be selected. We used the $10,000.00 prize to fund the initial start-up costs of our charity. Once again, or perhaps still, I was in appreciative awe of Tracy's talents and drive.

She showcased her infectious determination and resiliency many times as we moved forward together. An unexpected end to her first NH job presented difficulty in finding employment in her accounting field. Many places would not invite her for an interview simply because she did not have a college degree despite her decades of experience. Undaunted, she began taking classes aggressively to obtain her degree. While going to school full time, she continued to search for reasonable employment. In the meanwhile, she put her extra time to good use, at least from the perspective of my taste buds. Our tailgate food was particularly the beneficiary as Tracy is a tremendous cook and put her creativity to themed menus to the delight of our guests. This benefit was short lived because ultimately her diligence was rewarded, and she accepted work; different than her preference and skills might suggest as ideal, but she was determined to finish her degree for her next job.

In the world of over-achieving, Tracy stands tall. Working full time, attending college full time and co-founding 2020 Vision Quest made for quite the spring of 2010. This did not prevent me from complicating matters a little more. On May 1, 2010 we set out to climb one of Tracy's favorite peaks, Mt. Welch. The rest of our hiking team had been alerted to my secret plan to propose to her on the summit. Our dear friend and talented jeweler, Rachel Morris, provided one of her own crafted rings for the purpose. The ledges were very warm. Quinn and I were still developing our hiking skills, so that the work was physically and mentally very demanding. The summit rewarded us all with an idyllic 360-degree view which captured everyone's attention. Under the auspices of recording a podcast for the Teva Life Agent project, I asked for the right location and for Tracy to hold the recorder.

She chose a rock seat for me and warned me dramatically each time I reached for my pack as there was apparently an impressive drop off to my side. "It's too dangerous" she warned several times as I reached to remove my pack or even to get to the top pocket where I had the ring hidden away. I laughed at the irony of the warning preceding my proposal and began the recording. My romantic notions of leading her through our journeys and adventure to the proposal of a journey and adventure in marriage was emotional for me. I realized she was a little distracted by the views initially but, she soon caught my intense emotion. As the words of my proposal culminated I was met with only silence. Only a little concerned, I gently repeated my question "Will you marry me, I kind of hope to hear an answer?" A barely whispered response struggled to break through the sobs of joy I could now plainly and happily hear as she said, "Yes." I was overjoyed. Eventually she explained that her teary eyes and vigorous head nods had not relayed her initial affirmation to my sightless eyes.

Pictured: Randy and Tracy's engagement photo.
Summit Mt. Welch May 1, 2010

Our engagement atop Mt. Welch promised to add a year of wedding planning into the busy mix. June 1 saw the official start of 2020 Vision Quest, both of us along with a group of friends undertaking multiple roles. We were working our way towards the July 4 summit of Mt. Washington as the grand start of our quest to climb the NH 48 4000-foot peaks. We all worked as a team through the many tasks required to bring things together, and yet Tracy managed all of her other projects, all of our joint projects and provided me the support essential to my learning, enacting, failing and recovering in my role as the front person for our charity. She continuously read my mood and provided the challenge to push me harder or the empathy to recover when I felt I made one of several poor decisions in those early days.

The MS Mt. Washington Cruise Ship invited us on a free cruise in late July with the intent to make us an offer. Having heard of our epic adventure on July 4 and understanding we were planning our wedding, they wanted to offer their ship as a possible wedding venue. They had an opening on October 10, 2010 and while that would allow us only a few months to plan, a sunset wedding at peak foliage on a mountain lake might be just the right magic for us. The perfect sounding date of 10/10/10 made it all the more special. We agreed and with an astounding turn-out of all but two invited guests, 210 of our closest friends joined us on-board for a picture-perfect evening. Quinn in his tuxedo guided me to the front and as Tracy joined me we each spoke the vows we wrote for the other. I took the liberty of revising the lyrics to John Denver's "Annie's Song" slightly. I sang to my beautiful bride rather nervously but completely with a heart full of love for our partnership and for my sweet, caring, intelligent, determined and loving Tracy.

Pictured: Randy and Tracy kiss on their wedding day 10-10-10

The evening held many treasured moments including our first dance to the upbeat verse of Lucky and dancing with my mom to Color my World. There was a blur of friends celebrating with us until all too quickly the boat had docked, and it was time to depart. One more appropriate surprise awaited us. Our clever bridal party arranged for a bumper car extravaganza, including two cars decorated with "just married" for each of us. It was an apt demonstration of why I should not be driving and fortunately I wouldn't need to as we would steer our lives together going forward.

Our lives remained incredibly full with 2020 Vision Quest success and work both increasing beyond our initial expectations. My days were filled with Karate training, 2020 Vision Quest coordination and the increasing popularity of my school presentations. I supplemented this with hiking for our quest, a slow but steady progression of run training with Quinn and of course the usual social engagements of hosting, such as our Bardic events or Patriot tailgates. As our quest leapt from 5 mountains in the first year to 17 additional peaks in 2011, more media outlets were taking notice. With Tracy's support we arranged multiple radio shows, local television news and even a feature filming for Animal Planet.

Along with these successes we experienced transition in our all-volunteer staff. I tend to be hard on myself for my failures. Recognizing some of the poor choices I made due to inexperience, I sadly accepted the departure of frustrated friends from our charity. Blaming myself for the hurt feelings of friends, I particularly needed Tracy's support. Together we evaluated the opportunities to strategically rebuild and enhance the team, better positioning ourselves for the future. This was especially important as I launched into one of the most epic experiences of my life.

I met Bob Hayes at an Eastern Mountain Sports Club Day event in Nashua. He spoke with tremendous knowledge and experience of the White Mountains and in particular of how the terrain must present a particular challenge for my steps. He confidently stated his belief I would excel at winter hiking. My initial reaction was to discount his assertion, because snowshoes created extra width and had aggressive bottom grips, both of which posed danger to Quinn. But Bob was enthusiastic as he explained micro-spikes, often packed-down trails and other solutions. As I listened to him speak I was energized by his enthusiasm and confidence. We built a friendship and with his guidance I greatly expanded my running and hiking. Bob soon invigorated me with the notion of undertaking a single season winter summit of all 48 of the 4000-foot peaks in NH. At that point he was one of the 46 people who had accomplished the feat and suggested it would be an excellent demonstration of "Ability Awareness" for me to undertake this as part of our quest. He agreed to help guide me through the process and we set our sights on the winter of 2011-2012.

During the three winter months I would be away from home a tremendous amount of time in order to be prepared to hike when the weather allowed. The plan would need Tracy's full backing and she gave that and so much more. One week before the start of this new quest my Dad had a major stroke. During the many hours it took for him to come out of his coma and the early days after with his life hanging in the balance, I thought my quest might end before it began. As he became less critical I wrestled with my decision, feeling selfish to even consider the hiking attempt. Tracy was beside me for all of it, giving encouragement to any decision but emphasizing her willingness to cover me during the times I needed to be away. It is simply so much easier to pursue our dreams when we have a relationship of positive challenge, encouragement and support.

I was often away, departing on Thursday and returning on Tuesday most weeks. Each trip home Tracy ensured I maximized my time with Dad and during my travels provided thorough updates on his progress. Nightly phone calls celebrated each success and gave us the chance to discuss some of the real challenges. Interactions between Bob and I broke down during the midpoint of our quest. We attempted unsuccessfully to resolve them, and Tracy eased my nightly isolation, providing concern and perspective. February 10, 2012 was the most challenging in this regard and after the worst of Bob's sullen silence for a hard hike over Lafayette and Lincoln, I called Tracy in desperation. I knew this hiking partnership was too dysfunctional for me to endure. With 33 of the peaks accomplished, the goal was pushing me more than was reasonable. It was time for me to separate from Bob while I could still appreciate all the help and support he had provided. I took one last hike with him and his wife Geri up Mt. Carrigain. Afterwards, Tracy picked up me, all my winter supplies and my spirits which felt so low from the fear my dream of the winter 48 was over. She encouraged me to finish the quest with Justin and Dina. More importantly, she consoled me in my guilt, validating I had made the right choice in stepping away from an untenable situation.

One week later I set upon a Bonds traverse with Dina and Justin. This 24.5-mile trek would be the most remote of any of the winter hikes. It was the one hike most experienced hikers suspected would make or break our quest. We planned it as the start of a 54-mile, 7 peak stretch in three days. On a crisp and cold day with a light snow falling we started Zealand Mountain's relentless upward climb to overlook Zeacliffs briefly in the early morning. By the time we crossed the knolls of Guyotte a full-on blizzard had us temporarily evaluating if we might need to turn back as the weather had been forecast to be very good but clearly wasn't clear! By Bond's summit, however, it was blue sky beautiful and gave us the energy to battle the windy col of Bondcliff with only a long but steady descent through the Wilderness trail to Lincoln Woods and the miles of flat trail to our waiting vehicle. Those last miles seemed forever long. Even Quinn's tireless steps had slowed a little in the dark cold silence. Suddenly Quinn's pace increased, forcing me to push my tired legs a little more. His tail began to wag mightily, thwacking against my snow pants as I hastened forward. I heard a shout from the distance and recognition slowly came to my exhausted mind. Tracy was on the suspension bridge waiting for us. How well she knew me, the guilt I felt for not having been able to make things work with Bob, the apprehension of this significant first hike and the similarly daunting Owl's Head Mountain tomorrow. She drove up on her Friday night to celebrate with me, boost my confidence for the next day and most of all to showcase the love and partnership which makes our relationship so strong.

Far more than merely offering support, Tracy is an active participant in a life we choose to share. Later that summer I planned a 100 mile walk to celebrate the 100th anniversary of the New Hampshire Association for the Blind. By plan, I would arrive at their annual Walk for Sight at the finish of my endurance experience. I set out with Robert and Jennifer Liang as well as my nephew Chris for the first half of the walk, going from Concord through Durham and Dover to Portsmouth. There Tracy met us for the return trek, taking part in the rotation of guides to help me reach my goal. As Saturday's surprisingly cold and rainy weather made the early morning challenging, Tracy took the final long stretch of miles into Concord. The downpour encouraged us to pick up the pace to trot as we laughed nearly maniacally for the excitement of accomplishment, the magnitude of difficulty, and appreciation for undertaking such things together.

It was far more fun to share our delayed honeymoon together later that year, with our trip to the Grand Canyon and Sedona in October of 2012. Rick and Monique had generously gifted us a week's stay and Tracy's influence guided us to make it one of the most marvelous vacations of my life. I am often asked with the utmost of earnest well intentions, what I get from experiences which are so vitally visual. Standing on the edge of the Grand Canyon and hearing Tracy's emotionally laden "Wow! Wow!! Wow!!" certainly captured my attention and more so when she followed up with the vivid descriptions of what had taken away her breath and initial language skills! Tracy shares her sight with me, as do many of my friends and through those eyes I appreciate the majesty and beauty of many situations. There are, however, so many other aspects beyond the views which are often lost to those overwhelmed by the visuals. The sounds, fragrances, tastes, and even the feel or texture of the air are part of my experience. It was cold with light snow flurries on our first day, and I could feel the immense vastness of the air. I tasted a snowflake on my tongue, felt the brisk sting of cleansing air in my nostrils and listened to the ambient sounds ebbing into the void. Closing my eyes, I envisioned the images Tracy described in harmony with the fullness of my other senses. The synergy was richly rewarding.

It is the adventure of something new I treasure most though, such as our hike down along Bright Angel trail. All of our work hiking in the perilous footing of the Northeast was rewarded by the ease with which we managed the remarkably smoother pathways here. Every turn of the inner canyon unveiled new panoramas of the colorful layer cake geology and our desert hike surprisingly exploded into an oasis of cotton trees and foliage at the Indian Garden campground half way down. This was the end of our journey in the canyon for this trip, as down was optional and up was mandatory. We sat together in the cool shade of those surprisingly massive trees while mule teams came and went around us. There are so many wonders in the world and though I had experienced some incredible things, this felt like the first deliberate touching of the marvels by choice, and we basked in the moment. Those mountain peaks in NH had started a journey of experience and already this vacation suggested it need not have any limitations. Together we could and would plan more such experiences to enrich our lives.

Before we allowed Sedona to sweep us away there was one more gift from Tracy and the Grand Canyon. We went to one of the park buildings on the rim which held a raised relief map, so I could trace the tactile outline and comprehend the full details of the massive river canyon. As we neared the rim in the morning, the mist which often rose from the depths unveiled a pair of rainbows rising and settling on opposite ends of the Canyon. We were told it was a common occurrence but there was nothing common for us in those moments, feeling the moist wind rise to our faces and seeing together the majesty in that moment. We took the tranquility of that moment to Sedona's sunsets. We had our share of adventures such as the Devil's Arch and a day of losing our way on a desert hike; but most of all we had an epiphany of making the experiences we dreamed become plans instead of wishes.

Tracy returned home to a new job as the Controller at a Bicycle Adventure Company. Our film, Four More Feet, was being shown in various places around New England, helping to garner more attention for our charity. Our school presentations continued to grow in popularity while we began to receive steadily more interest for corporate keynotes as well. I developed our core keynote presentation, "Reaching Our Peak Potential." Our annual charity fund raiser, the Peak Potential Dinner and Auction, sold out for November 17 and while busy, life was exciting and promising. With all these things going so well, I had little reason to expect the heartbreaking news just a little way ahead. My Dad had recovered from his prior year's stroke and while still tremendously challenged he kept his spirits high continuing to give smiles and encouragement to all those around him. Dad wasn't healthy enough to attend our event but looked forward to hearing all the stores I would share with him.

On the morning of our big event I received a phone call at 5:00 a.m. from Kyrra, one of Dad's beloved caregivers. He had died in the early morning hours, and although I knew the prior year had been a gift of time to savor and share, it was little succor to the grip of grief on my heart. I sat on the edge of the bed in stunned silence, holding the immense weight of the phone in my hand. I bent my head and sobbed. We had used all the extra time together well, in loving compassion. I loved him, especially for all the growth he made in his later years. Dad made his love and pride for me crystal clear, particularly in our final year together.

The finality in losing a parent is transitional and I paused on the pinnacle of this moment, unable to go back and unwilling to go forward with the responsibilities which must begin immediately. Tracy's hand fell gently on my shoulder and kneaded tenderly. Her touch pulled me back enough to hear her own quiet sobs even before her voice reached out to tell me she was so very sorry. I let my shoulders sag just a little more, let her be strong for me for a few more moments as I mourned my Dad's passing. Then putting my hand atop hers and turning to embrace her in a hug I allowed us to build our strength together for the tasks of the day: calling to inform my brother Rick and then making my way to see Dad one last time.

There are so many distracting details in the loss of a loved one. Coupling these with trying to manage the details of our Peak Potential Gala that very night was unimaginable. Tracy, amidst her own grief, supported the effort and coordinated our incredible community of friends to manage the rest of the details. Standing before a packed hall in a dazed grief-stricken state would have been too much except for that support. Together we gave a tribute to my Dad and the resourceful ingenuity he inspired within me. He loved to tell tales and I suspect some of my story-telling spirit comes from him even as I know coming away from his loss is a journey I would not have wanted to make alone.

The adage "life moves on" holds true for all of us. I struggled many times, but I also had old stories to tell and new stories to make. Bruce Albiston called to invite me to speak at the New England Visually Impaired Ski Festival at Sugarloaf, Maine in February of 2013. He enticed me with a different method of interacting with our New England peaks, coming not from hiking them but from learning to ski down them. Brent Bell and I made the journey, warmly hosted by Bruce and his wife Annemarie, meeting yet another wonderful community of friends. I learned the exhilaration and freedom of gliding atop the snow completely untethered, using only the sound of Brent's voice to guide me. He skied about 10 to 15 yards ahead of me, providing instruction on technique and direction. I could also determine the location of his voice as he moved left, right, or suddenly down at steeper points. It was three days of magical learning which we proudly shared through a little video work.

On day one Tracy delighted in seeing me slowly snowplow on the bunny slope. Day two brought wedge turns and steadily more comfort as we took higher runs on the mountain and felt the first signs of real speed and freedom on the slopes. Day three culminated in Tracy's request to please stop sharing videos as she didn't need to see her husband hurtling down the mountain any faster! This newfound adventure was invigorating in many ways and there was a plan and control to the seeming chaos of the sightless surge down the slopes. The NEVI program aided Brent and I in learning steadily more skills as guide and blind skier. I hoped to return many times to the people and potential of this different dance with the mountains.

My hiking that winter was not going as smoothly. There was a steady pain and tingling in my right shoulder, arm and both legs. I evaded getting it checked out until the persistent discomfort convinced me it was time to explore. Just one week after my ski expedition, I arrived at the Lahey Clinic to some difficult news. My condition had caused a significant amount of neuropathy below my knees in both legs and to a lesser level below the elbow in both arms. After repeating the nerve conductivity tests multiple times, I was diagnosed with chronic demyelinating poly-neuropathy. The loss of sensory nerves in my legs enhanced the challenge of walking and certainly hiking. With an ambitious summer schedule intended to bring an end to our quest for the 48 4K peaks in the non-winter months, I would need to lean on Tracy's support once again.

The medical team felt I had received too much Solumedrol in my past and suggested a new treatment approach to this nerve deterioration. They gave me infusions of Intravenous Immunoglobulin (IVIG). This was administered alongside patients receiving chemotherapy for cancer and certainly provided me immediate perspective as I compared their challenges to mine. In fact this perspective was eerily reminiscent of my time in the neurological ward during my initial treatments when first losing my sight. Still, I felt my own struggle with acceptance of my situation. Why was I facing a new and difficult challenge in addition to my already demanding circumstances? This time Tracy was there to remind me the 'why is this happening" is not as important as the "how do I respond".

Hiking proved to be difficult from our first double day launch of Cannon Mountain to crossing the notch and climbing up to the Green Leaf hut for an overnight. Quinn and John Swenson teamed up to guide me over Lafayette, Lincoln and down the perilous path of Falling Waters Trail. We often joked it might be more aptly named falling blind guy except my guides were so attentive I did not fall. My feet did take more abuse than normal as I learned to manage the neuropathy by paying attention to the trail through the feeling in my knees and thighs instead of my feet. I simply could not feel anything below my knees as if they had fallen asleep and would not wake. I learned to ease my foot into each step before verifying the stability of that placement by leaning my weight onto the leg. This was arduous and slow. Fortunately, our entire team's pain and exhaustion was alleviated by arriving to the trailhead to find lawn chairs, a barbeque grill full of steak tips and burgers as well as ice-cold beverages for we weary hikers. Who else: Tracy providing the extra special reward to lift our spirits.

The next few hikes were brutally exhausting. My steps were slow, my strength low and it seemed something more than neuropathy was awry. In the follow-up explorations a blood test discovered the source. I'd been suffering with Lyme disease all summer and my other neurological condition had hidden the effect. A strong course of antibiotics for a month had me back on track to end the summer season and our epic quest in style. On August 24, 2013 we were poised to finish our original 10-year quest in just 37 months. Although we'd achieved the single winter summit of all 48 in the midst of this, the more challenging footing of the summer had me proud for the accomplishment. Better still, I was celebrating the official achievement with John Swenson and Tracy who were simultaneously achieving the goal for themselves. In fact, Quinn, John, Tracy and I took the final steps to the summit of Flume together with tremendous appreciation for each other and the wilderness miles we'd shared.

Too soon thereafter, Quinn's journey with us was brought to its tragic end. Tracy's presence with me on the journey made the heartache and loss more manageable. When he was gone I not only mourned the loss of my beloved friend, I was without my trusted guide to help me navigate the routines of my everyday life. I begrudgingly retrieved my blind cane and used it as needed, building up some of the skills lost to neglect and often supplementing them with Tracy's sighted guide assistance. While grieving for Quinn I missed his emotional support and Tracy filled that role even amidst her own grief.

After two long-seeming months both of us set our sights on an impending positive arrival. While Quinn was ill I told my guide school that I would not leave him to train with another service dog. This limited my options as they could not truly consider me for a candidate match until after he had died. My wait was shorter than it might otherwise have been because they had a high energy 'spitfire' named Autumn who they felt would be a great match. There wasn't a space in class for us but a home school opportunity was available on March 16 and so we prepared our home and hearts for our new arrival.

Chrissie Vetrano, Quinn's trainer, called to tell me she would be providing my home training. She informed me Autumn was a Black and Tan Labrador Retriever with very high energy and a loving disposition. As usual my excitement was mitigated by unreasonable but oh-so-natural feelings of guilt. It is no disservice to my love and appreciation for any of my past dogs to welcome a new pup into our home and yet I still feel the pangs of disloyalty. I prepared Tracy for an even harder sacrifice on her part. Since the building of the bond between blind handler and guide dog is so critical, it would be essential for Tracy to initially keep her distance from Autumn. We would slowly integrate into the full family connection she had experienced with Quinn but only after Autumn and I established and strengthened our bond, which is the key to the working relationship. So, going into this time, still fresh from the sorrow of Quinn's loss, Tracy would willingly step back, allowing me all the fun and frolicking of a young dog while getting little to none of that for herself. Such is the depth of her love and support for me and my particular needs.

Autumn arrived, bounding across our Patriots room, unruly in her leap-lick-assault into my arms. She was a joyous burst of energy and pranced or snuggled every moment of that initial meeting. Her spirit was beautiful, and I instantly knew that she would be an easy dog to love. As Chrissie joined us for dinner that evening, Autumn showed some early warning signs as she did not settle particularly well under the table. Many firm attempts to remind her to return to the down position under the table lasted only until the next bite of food reached my lips and she sprang up to test the leash which was wrapped around my leg. Finally, Chrissie ducked under the table to have "quiet words" with her under the table and things improved.

Our first day of actual training had some additional challenge as it fell on trash and recycle day, lining the sidewalks with extra obstacles for her. I realized that from Autumn's perspective, I was new, the area was new, the distractions were all new and she had to work hard for her focus. She understood her job, but it was not a smooth and easy transition from the effortless work with Quinn. It's always hard switching from a well-traveled experienced partnership to a brand-new team's early introductory phase. Much of this was to be expected. Over the course of our ten days I learned areas where Autumn was strong as well as the things which challenged her. Her confidence was a unique strength as she would boldly follow each command without regard for any of our companions' actions. Her commitment to following commands and our teamwork is a liberating gift since it enables us maximum independence. On the other hand, when not sufficiently challenged she would actively seek out distraction. Like a bored schoolchild, these distractions led her to drift away from a curb or meander when straight line targeting was desired. Through her strengths and challenges we learned to work together and quickly fell into full appreciation for each other outside of work. When Chrissie departed, we knew there were still

Pictured: Randy and Autumn sharing a bit of fun with the camera
Photo credit: WBUR Radio

skills to work on and it was important to keep her work simple for a while although the foundation was there to build a great team.

Tracy witnessed the stark contrast between my work with Autumn and the skills she'd observed with Quinn, having met Quinn and I at the peak of our teamwork. She was worried for my well-being at times and had to learn to trust Autumn and I to work together to build our skills. Tracy developed systems to allow her to help with Autumn's training and the improvements showed each time the three of us practiced together. During this time, it became very clear Autumn was totally a Daddy's girl and Tracy was free to fully develop her own relationship with our girl. I think the point of my full acceptance came one morning several weeks into our time together. Guide dogs are not allowed onto furniture typically and I keep to that rule very well for the benefit of consistency, ensuring her respect for public places. The exception we choose is that some nights after the early phase of adapting to our home is done, I will invite my guide to sleep on our bed as a treat to us, as much as them. This particular morning Autumn had been on the floor beside the bed. As Tracy rose for work I lingered, inviting Autumn to come up on the bed. I knew Autumn loved to crawl on top of me and to give me kisses. Being somewhat groggy I had not fully prepared, so my arms were beneath the covers. Thus, when Autumn climbed on top of me she pinned my arms under the covers and I had no defense for the kiss onslaught. I laughed heartily, deeper than I may have laughed since Quinn left me, as I struggled to free my arms to control the storm which is Autumn's affection. Tracy joined in the laughter, happily sharing her appreciation that my laugh had ushered in the true and full welcome of Autumn into our lives.

Almost immediately, Autumn and I were on the school presentation path. A special school in Maine involved a collection of "rock stars". These high-achieving students had earned the reward of choosing a monthly activity as a reward. All through the fall of 2013 their reward requests were to hike with Quinn and me. When they learned of Quinn's situation they sent many very kind cards. On hearing of Autumn's arrival, they began hoping I would bring her to hike with them. Quinn and I were a team for three years before we hiked mountain trails and it seemed unlikely to think Autumn could hike so soon into her young working career. Each month their touching requests enticed me to try and find a way.

Three months into our work together, I committed to join them with Autumn on Mt. Agamenticus, a short drive from their school. The plan was to take the most mild of paths in the morning with a hiking partner, and if Autumn did well, to explore further. If she struggled in any way we'd use the road to reach the summit and though a road walk would be different we'd share a summit with the students just the same. The aptly named Laura Mountain joined us and celebrated with me when Autumn found an epiphany on the trail. Autumn set out rapidly, highly excited, taking straight line routes and stopping for the near constant obstacles. As I stumbled my way to working through those steps she began to realize the purpose of her work differently. Her training was simple, stop in front of changes in elevation or other obstacles until the handler taps them in acknowledgement, earning the rewarded of their happiness and praise

As she observed my stumbles her intelligent brain began to quickly realize that I didn't see the obstacles and it wasn't just for my praise and happiness but for my well-being that she needed to attend these tasks. She immediately started adjusting her body position to give me better approaches to every rock, root and branch adapting her basic training to these new circumstances. Within fifteen minutes we were working the trail smoothly! We drove to the school and provided our usual presentation about ability awareness, believing in possibility, achieving through adversity and overcoming obstacles but the highlight came when I told them we could hike any and all of the trails up to the summit. That very afternoon, on a beautiful June day, they watched in awe as Autumn guided me around the obstacles or positioned me perfectly to manage them with my hiking stick and strides. We kept pace with the class and proudly began Autumn's hiking career.

In December we planned a family trip, confident Autumn's skills were up for the challenge. We were heading to Sacramento for the USABA National Marathon Championship and also for a week's vacation afterwards. We did have to entrust Autumn into the care of a carefully selected host while Tracy and I ran the marathon but reunited at the finish for the celebration of our National Championship. The excitement propelled us into our tour of the Sonoma Valley and several majestic vineyards. Autumn continues to delight in any travel outside and so it was no surprise the Muir woods and the Giant Redwoods were a wonder to her as well as Tracy and me. We took our journey further into the mountains and the Sequoia National Forest. It's hardly hiking to stroll down the smooth, paved paths leading to General Sherman, the world's largest tree. Still in awe of its massive size we started our hike back to the top of the park only to encounter a black bear and her two cubs walking down the trail towards us! Autumn was curious and enthusiastic but wisely acceded to my command to wait as the bears turned into the woods away from us. Always confident and curious my friendly and exuberant girl just wants to experience the world, and we were well on our way to doing just that.

Unfortunately for Autumn our next epic adventure would not include her. We had chosen a location with altitude so high it created unacceptable risks for her. Since our hike with Tedy Bruschi to help him prepare for his climb of Mt. Kilimanjaro, I'd had the notion in my mind of climbing it as well. Invited by another hiker to join their trip to Kilimanjaro we quickly realized we had a full contingent of our own to plan the trip of a lifetime. With our sights set on fall of 2015, we had a year of intense planning and preparation. Tracy showcased her impressive planning prowess as the 7-day summit adventure with our guides, Climb Kili, as the focal point. To this we added a safari into the Serengeti plains of Tanzania.

Tracy's time with an adventure company, her organization, and her patience allowed us to assemble a team of ten and expand it to eleven at the last minute. With the lion's share of logistics managed invisibly and masterfully we could focus on simply savoring the trip of a lifetime. At least it might have been the trip of a lifetime for many even extraordinary lives. We live, however, in a constant preparedness to accept and embrace opportunity. Along with this is Tracy's addition to my life by making the deliberate strategies for the experiences we want to savor in turning wishes to plans.

Thus, it was only two years later we found ourselves on yet another grand expedition. This time we had set our sights on Machu Picchu. While Greg Neault would run point on the group planning, Tracy coordinated all of our details seamlessly. For his part, Greg inspired one of the more marvelous decisions by talking us away from the normal approach of a 5-day jungle trek along the Inca trail. Instead we designed our trip to include the marvelous ruins of Machu Piccu, the dramatic and perilous climb up Huayna Picchu and to also include a four-day trek through the remote Andes, ending with a stunning overlook of Vinicunca, or Rainbow Mountain as it commonly known. On hearing reports of Peru's hosting one of the world's most unusual lodgings, we enhanced our plans still a little further. The Sky Lodge is a transparent pod 1800 feet up a cliff face overlooking the Sacred Valley of the Incas and it is reached by scaling a via ferrata (a fixed cable on a climbing route) and then zip lining out the next day! I love having a partner so eager and willing to embrace adventure, experience and the planning necessary to achieve it. I also appreciated her wisdom in suggesting that a quiet week of actual vacation to relax afterwards was a reasonable and appropriate end to our adventures.

Pictured: Randy and Tracy at Machu Picchu in 2017

The rewards were as grand as planned and with adrenalin still as high as the peaks we'd achieved, our team piled into the vans ready for relaxation. Tracy caught a bit of phone signal and a strange message from Monique urging me to check my messages. Thousands of miles from home I heard my brother's voice in a series of shaky messages. My Mom had undergone emergency surgery and survived beyond expectation but was still in critical condition. I crashed from the incredible euphoria of our accomplishment to as low a point I could imagine in seconds and my equally stunned, caring and respectful friends fell silent. I vaguely heard some expressions of love and support, I realized Tracy's hand was on mine, but I was at a total loss on what to do. The emotional crash left me dumbfounded and the only thing I knew with confidence was I could turn it over to Tracy and she would guide me through until I could process a little more.

Despite an abysmally callous response from American Airlines, Tracy simply did, with loving efficiency, what was necessary to get us home as quickly as possible. My only hope was to reach my Mom one more time while she lived. Few things went smoothly, and yet all I had to manage was thanking Tracy and following her encouraging lead. Every update kept our hopes alive and we arrived to find Mom in rough condition in the Intensive Care Unit of Mass General Hospital. Monique brought us home late that night and for several days we made trips to visit Mom and watch her hopeful progress forward. Surprising the medical teams, she continued to heal and improve despite the frailty of her 88 difficult years. We even celebrated her transferring back to NH to a temporary assisted living situation.

But the visits there were discouraging as she was struggling, and it took only a few days of slide to get a call requesting permission to transport her by ambulance to the hospital. Tracy and I were off to get there quickly when the call came in from an unknown number. "Is this Randy Pierce, son of Georgette Roy?" I croaked out my "yes" thinking no, no, no this sounds so very wrong. "Is there a DNR?" In my head the stream of thought explodes: No, no, no this isn't a fair question to ask me, I know there is a Do not Resuscitate order, I know that is her wish and I know that if I have to tell you it means I have to make the decision to not save my Mom and damn it that's exactly why she processed those papers in the first place. Throat constricting, tears overflowing and dreading my own response, I honored my Mom's wishes: "yes."

There was a long silence before I could ask for more. All the details I learned on the rest of that short phone call and at the hospital when we arrived and were rushed into a family waiting room couldn't assuage the knowledge my Mom was gone. We didn't get to go to her for another half an hour, with only Tracy's calming attempts keeping me close to holding it together. Losing a second parent has a generational finality which I'd been warned to expect. This struck with the force of the pain my tremendous love for my

Mother brought as well. Along with the hurt I felt a loss of connection to my past. The night before Mom's graveside service I could not sleep and found my brother Rick was online similarly sleepless. We called and talked for hours, including putting together a plan for him to play his flute and me to sing a slightly revised version of Color My World by Chicago at the service the next morning. Mom brought music to both of our lives and valued her family being together most of all so this seemed a fitting tribute.

We stood side by side and he played the instrumental absolutely beautifully. For my part I did not manage so well as the emotions and exhaustion frayed me too far. In my mind I was dancing with Mom as I did at my wedding to that very song. I did not see the last 18 years of age upon her as my sight did not allow, and my vision of her was of her red hair and remarkably blue eyes. Just as it happened on our wedding day, my dance with Mom ended and I turned to Tracy. So too at the graveside as the song ended with Rick's haunting flute melody lingering over us all. I turned to Tracy now, clasping her hand tightly, grateful for the family we forged together.

The combined strength of our union took me past the loss of both my parents and the Mighty Quinn. It took me through a few medical crises and it will, no doubt, be tested many times in the future. The beauty of trust is how strong it grows under such extreme testing. The beauty of Tracy is our love, trust and partnership so well united in vision for savoring the present even as we plan our future adventures.

A Vision for 2020 Vision Quest

"I am only one; but still I am one. I cannot do everything; but still I can do something; and because I cannot do everything, I will not refuse to do the something that I can do." Reverend Edward Hale

Finding Purpose

June 2008: I entered the boardroom of the NH Association for the Blind with a considerable amount of trepidation. Listening to the voices of so many respected business leaders, I felt entirely out of place. Why had they invited me to join their Board of Directors? Was I a token blind presence? There were a couple of other clients on the board and I respected both of their talents. I observed their competent board interaction but I simply felt out of place, uncertain of what my role would be within this organization. But I believed very much in the organization's mission and wanted

205

to be more involved in making a positive difference. I resolved to listen, learn and watch for my opportunities.

Any optimism I might have felt suffered an immediate and significant blow as the financial report painted a bleak picture. The economic downturn of spring 2008 affected the endowment earnings which provided a significant portion of the annual budget. I sat stunned and surprised as the president told us staff would, unfortunately but necessarily, be downsized. As an uncomfortable silence held the room, Quinn rolled onto his side under the table and as he occasionally did with such a move, let out a long slow groan. While likely protesting his boredom at being under a table instead of out exploring the world with me, it seemed as if he too was reacting to the dour news, creating just enough levity for us to resume the meeting. The situation was incredibly serious though, and I was devastated. People who helped me in my transition through sight loss, helped many like me, were likely going to lose their jobs because of this harsh fiscal reality. I was attentive to all of the meeting details even as my mind began to evaluate how I could help prevent such a terrible thing in the future and have a positive effect on the long-term stability of the organization. I still felt inconsequential compared to the business minds present in the room but the problem solver within me established a goal.

What were my assets? I had a fairly diverse and deep collection of communities linked to the various hobbies and pastimes of my life. My New England Patriots notoriety as "Fan of the Year" brought significant attention and community while providing some possible media connections as well. I also had the luxury of time as my sight loss had led to the Long Term disability which provided my essential medical benefits and a base income. Certainly I had skills which, despite several attempts to work with social security and the Long Term Disability provider, had made clear there was no reasonable option for me to use in a return to work.

In the past, I gave time to volunteer work, which I had found rewarding on several levels. One of the best ways to feel good about yourself is to help others. For me, it is a demonstrable reminder that I do have value. I kept reasonably busy with my various pursuits and pastimes but they were all schedules I effectively controlled. Inspired by several factors in my life, particularly the situation at N.H.A.B., I evaluated the many allocations of my time to consider how I could make a more positive influence on the world.

During my early exploration of hiking with Quinn, I developed the notion of climbing "the NH 48", the peaks which rise over 4000 feet. Completing this list of peaks has come to be a significant hiking achievement. I thought perhaps it might be a method of gaining attention for the N.H. Association for the Blind. It was, in fact, that very organization which alerted me to a pivotal opportunity in October of 2009.

Pictured: Quinn, Randy and Tracy share a summit photo from a very difficult first blind 4000' mountain hike. 2009

Fresh off two significant and exciting hikes on Pack Monadnock and Osceola, Tracy and I attended a presentation by Erik Weihenmayer, a blind hiker who had successfully climbed the tallest peak on all seven continents! He spoke about the Adversity Advantage, his impending second book, and his concept of alchemy: turning something less valuable into something more valuable. His talk was excellent for me in several ways. I already practiced many of his messages but hearing concepts in different ways often helps them to resonate more powerfully. It bolstered my confidence to compare my own presentation ability comfortably and favorably with his, although I certainly fell well short of his impressive life accomplishments. After the presentation we had some time to talk and an easy natural comfort developed. He was curious about my martial arts and my quest for the 48. He well understood the trail challenge in the White Mountains and told me frankly it would be a difficult and worthy achievement. So much of a challenge, in fact, that he strongly suggested I consider using it as powerfully as possible. Given my immense respect for his accomplishments and approach to life, the determination deepened within me to do something more. I already had the notion of taking ten years to hike those 48 peaks with a goal to finish by the year 2020 so I could play on the concept of 20/20 being perfect vision. What I needed to do now was expand my vision into something which not only raised awareness but also funds for N.H.A.B.

Just a few weeks later Erik called me and asked if I'd consider meeting with him to talk further, and perhaps for a hike. He had a small time window prior to a commitment in Beverly, MA for a presentation. We determined the morning of December 8 was free for us to meet, hike and talk about our various lives and goals. I reached out to my friend Professor Brent Bell who was teaching outdoor education at the University of New Hampshire. Brent suggested Mt. Agamenticus, committing to join us and manage the details of trailhead and route up the easy mountain which represented the only sufficiently close elevation to be viable for Erik's time frame.

I arrived with my friend Kara to help support my work with Quinn, and Brent had charged a student, "Sherpa" John, to help coordinate logistics. We all met on Newcastle Island at Erik's hotel and my nervousness at hiking with a legend was hard to mask. Erik and his human guide Skylar were relaxed and soon put all of us at ease. An early storm had dropped an icy few inches of snow but crisp air and clear skies promised an excellent day. I was excited to have Kara observe Erik's technique of using two trekking poles while following Skylar, who wore bear bells and turned to give simple verbal guidance along the path. Quinn seemed to sense there was a spirit of competition and was proudly showcasing his excellent work. Ironically it was hardest for Erik and I to talk as we needed to give each other clearance to explore the trail. Despite each of our appreciation for what the other accomplished, there was also a desire to demonstrate our own competence. On a particularly icy ledge the rest of the team stepped off the trail and into the scrub brush for traction. Quinn, evading the brush, indicated he wanted me to make a long stretching stride over the steep icy slab. Taking the step caused the entire ice ledge to slide out and we both slipped several feet back to our starting point but somehow stayed on our feet. It was probably a good location for MICROspikes which none of us had brought for this generally simple hike. Brent provided the solution by using trekking pole as traction, supporting my long stride across the tricky ledge. This highlighted an additional challenge of winter hiking, but also established Brent as a partner in hiking solutions. At the summit we climbed the viewing platform where Erik delighted in taking the picture of the group. I had my opportunity for a longer conversation with Erik and once again he encouraged me to make the most out of the opportunity and to let him know if he could help. We made rough plans to share one of the hikes along the way if our schedules allowed.

Pictured: From L to R Kara, Brent, Randy,
Erik and Sherpa John atop Mt. Agamenticus
(photo taken by Erik's guide Skylar)

On the descent Sherpa John enthusiastically told me about his trials and triumphs while completing the 48 previously. He filmed the journey producing a documentary about his experience which he used to raise money for diabetes, in honor of his girlfriend. He shared some of the pitfalls of his fundraising experience and excitedly told me of the parts of the hikes he thought would be most challenging for me. For example, Owl's head was an 18 mile round trip with two difficult water crossings just before a very challenging scramble up the slide which leads to the summit. The Bonds were very remote and would probably be a multiple overnight for me in the heart of the Pemigewasset Wilderness. I didn't fully understand the magnitude or details of the challenges he described but I was eager to learn.

Brent was inspired by the limited experience we shared on the trail and invited me to be part of his spring course, KIN 551, on backpacking. Attending the weekly course would teach me many of the skills for successful backpacking in the White Mountains, as well as providing a five day "Pemi Traverse" just before Memorial Day weekend. I leapt at the opportunity and soon discovered Sherpa John would be the teaching assistant for the class, adding to our skills and knowledge each week leading up to our impending spring hike.

There were so many questions to answer: What is the right gear for a day hike or overnight hike? What nutrition is needed for the varying types of trips? What backpack is best and how do you adjust them to properly fit you during a hike? How do you pack to ensure gear is properly accessible and the load is going to work right for you? How do you plan a trip, read a map, evaluate risk, manage first aid and so many other basic concepts essential to being a responsible hiker? Now how do you do all this while factoring in the challenges of blindness; both personally and to the group?

Meanwhile, I met with my friends on many evenings to continue creative thinking about how to make the most of my planned quest. We were fairly certain we needed to establish a foundation or charity of some type. I knew so little about how to build a business but I had many talented friends willing to share their knowledge. I gathered a diverse collection of friends for a multiple hour strategy session. We coordinated all the ideas into a very rough business plan that we thought would harness our strengths into an awareness- and fund-raising effort for "2020 Vision Quest."

One of the most significant and obvious parts of the plan was to recognize and appreciate the incredible work of my guide dogs. Ostend and Quinn had been absolutely life altering positive influences for me and the organizations who provide people these incredible guide dogs do so by raising charitable donations. Our inclusion would not only showcase Quinn specifically in our early efforts but expand the appeal for support well beyond the scope of the excellent work done by the N.H. Association for the Blind.

A core mission was thus to raise funds for two remarkable organizations in Guiding Eyes for the Blind, and N.H.A.B. I, however, had a significant problem: I'm incredibly uncomfortable with the notion of asking for money. But I am comfortable in providing partnerships where everyone receives something in exchange. I expressed my difficulty to the team and one of the suggestions was to integrate the appeal with the school presentations I had been providing since 2007. The idea was simply to suggest that our enhancement to the education process was helping to build a better future for all of us. By supporting our charity, donors would directly support this investment in the future while simultaneously providing funds to the worthy charities we supported. In essence we added value to their donation with our school outreach as an additional incentive for them to donate. Since we were an all-volunteer organization we hoped it would serve to inspire their generosity.

We crafted our mission statement to reflect all of our goals and include our many inspirations:

> 2020 Vision Quest leads and inspires students and professionals to reach beyond adversity and achieve their peak potential. We believe in leading by example, in climbing the highest peaks, and in sharing our successes and challenges with each other. Funds raised through these endeavors will be given to two remarkable organizations which benefit the visually impaired community: the New Hampshire Association for the Blind and the internationally renowned Guiding Eyes for the Blind.

Since 2007 I had been making regular visits to several schools to share an assortment of messages, initially focusing on guide dogs, disability awareness and managing adversity. Two individuals in particular inspired my school presentations. Joy Weiss, a friend and teacher at the JR Briggs Elementary School in Ashburnham, MA invited me, annually, to her school for 6 presentations throughout a long and meaningful day. I was invited by teacher Cheryl Mousseau, to visit the Memorial School in Bedford twice each year. It was fun to share the incredible things Quinn enabled me to accomplish and it soon became an enjoyable challenge to answer the pupils' suggestions on what a blind person might not be able to do. "You can't read": Led to discussions of Louis Braille's ingenuity while he was only 14 years old. "You can't enjoy sports": Allowed me to share my methods for martial arts, basketball, hiking or virtually any example they asked, whether I had direct experience or simply brought creative imagination to the necessary problem solving. By the time they asked "How do you drive?" I knew I had them fully believing in possibility!

As my comfort grew with these presentations, and common questions showed patterns of curiosity, I realized my natural problem solving approach was something I could share directly. I began to emphasize ability awareness as an appreciation for what we can all accomplish. Word spread steadily, and schools throughout the region invited Quinn and I to join them.

I interwove a few memorable quotes to augment the messaging, such as one of my favorites from Henry Ford: "Whether you think you can or you think you can't – you're right." It so well expressed my hope to illuminate a simple message for the students which had been invaluable in my own life. When I first struggled with blindness and thought I would never do anything fun or meaningful, that was very much my reality. When I started believing in the many possibilities available to me, I had taken the first step to success. I feel strongly the same is likely true for anyone, certainly for these students and teachers who seemed captivated and motivated by my presentations.

Another quote I love to share originated from Ben Franklin and was revised by John Wooden: "We don't plan to fail, we fail to plan." These are not trite platitudes but rather words I choose to live by as evidenced by the thorough planning involved in establishing our charity, 2020 Vision Quest. The last major component of our strategic planning was to build community from the hiking events involved in my quest for the 48. In order to achieve this we needed to develop a website, social media and blog, along with a strategy to keep these active, relevant and worthwhile to as broad a group of people as possible. I had several strong communities likely to be supportive, and provide a foundation from which we hoped to expand significantly. Identifying who were the most likely to be interested was important but difficult. Quinn's participation ensured dog-lovers had a reason to be connected, hiking opened up an entire avenue of outdoor enthusiasts, and we also hoped to appeal to the visually impaired communities as well as educators.

It was clear we were creating a full-fledged organization, albeit volunteer based. The spring strategy session identified key positions for the organization and I reached out to various qualified friends to entice them to join the team. It was exciting and fun to be at the ground level, building our charity. A benefit of our staff being all volunteers is that we are all driven by the desire to do good. It also meant we don't have the burden of pressure to earn a minimum amount to survive.

We needed to create a legal entity, and thanks to my connections to the N.H. Association for the Blind, I was able to seek advice from a fellow board member and highly respected attorney, Michelle Arruda. Her support and guidance were invaluable in the decision to legally connect our charity with NHAB.

The latter did require Michelle and I to recuse ourselves from the NHAB Board vote to approve the contract, but the support for our mission proved unanimous! We established the minimum legally-required five person Board of Directors which consisted of Tracy and I along with Jenifer Tidwell, Rachel Morris, and Kara Minotti Becker. We would meet annually to oversee the 2020 Vision Quest organization. The day to day business required managers to coordinate their varying responsibilities such as Finance, Marketing and Fund Raising. Each founding member of the board also took a staff role and I reached out to other friends to fill the remaining positions. It came together so quickly that spring that suddenly I found myself president and founder of a charity and Chairman of a Board of Directors. Many of the organizational responsibilities were mine to manage as well. We planned to officially launch by June of 2010. All of this was daunting even before I included the hiking.

Hiking was a significant inspiration in the founding of 2020 Vision Quest and as the spring course at UNH progressed, my skills and comfort steadily improved. Carrie McMillen took on the role of Hiking Manager for our fledgling organization and while she lacked experience in the challenges of blind hiking, she hoped to start smaller and work our way towards the more challenging hikes. The Teva Life Agent application process caused an escalation of our plans. They required a singular dramatic event as part of the goal to be achieved and so with some appropriate hesitancy and resistance,

I convinced Carrie we'd launch our 2020 Vision Quest with an attempt to climb Mt Washington on July 4, 2010, Independence Day! On the strength of that goal, our overall mission and Tracy's impressive community rallying efforts; TEVA announced us as their Life Agent, awarded us the starting funds for our charity and locked us into Mt. Washington as our first hike.

Before this I had one very significant test with the UNH program as we attempted the rigorous "Pemi-Loop" hike over the five days preceding Memorial Day, 2010. I took all the hiking knowledge I learned in Brent's class and limited practical application to Lincoln Woods as an unseasonably hot and humid weather pattern settled over the mountains. Most of my treks had been day hikes and the additional gear was impressively heavy in my pack, especially since I carried food for both Quinn and myself. Sleeping exposed at elevation meant a real possibility of cold nights and we learned Quinn required a sleeping bag as well. Finally, water in the White Mountains is often contaminated with a parasite, giardia, which can cause long term health concerns for both people and dogs. This necessitated I carry water for both Quinn and myself. All this gear meant hoisting a pack well over 60 pounds: possible but taxing!

Fortunately, the first day was a short one while we were strong and hiking along the generally easier trails of Lincoln Woods, the Wilderness trail, and camping at the base of Bondcliff Mountain. As we reached the higher elevation and more challenging terrain of day 2, each stagger in my step for balance and every re-step to find the right footing increased the wear and exhaustion on me, particularly my stabilizing muscles. Exacerbating this was the consistent learning Quinn and I were still doing on just our second 4000-foot peak. I was incredibly slow as a result and this took a toll on the entire team. We were well behind schedule for our plan to arrive at Guyot campsite.

Stepping above the tree line, I was rejuvenated by the sudden steady winds which cooled my overheated body. A larger burst of energy came as a result of the exultations of my fellow hikers "We did it! We are on the summit of Bondcliff!" We had an incredible celebration surrounded by majestic scenes in every direction. Sherpa John shared named all the peaks around us as easily as old friends and I hungered for the same relationship with these mountains. I already felt an impressive kinship with the group who had spent just a single night together, but quite a day of hiking and supporting each other through early struggles. We shared lunch, relaxing and preparing for Mt. Bond just ahead. We also found a windy refuge from the black flies which had ravaged us on the lower trail. Just before departing Sherpa John took my arm and traced the outlines of the mountains for me, stopping at 'George'. "That's Mt. Washington, where you are heading next. It will be a lot harder than today" he said ominously, "but we'll get you ready for it."

Pictured: Randy collapsed in exhaustion while Quinn lays beside him in support

The rest of our day was arduous, and I was pushed to my limit several times. Quinn also showed signs of reaching his limit. He took longer pauses even for obstacles which did not warrant such attention. Brent noticed his normally powerful tail wag droop to barely a twitch, he was simply tired and needed a break from guiding. This created an opportunity we had discussed but never practiced, human guiding. My guides found that a mere hour of this work was mentally exhausting. They were being asked to look at the trail differently and also to describe the plethora of hazards awaiting me, while maintaining a slow but steady pace. We all ran out of water because of our reduced speed and the incredible heat. Dehydration weakened us and intensified the challenge. Still, as we hiked down the north side of Mt. Bond towards Guyot shelter we encountered the first of a couple surprises. Snow! The trail was covered by several feet of snow and a playfulness refreshed our warm and weary company.

We all paused for our second wonder as South Twin Mountain to our West was completely illuminated in a bright pink aura! A chorus of voices exclaimed their amazement, soon followed by eager descriptions of the scene to me. On rare occasions, after the sun has set, when its direct light no longer strikes a mountain, the rays of the sun may reflect or refract off ice particles in the atmosphere, illuminating the mountain in this colorful phenomenon called alpenglow. This night, it was so bright as to light our faces and the snowy trail ahead with this beautiful and rare treasure.

After a 15 hour day, I finally stumbled into Guyot camp in complete exhaustion. I could barely eat, virtually collapsing beside my soundly sleeping Quinn. I woke aching from the prior day's exertions and still weary from a fitful night of sleep. Day 3 was another relentless 15 hour trek over South Twin Mountain and down the perilous descent to Galehead hut. This forced us to rethink our plans. Instead of finishing the loop over the Lafayette Ridge we would stay at Galehead for a day of recovery and hike out the Gale river trail. There was tremendous wonder and accomplishment in the five days we spent in the wilderness, along with the humbling concerns for how much my pace and physical limits affected our group. I wondered how much of a challenge I was inviting, all the more for the realization I that would be repeating all of these mountains again, since my quest did not officially start until our July 4th hike of Mt. Washington.

There was more work to be done before that official climbing could commence. One of the most critical aspects of our project was crafted through the talents of Jenifer Tidwell, who literally wrote the collegiate book on user interfaces. She designed and produced our website and it was absolutely beautiful. It captured the mountains and illuminated our mission from the complicated thoughts and goals of our young staff, even as we ourselves were still fully identifying that mission. It connected our blog and social media to an internet base of operations with a blend of professionalism, mountain majesty and mission. She exceeded our expectations and in time for the marketing push of our first epic climb. Thanks to Tracy's social media outreach we also had television, radio and newspaper coverage leading into the launch of our efforts. The entire region seemed invigorated by our quest.

In preparation for our inaugural Mt. Washington hike, Tracy and I met with video producer Kat Alix-Gaudreau. She impressed us with her insight and passion, immediately convincing us to invite her to film the first trip. This would highlight our challenges and showcase the possibilities in which we believe. Given the success of several other film pieces from my Patriotic past, I thought to reach out to the companies involved, but here I had an inspired and capable friend who won us over. She envisioned a short piece we could use to augment our website and showcase our mission, as well as a longer piece that might have a myriad of uses depending on the results of the climb.

The Quest Officially Begins

Quinn, Tracy and I arrived at the AMC Highland Center in Crawford Notch on Friday, July 2, 2010. Our team planned to gather here in preparation for our epic climb. It was a beautiful evening and we proudly gave a well-attended presentation to an audience of hikers in the auditorium. I was encouraged by the many eager questions regarding our preparations, expectations and purpose even before our quest officially began. I felt surreal disbelief as we received reports of 6 inches of fresh snow falling on the summit, in July! This freak storm highlighted the magnitude of the mountain's well-deserved reputation for some of the worst weather in the world. Record winds, freezing temperatures and the rapidly changing weather conditions add up to a dangerous unpredictability.

The team assembled throughout Saturday for some advanced filming, with building excitement for our early morning departure on Sunday. Equipment was checked, bags packed and we all enjoyed one final night of sleep before our trek began. Quinn and I were bristling with enthusiasm as we set out on the clear, warm morning, but the trail soon calmed us into the carefully placed steps necessary for my hiking. We made steady progress along the lower trail, thwarted only when a scrape to my right knee against a sharp-edged rock caused an excessive amount of bleeding we had to tend. Roughly one hour into our hike, shortly before Gem Pool, we encountered the timing challenging our learning process created. My slower pace often results in a traffic-jam style backup of hikers behind us. Normally, we step to the side and allow them to pass us, especially on popular hiking days such as July 4th. When I am in the

217

middle of a particularly tricky section of trail, it is often difficult to find the opportunity to allow others to pass. On this short but tricky scrambling descent, I needed to use my hands on the terrain and apply significant caution. As the team meticulously described how to navigate the obstacle, we were developing essential communication skills. Unfortunately, during this time-consuming process a large number of mostly patient hikers piled up behind us. Learning how much information is too much was an important part of hiking blind. Doing so with safety of the moment and understanding the overall impact on timing was complicated.

As the subtle nuance of Quinn's work was repeatedly demonstrated we took additional time to ensure it was captured on film. Pausing before a narrow passage between boulders, Quinn waited for me to tap the rock signifying I knew it was there. We still needed to work together to pass through this constricted section of trail. He waited for me to step behind him so he could lead single file, differing from typical guide dog work, but essential to allow passage. Yet another example of excellent work involved Quinn's pause, crouch and jump for tall boulders we needed to climb, the depth of his crouch and height of his jump both giving me crucial information for my steps following him. It also made for great video!

By the time we completed the unyielding steep steps above the pool, we were significantly behind schedule, routinely halting to allow groups of hikers to pass us. The final scrambles rising to the krummholz, the region of stunted, twisted trees at high elevation, were demanding mentally and physically. My legs, bruised from the miscues with the boulders below, were scraped by the branches, unavoidable due to my inexperience. Exhausted, I heard the sounds of fatigue from my companions even as we reached the Lake of the Clouds hut to considerable rejoicing. I knew there was a decision coming about the trip. Our original plan was to reach the hut, briefly rest and remove some pack weight, summit and return if time permitted, so that we would be poised to hike down the next day. Our 8 hours to go this distance suggested we would not reach the summit and back in daylight. Likely tomorrow we'd have trouble summiting then descending back to the base without a very long and taxing day for the team who then face an additional long drive home.

Kat pulled me aside prior to filming the discussions and decisions. "One of the problems I'm having, Randy is that while the scenery is astounding and your teamwork with Quinn amazing, there's no conflict. Everyone is simply reacting supportively and the best film pieces generally rely on conflict and resolution." Knowing Kat, I suspected there was a mix of mirth with her intent to draw me out. The truth is there was plenty of conflict in my mind. I was internalizing my desire to push on for the summit and just make it work, my reasonable belief that was a poor choice, and my absolute empathy for the consequences of any decision on the entire team. Carrie and Kara as trip leaders presented the most safety conscious options and suggested it would be unrealistic to summit Washington that night. They similarly suggested it would be impractical to attempt the summit and full descent the next day given how long we'd spent on the trail today. Other possibilities included heading out over Monroe and Eisenhower via Edmund's Path on the next day. This would allow us to claim success on two 4000' peaks. Another option would be to summit Washington the next day but depart by the Cog Railway which would mean it would not count towards the 48 which requires a hiking ascent and descent of the peak on the same trip. Cliff Dyke's impassioned speech inspired the group to overwhelmingly choose the summit of Washington. We did, however, decide that before dinner we would leave our packs while most of the team made the short trek to the summit of Mt. Monroe and back, then summit Mt Washington the next morning.

Free of the weight of our packs and hiking above the tree line we made quick work of the trek across the ridge. We were very efficient, I used my hands on the more difficult scrambles, applying the day's lessons to great effect, and soon we stood on the windy and cool summit of Mt. Monroe. All through the side trek I was coming to terms with our decision. Part of me wanted to believe we could rise very early, achieve the summit of Washington and work through the grueling descent by trail to earn the complete victory. I knew descending was generally slower and harder for Quinn and me. I also knew that a second day was usually more difficult because of the weariness and soreness from the prior day. The prudent decision made more than enough sense for me to agree with it, but that did little to quell the emotional disappointment at starting our quest with some level of failure.

I was, however, trying to frame the failure around all the successful aspects of the entire trip. The mountains will always be there and by proper risk management we will be assured the opportunity to be there to appreciate them. If we were going to be worthy of our tagline "Achieve a vision beyond your sight" we had to demonstrate the mindfulness of vision in just such moments. We could not allow setting our sight on a summit success to be more important than the vision of our full mission.

In this decision I found my comfort quickly. Back at the Lake of the Clouds hut we all gathered for a rare perfect weather evening and one of the most glorious sunsets any of us ever experienced. Various members of the group described the majesty and splendor of the scene, painting a picture rivetingly vivid for even my sightless eyes. Later, we sat outside listening to the wind whistling in varied patterns at the higher summit, along the multiple ravines below us and even across the icy tarns beside our hut. As full darkness fell across the land, bursts of colorful explosions unfurled across the landscapes all around us. It was the Fourth of July in a world which seemed impossibly distant from our remote wilderness retreat. As we all celebrated Independence Day and the independence this climb symbolized, we now tried to determine which communities throughout New Hampshire, Vermont and Maine were the source of the fireworks erupting throughout the night. We may at times over-use the term awe-inspiring but it definitely fit this day and evening. Listening to my friends, I patted Quinn's head, thanking him for the freedom I celebrated with him beside me.

Positive moments of a glorious sunset and shared accomplishment helped lift our team along our route to the summit of the great rock pile of Washington the next day. The moment felt epic regardless of the rules of the 48. Our celebration was far too short on the chilly summit, as most of the team did indeed descend by the cog railway. Tracy, Kat, Quinn and I had the great fortune to ride the auto road down. Our good friend, Bob Dunn, followed our live online map broadcast by the satellite technology we carried for that purpose. Observing our approach to the summit he drove up to meet and celebrate with us in an incredible display of friendship. We rode down with him so I could show Kat the famous raised relief "Washburn Map" which is located at the Joe Dodge Lodge in Pinkham Notch. Our team separated in hope to return together to reach this peak successfully in the future, and though we all meant it with fervor, it is hard to bring such teams and moments back together again.

Pictured: At the Summit - Front L-R: Jenifer, Kara, Carrie, Kat, Tracy, Randy
Back L-R Ben, Cliff, Dave, Jessie

Our First Successes

Three weeks later a different team earned our first of the 48 on Mt. Hale, named for Reverend Edward Hale, the author, abolitionist, and historian, remembered for the quote I use to introduce this chapter. Another couple of weeks and we enjoyed camping overnight along the ridge line while adding Mt. Tom and Mt. Field with further spectacular moments and memories. On September 11 "Flags on the 48" allowed us to commemorate the anniversary on the summit of Mt. Liberty. Finally, our first year of hiking the 48 ended one week before Tracy and my wedding, on Mt. Pierce. We were joined by one of my most inspirational teachers, Bill Schomburg, from Colebrook Academy. As my High School English teacher he had exposed me to so many writers and thinkers, with a passion such that I recall them in his voice still. On our hike, he hopped spryly from rock to rock, marveled at Quinn's guidance, guided me himself over bog bridges and gave me a most powerful compliment, "My friend, you are indeed living deeply and sucking out the marrow of life, not just writing about it like that Thoreau guy!"

Our first season brought us only five peaks in pursuit of the 48 and with my ten year goal we'd need to certainly step it up in the future. In the present though, Rachel Morris had a more pressing goal as she shouldered the unenviable position of managing our fund raising. She developed a pitch with me which we took to her family for our trial run. Bob and Celia Morris offered excellent feedback on our approach, highlighting the key value of our presentations. They also provided a base donation and matching grant to launch our initial efforts in both the charity and community building. This led to Rachel pitching to me and the team her idea for an annual Dinner and Auction event. I didn't like it at first. A posh event may be what works in the fund raising world but it didn't immediately resonate with me nor, I thought, would it work for our community. This type of event would involve a lot of preparation work for a hall, meals, entertainment, auction items and I wondered, for how much return? I had some hesitation as a result of my concerns, but Rachel was confident, passionate and well informed with research. I always want to be supportive and encouraging of my friends as my own goals and aspirations were so often made possible by their willingness to do such for me. I did my best to quell my reluctance and put my full support behind her efforts.

In creating our signature event, we sought a name evocative of our mission and selected "Peak Potential Charity Dinner and Auction" or "Peak Potential Gala". Rachel was the overwhelming and incredible force behind our first event. Tracy and I gave our support and many in our community stepped up to make it a success beyond my expectations. Standing in my suit at the Derryfield Country Club before a room full of friends and supporters I was overcome with gratitude.

Our vision had blossomed into something vivid and real. At the podium I paused to just listen to the room full of laughter and talk. Did they even realize what they were doing here? One year ago none of this existed, I hadn't even hiked with Erik yet, but now the reality was beyond my initial notions. I thought we must be on the right track if we could encourage or cajole a hall full of people to be aware of the need which inspired our mission and to also embrace a path towards resolution. I shared a brief presentation expressing my appreciation for their presence, an overview of our mission and some highlights of the first season:

"Here we are in 2010, I have learned there are 4.4 million severely sight impaired people living in the United States. By the time I hopefully finish my quest to climb all 48 of these majestic peaks that number is anticipated to rise to nearly 32 million! Why? Age-related Macular Degeneration is the top cause of blindness in the United States and we understand what percentage of the population is likely to experience this illness. Presently a very large population spike, the Baby Boomers, is heading into the window of sight risk. Each of those people will potentially face a challenge similar to what I faced and I know the difficulty very well. I hope to ensure those feelings of hopelessness and helplessness are eased by the training and services we support. Thanks to all of you we are taking some very positive steps on all of our quests from the charities we support, the mountains we are climbing and the schools where we hope to inspire future generations."

We launched into 2011 on many high notes. Our first corporate presentations were requested and developed for Primex and the Laconia Savings Bank. I adapted the messages of achieving through adversity, goal setting and problem solving into a flow with an emphasis on achieving a vision, using a description of the sunset on our Mt. Washington summit. I describe the powerful imagery as it was given to me: Sitting beside the Lake of the Clouds hut and facing west on a rare idyllic evening, we were granted an incredible gift: Seven mountain ranges stretch their ridgelines from south to north before us. Close up the Willey range, the Bonds and the Lafayette Ridge, further into the west, looking smaller, are some mountain ranges in Vermont. Further still on the horizon, several hundred miles distant and seeming so much smaller despite looming over 4000 feet, are the Adirondack Mountains in New York State. As the sun sets those distant horizon summits seem to shimmer purple like the lyrics in the song: "for purple mountains' majesty." Closer, the Vermont peaks have a blue hue to them, and our NH peaks are the lush green of July cut only by the stark grey granite cliffs. In the sky thin wispy cirrus clouds streak horizontally above those peaks. They do not block the sun but rather capture it resplendently. As the sun sets there are streaks of deep crimson red across the sky while higher the clouds showcase the orange of an oak leaf in autumn and higher still shades of pink and purple finish nature's masterpiece before us.

Pausing in my description I always ask the audience if any of them pictured the scene I had described and overwhelming shouts of yes encourage me to share further. How is it possible they have pictured it, I ask? They didn't see it and I didn't see it: It is our imagination. Our brain puts the images together and our eyes are simply only one means to get the information to it. Read a good book or listen to an impassioned blind speaker for a similar effect. The reality is that sight allows you to see everything around you right now and I do not have that skill. Vision allows you to see everything around you in a different manner. More powerfully, vision allows you to see it and all the possibilities for those things around you. Vision is the choice to look at the world differently, deliberately, mindfully. You don't need to have sight to have vision, but you do not get vision simply by having sight, that comes from the choice of mindfulness.

The presentations were well received and our 2020 Vision Quest team began to work these into the plan for our charity efforts. Requesting an honorarium from presentation clients supplemented our fund raising. As our first year came to a close we had paid all the startup expenses of legal fees, insurance, website, documentary and proudly donated $2020.00 to each organization. We reserved the funds to operate for another year, and hopeful to make a more significant donation every future year.

Our second hiking season began with a flurry. Before the official season started we were honored and excited to hike with Tedy Bruschi, my friend and New England Patriots hall of famer. We hiked through the Belnap range in preparation for his Kilimanjaro attempt in support of Ability Awareness and the Wounded Warrior Project. Sharing the beauty of the NH mountains with Tedy was incredible. Playing snowball baseball atop Mt. Gunstock and letting him enjoy the tug of war reward for Quinn were highlights of an epic day on the trails with a legend or two. Tedy's legendary status is clear and Quinn was carving out enough of a niche for his own legend.

Powderhouse Production approached us to film a pilot for Animal Planet focusing on Quinn and his work. Ethan Zohn, winner of Survivor Africa, was hired to be the host. We started our day at the Hidden Valley Boy Scout Camp to provide a presentation before our climb up Cannon Mountain together. Quinn's incredible work was highlighted on dozens of balance-beam-like bog bridges around Lonesome Lake. Half the production team turned back before we continued climbing to Coppermine Col and tackling the extremely difficult scramble on to the summit. At the summit, Quinn, Ethan and I sat with our legs dangling over the Cannon cliffs. We talked about his battles with cancer, the power of overcoming adversity and, in fact, achieving through adversity can have in all of our lives. These personal moments are the essence of each hike for me. The natural scenes gifted me through my remaining senses and the eyes of my friends are simply the extra benefit of an experience already well worth the undertaking.

As our real hikes began we pushed through 17 summits that season. Through it all, my communication with Quinn became almost seamless. I understood the subtle shifts in his body and I angled my own to successfully evade bumping knees, shins, or feet as we built a more consistently steady pace even on challenging stretches. The extra conditioning of running helped provide more energy and I felt full confidence the goal would be reached, most likely well ahead of our original 10 year schedule.

Not everything was seamless, though. The initial surge of considerable volunteer work had carried us through a successful first year. In our second year many of the mistakes I made in setting up the various roles created challenges for the 2020 Vision Quest team. My diverse friendships ensured kind hearted good intentions, but an assortment of approaches at times created tension, frustration and arguments between members of the team. My inexperience did not help us navigate through these with ease. As a result, some team turnover took place. I spent a considerable amount of time and effort evaluating my missteps, forging ahead with better decisions and connecting with all those affected. This was a difficult but valuable learning experience and 2020 Vision Quest benefitted as both our board and staff grew to accommodate the changing needs. Despite the turmoil on the inside, we all worked productively to keep a healthy connection to our ultimate charitable mission and the less important but more visible hiking goals.

In fact, by our second Peak Potential event, which sold out, I was able to announce a bonus hiking goal to all in attendance. Bob

Hayes and I were going to attempt the Single Season Winter Summit of all 48. I explained that snow provided many new challenges but smoothed away my most significant challenge, twisty, rocky, rooty, and thus uncertain steps. It was an ambitious goal as before that winter only 46 people and two dogs had reportedly succeeded in this quest. Quinn's task would be monumental in guiding me for much of it but human guiding would be needed as well. I confirmed we would also continue with our original quest to complete the non-winter peaks.

The Winter Quest

On December 22nd we set out on Mt. Tecumseh, coincidentally our most recent peak in the non-winter. I was proud to have Glenn Gunn, my mobility instructor from NHAB along for the hike. I also was enthused to meet Dina Sutin, a hiking friend of Bob's who had asked for permission to film the hike. Not enough snow had fallen and so unfortunately the trail was every bit as challenging as my summer hikes, with the additional detriment of icy patches. MICROspikes are a simple traction device which stretches over the bottom of a hiking boot for just such conditions. The entire summit slab was a sheet of ice and I broke my first of three pairs on this hike, because of the torque my feet experience on difficult trails. We were fortunate our plans called for shorter hikes initially. We planned to gradually increase in difficulty and duration to help us prepare and to hopefully allow snow to accumulate and thereby ease my footing.

Christmas day we managed another ice-sheet summit of Mt. Jackson. The hike took too long as my speed in some of the rockier points was a factor. Daylight hours are so much shorter in the winter, it would be common for us to start in the dark and finish in the dark. While that isn't necessarily a challenge for me, Quinn benefits from daylight as do my hiking companions. Headlamps illuminate the snow nicely for most situations and Bob was more than sufficiently skilled to manage, but darkness was a consequence of my pace if I didn't continue to develop.

Our third hike of the winter showed encouraging signs of increased speed as we tackled Mt. Hale on a lovely day with surprisingly high amounts of snow on the Fire Warden trail. Hiking towards the "skinny tree" landmark for the unmapped trailhead, we met Greg Neault and Aaron Sakash just realizing they had entered at the wrong location and on the wrong side of Mt. Hale. They were hoping to climb it anyhow but had discovered to their dismay the map showed no trails up this side. They were thus delighted to learn we were climbing up just such an unmarked trail. In the quick friendly introduction there was a sudden realization of my blindness and a playful suggestion from Greg that a blind guy was helping to direct the lost sighted hikers. While far from the truth, the reality is we spent the next handful of hours chasing each other up and down the snowy glades and switchbacks of this beautiful trail. In order to pick up the pace Bob did more sighted guide technique than we used before and the smooth footing allowed us to run on the narrow track of trail. This resulted in a couple of laughing falls and pile-ups as we pushed ourselves beyond a reasonable pace in the interest of keeping up with our newfound friends. Three peaks in five days certainly had me encouraged, especially with the amount of sheer joy on Mt. Hale.

Two hikes later we took on Mt. Garfield and Bob introduced me to a friend of his, Justin Fuller. Bob felt we would benefit from an additional human guide, enabling us to increase our pace. He and Justin had many prior hikes from which he expressed confidence in Justin's ability and approach. During our hike the two of them were old friends reconnecting and I almost felt left out, excepting I had Quinn's companionship while managing the trail with glorious ease. Just before the switchbacks began we paused and Justin noted I had lost a MICROspike. The summit cone would require them and I was dismayed at my failure to notice. My going back would delay us on this longer hike, but Justin suspected he knew the spot it had been lost.

Acknowledging his youthful speed he offered to retrieve it and trotted off, promising to catch up with us. He delivered on both promises in impressive time as Bob, Quinn and I continued to make good progress. On the journey down, Justin and I became fast friends, extending into the overnight at Bob's camper where we shared the living space after Bob retired for the night.

In those four days we completed six peaks and connected with a host of friends old and new to celebrate the progress of our quest: 11 peaks behind and 37 ahead with plenty of optimism for success. By January 22nd we were ready for a southern presidential traverse and the weather granted us a bluebird day. Absolutely no wind and crystal clear skies allowed a large group of friends to hike up the Ammonoosuc Ravine trail together. Pushing the pace up the steady steeps to arrive above the tree line I was gifted with a liberating experience. The wind and cold had hardened the surface everywhere into a solid, rough snow crust which allowed me to walk absolutely anywhere with complete freedom. It was sufficiently smooth to make Quinn's guide work virtually unrestricted and the only points for concern were the "gems", as Cathy Merrifield described the fist-sized chunks of rime ice which surrounded us. In the bright sunlight these gems sparkled in every direction, creating an even more spectacular winter wonderland than the snowy mountain summits already provided. We scrambled up the steep summit cone of Mt. Monroe and Justin shouted out that he had captured a picture he thought was iconic of Quinn guiding me up the steepest point with pure joy on his face.

We continued our trek deep down into the col, the low point between two mountain summits, before rising up to Eisenhower and then over to Pierce. The snow was fairly deep and at one point the hard pack gave way under my weight and I once again managed to lose a MICROspikes without realizing it until far too late. Though some looked, none could find it. I managed with the more slippery boot tread and emphasized the traction foot when needed. At the summit of Pierce, Bob challenged Justin and I to showcase human guide work on the descent. The Patriots had a playoff game in one hour and if we could get from summit to trailhead in that hour he'd let us watch it at his camper. Justin was new enough to guiding me and tended towards caution, so our pace was likely a little short of what we needed. Bob had developed those guiding skills very well and so I challenged him to give me everything he had guiding and I'd keep pace. He accepted and what followed was a full-on run down the Crawford Path which took 45 minutes to complete! This included two wipeouts due to the boot without a MICROspikes. The Patriot playoff victory over the Denver Broncos only sweetened the feeling of success. When a friend of Justin's posted to a hiking group reporting finding a MICROspikes belonging to a giant in the col of Eisenhower, we connected to get it back right away.

Just when everything seemed perfect, the first crack in the teamwork appeared. At breakfast Bob announced he didn't think we could succeed in our quest and that he thought I was too slow. His words hit me like a sledgehammer. There was no sign of humor in his voice and when asked he confirmed that he was completely serious. We nonetheless set out for the summit of Carter Dome with reports of an impending storm requiring us to hurry, or possibly turn back if the signs warranted. Early on the trail we exchanged unpleasant words for the first time. We spaced ourselves further apart on the trail to reflect privately as the trip took on a somber and defeated tone. Ascending the 19 Mile Brook trail put a dangerous drop off to my right side. This was Quinn's least favorite way to hike as on the narrow trail he had no way to indicate to me how close I was to the edge. This resulted in a slow sidewinding step up the long stretch of trail. I didn't want to ask for a human guide given the prevailing mood of the day, and Justin was encouraging but caught in the middle of an awkward situation.

Just below Zeta pass I wrestled with possibly quitting the quest. I didn't want give up but I couldn't continue with 28 more peaks in this mindset and my support system effectively broken. I didn't understand what had gone awry and Bob seemed unwilling to communicate, or I was ineffective at the attempt. In the midst of this emotional turmoil Bob told me to hurry, as if I wasn't giving what I reasonably could to the pace. I told them to go ahead, get their peak without me. I'd continue as best possible and accept the missed peak if the weather didn't allow for my going onward. At that moment as I was accepting it was over for me, Justin came back and asked how he could help. He took over human guiding and we used the trekking pole to allow us to step more freely and swiftly without risk of my MICROspikes catching the back of his foot. Quinn trotted behind us seemingly relieved to have Justin handling the difficult section of trail. My crushed spirit did not lend strength to my hiking Carter Dome but Justin's kindness and determination carried the day. We finished just before the storm and headed home. I had one more overnight alone with Bob to try and understand what went wrong. That day he had informed Justin the camper was too tight with three of us staying there and it would no longer be available for him to overnight. I asked Bob directly if there was more involved with Justin or me and could not get a clear response. What I could reasonably discern was that he believed I was too slow, needed more of his guiding than he intended to give, and that ultimately we could not succeed on the longest and hardest hikes still ahead. What confused me most was Bob stated willingness to continue despite his conviction of impending failure.

Four days later we were back on trail together for the Tripyramids. Dina was still filming as often as possible and I was delighted to see the early signs of a relationship between her and Justin. The interactions with Bob were not improved and only the support of other companions provided distraction from the tension and an overall positive experience. Bob's hiking skills still lent tremendous help, such as teaching me to shorten trekking poles to become two hand-held ice picks for scrambling up steep, icy sections. We were still staying at his camper at Twin Mountain but Bob openly expressed his unhappiness and no resolution was in sight.

The negativity intensified on Thursday, February 9, 2012 with our hike of South and Middle Carter. Once again on the 19 Mile Brook trail heading to Zeta pass, Justin and I were working together comfortably. As Justin and my teamwork and communications flourished it seemed Bob's antagonism grew proportionally. We parted ways at the trailhead with a loose plan to meet Justin at the trailhead for Mt. Lafayette the next morning. Bob was angry that evening and he shared a surprising story, claiming that Justin had abandoned him on a previous wilderness hike. He said he never trusted Justin or considered him a friend and no longer wanted to hike with him now. Those concerns stood in stark contrast to what he'd told me when introducing Justin to our hikes, and to everything I'd experienced with Justin. At least I now had a potential source for the problem. This source, however, did not address how badly Bob had been treating me. Bob simply refused to tell me what I had done to cause that treatment or what could be done to improve our interactions.

The next morning there were few words spoken and I couldn't determine if we were hiking or not. At the last minute he said "get your things and let's go" and so I quickly assembled my gear. My cell phone was left behind in the rush and Bob refused to call or text Justin with any of the information for our timing or route. We set out in the opposite direction most hikers take this loop hike, choosing to ascend Lafayette and thus descend the difficult Falling Waters trail. I learned later that Justin found our vehicle but guessed the loop direction wrong. Bob and I didn't speak a word on the trail, but Quinn was so strong and capable he guided all of the Lafayette trail with tail-wagging determination which kept my spirits striding forward. At the summit of Lafayette I knew I'd likely need some guidance down Falling Waters and Bob confirmed he'd help me there so we continued, awkwardly passing a reticent Justin at the summit of Mt. Lincoln. Bob met the bare minimum of that commitment and I finished mostly unscathed. I knew my time with Bob was over and I just needed to make it official. I called Tracy that night and she made an offer to come up and get me but I suggested she wait until the next day. Bob's wife Geri was joining us that night and she had remained warm and kind throughout. We were scheduled to hike Mt. Carrigain for our 34th peak. Having the Saturday to drive up in a more leisurely way would be easier on Tracy's schedule and afford me the time to pack all my gear. I made a similar phone call to Justin and Dina and commiserated over the potential end of our Winter quest. They had joined us for so many wonderful hikes, built a tremendous friendship and still had a desire to try and finish these peaks. We agreed to meet after my hike of Carrigain with Bob and Geri, to have dinner and talk about the possibilities.

At our dinner meeting, we found solidarity on the incredible good Bob had wrought in bringing us together in friendship. He also helped me so far along on this quest. We determined to finish the winter quest together and five days later embarked on one of the hikes Bob had called impossible for me, the Bonds traverse. We parked cars for the start and finish, nearly 40 miles apart by road, and then set out on the 24.5 mile winter traverse of multiple peaks through the remote wilderness in the White Mountains. In the early morning hours a light snow fell over Zealand's closed road access and through our flat forest walk to the slight rise where breakfast was just being served at Zealand hut. The steady steep climb to Zeacliff was through heavier snowfall, and as we descended deeply to climb Guyot a full-on blizzard arrived. We paused atop the windy, snow crusted peak of Guyot struggling to find a cairn, only to discover Quinn was pointing his body and pulling me directly towards it. Here, we needed to decide if the promised good weather was trustworthy enough for us to continue. Clearing the summit of Guyot, the weather instantly eased and by the West Bond Spur it was no longer snowing. Deep snow on this remote outcropping had us working hard but full of pride for passing the half way point! By the summit of Bond we were greeted by clear skies. Justin and I stood back to back in a "gangster" pose as playful enthusiasm buoyed our spirits. Quinn guided me down the windy channel to Bondcliff and over the edge of what I like to call the Hillary step. Now just the long steady slog out remained, as the sun descended and darkness swallowed the woods. During our long weary walk through Lincoln Woods I thought of the next day, where we'd take the Black Pond trail before bushwhacking our way to Owls Head Mountain. I felt we were close to that turn off and wanted to gauge distance for tomorrow's trip. I inquired how close we were to the Black Pond trail when Justin halted me abruptly to point out that my trekking pole was within one yard of the trail sign. I think he questioned my blindness for a few moments until I reminded him of how many times I "let" my head hit a branch! We triumphantly achieved our Bond Traverse, Owl's head and two more summits the following day in an epic 7 summits, 54 miles in three days. This left us only seven more summits to the finish!

Cold and stormy weather halted all hiking for two weeks. I started to get nervous for our success, knowing we only had until the official end of winter on March 19th. Finally, March 6th promised clearing conditions and our schedules enabled an attempt of the Northern Presidential traverse. Both Justin and I had worn out our boots and used the time to break in new boots at home. Thus as we hiked up Valley Way we set a punishing pace which had Dina suggest she should turn back. We slowed a little and encouraged her to keep our team together. On clearing the tree line by the closed Madison Spring hut we did not pause for shelter even though the winds and temperatures were severe. We confronted Mt. Madison, determined to re-evaluate the disconcerting weather after the shorter peak. As we crested the summit of Madison the first gust of wind was the most bone chilling I'd ever felt. It nearly lifted Quinn off his feet even as he guided me in harness into the wind. We angled our way to the actual summit, taking a quick photo before using the peak as our windbreak while descending back to the hut. The wind was still from the north which wasn't ideal as better weather would arrive from the west, so we chose to tackle Adams by way of the less common east approach. We quickly learned that was a mistake. Our route sheltered us from the wind, but the snow drifts were incredibly deep. We spent a tremendous amount of energy in the attempt while working our way back to Airline Trail, which had been broken out enough to show the path. At this point I realized my right achilles was in a lot of pain. The new boots were broken in for flat walking, but the angle of Valley Way exposed my stretched achilles and I suspected had rubbed it raw. Every time I placed the right foot at an angle it hurt. So as we climbed Mt. Adams I began to kick my right foot into the ice-crusted snow to get a step for traction. I couldn't kick with my left as Quinn was there and I didn't want to risk catching him with a MICROspikes. Atop Adams the weather broke and so we delightedly dropped into Edmund's col where the snowdrifts were again incredibly deep. I had borrowed snowshoes because mine had been unfortunately left in Bob's camper and we were having difficulty in arranging a return for them. Justin evaluated the snowshoes as too likely to become skis for me due to their metal outer ring and lesser tread. Thus Dina took the lead, strenuously churning through waist deep snow and establishing a path up Jefferson. With Dina breaking trail, Justin packed it down further in her wake, making it easier for Quinn and I to manage without snowshoes. It was hard work and by the time we hit the snowpack of the summit cone I was glad to kick my right foot in for traction again, though noting with concern that my right toe was becoming sore.

On toward the summit of Washington we approached the juncture with the Jewell Trail. My friend Brent Bell had suggested he might meet us near this point but we were behind schedule and it was colder and windier than expected. As Quinn's tail wagged furiously and he surged forward with joyful enthusiasm I knew Brent was there and my spirits rose greatly. Brent Bell and a friend had climbed up with skis and they added a tremendous burst of energy during a particularly tough point in the traverse.

Spirits lifted, we set forth for the final upward leg of our journey which proved still more work than I expected. I knew we were close to our goal and Quinn was leading confidently but I paused him to rest and seek inspiration from my companions Justin and Dina. Shouting over the wind "How much further?" Justin's response surprised, delighted and energized me anew: "Four more feet!" I had stopped Quinn just one long step from our summit goal! What had changed from my exhausted pause moments before to my energized final step? Only the knowledge that my goal was a mere stride away. Often the greater part of strength in striving for and achieving our goals is the mental confidence that they are within our reach. I now had an outlook for my approach to goals and Dina had the name of her film telling the story of our winter quest, "Four More Feet".

People often ask me for superlatives; best hike, favorite hike etc. It is hard to top that descent of Washington, we had the most magical experience. Striding past Lake of the Clouds on the adrenaline surge from the summit we reached the long steep stretch above Gem Pool for the glissade of a lifetime. Glissading, at least colloquially in New England, is the term for deliberately sliding down a hiking trail on your snow pants. Doing it by accident is falling and I managed that a few times that winter, as well. On this stretch it was deliberate, with the curved imprint of all the prior hikers serving to guide my slide even as Justin tried to run ahead of me. Quinn meanwhile galloped behind me determined to pounce on me if I slowed enough or dared to come to a stop. Laughing like children, we covered nearly a mile in all too few minutes of exhilaration. Standing on the trail again I was halted by Dina and Justin's exclamations of awe and wonder. The Lafayette Ridge was alight in alpenglow brighter than they had ever seen. More impressively the rime ice around us was capturing the pink hues and reflecting it everywhere in a colorful splendor that was a breathtaking end to an epic hike. Except it wasn't quite the end. As the glow faded and they resolved to dig out their headlamps, the full moon rose from behind Washington and lit up the forest in an eerie white faerie glow for the rest of our walk to the trailhead. How can so many magical moments condense in an already epic experience? Because, I believe, of the choice to actively participate in the moments of possibility. They may not all be full of rewards but when they do those gems will sparkle for the rest of our lives.

Back at our room for the night, the payment for those wonders came due. The agony of removing my boots and showering revealed the damage of the day. My achilles was worn bloody raw with the soft tissue underneath visible. The toenail of my right big toe had been pushed back through the skin behind it by my relentless kicking on the ascents of Adams, Jefferson and Washington. It was a mess and Dina's assessment was that hiking tomorrow was unlikely. She helped me wrap the wounds and suggested we decide in the morning. Justin's knee was balking from a freak twist in the parking lot at the very end of our hike, and he was going to have a tough time as well.

March 7 dawned with wonderful weather. I woke early with my right foot throbbing. I washed, wrapped and packed it into a hiking boot waiting for Justin and Dina to wake. I said I could give any one day hike a go and would then seek medical treatment back in Nashua. They acknowledged the ridiculousness of this suggestion and of course agreed! Wildcat A and D awaited us. I had received advanced special permission to descend Polecat Ski trail. I had the note tucked in my pocket for verification and ready to show the ski patrol before our descent. Justin and I were hurting and slow, each giving the other an excuse to pause every several hundred yards. Dina was in her glory, virtually dancing around us with her unsympathetic vitality.

The pace was a crawl at points and we laughed at ourselves for the challenge these easier peaks in perfect weather provided us despite all we had accomplished previously. Our pain would not stop us however and by day's end only a single peak remained between us and historic success.

At home the podiatrist delivered two bits of great, from my perspective, news. First, surgery would not be needed to extract the toenail, I'd done enough damage he could pull it right off. Second, while I would likely need a small surgical repair later, there

Pictured: Randy and Justin point out their matching injuries on Wildcat

was no reason someone stubborn enough to inflict that damage and continue hiking couldn't complete their final hike. The 2020 Vision Quest press engine worked overtime and we set forth on another perfect weather day, March 10, 2012 to reach the summit of Cannon Mountain. Once the home of the Old Man of the Mountain, symbol of NH, this peak was a shorter trail to allow plenty of time to celebrate. It included a tram virtually to the summit so all my non-hiking yet adventurous friends could choose to join us. It had parking sufficient for all who wanted to be a part of the celebration and so we set out for the final summit. It was an enormous crew of nearly forty who showed up to hike and celebrate that morning, and the excitement was palpable. A couple of reporters joined us and also Cath Goodwin, a legendary hiker for her own incredible accomplishments. I felt strong and confident with no sign of pain from my still damaged foot. I can only assume the sheer joyful exuberance I felt completely masked the reality of my injured foot. There was laughter and awe for those who hadn't seen much of Quinn's work and a rare moment when I caught my dear boy with a misstep, something I hadn't done since early in our work together.

We regrouped and settled into our groove soon leaving most of the team behind as the work we'd put in all winter showed. "Practice makes progress" is the saying I prefer over "practice makes perfect". I learned it from the students at South School in Londonderry and it was on display this day. Quinn, Justin and I reached the summit of East Cannon ahead of the rest of the team. We thought about going on and had an epiphany. If we continued the summit of Cannon where a crowd was gathered it would leave some of the team feeling left out of our celebration moment on the summit. This was unacceptable to me. I treasure the support of teams throughout my life and every hiking team for every peak winter or summer is on that list. This day was filled with people who deserved my appreciation, respect, encouragement and support. Having them feel left behind or devalued was wrong on so many levels. I thought of the quote I learned from Maya Angelou "I've learned that people will forget what you said, people will forget what you did, but people will never forget how you made them feel." When I build and sustain teams in my life I always want to place that quote at the forefront. There are sadly days I put my eyes on the prize and allow my goal-driven approach to let me neglect a bit of this belief. On this day I didn't forget and I'm happier for it. I choose to use the positive encouragement I received by all those on the trip as the reminder why I should always strive to live by Maya's words.

At the summit there were so many wonderful warm greetings. I heard my wife's woohoo from some distance away. I heard Kathy Dunn playing "Beautiful Day" by U2 in honor of the song's meaning in my life. I heard the tremendous roar of so many friends with me and waiting to celebrate a winter of work and accomplishment. There are so many aspects of the moment worthy of standing out, and yet one stands out most of all. Cath Goodwin was there to give Quinn an award. He was being named as the fourth member of the Four Legged Explorer Association, yes F.L.E.A., and receiving the membership in the Order of the Golden Biscuit. We placed his meaningful Golden metal award around his neck and he sprinted laps around the summit in joy for the excitement in the air. What made me so proud, so joyous was his getting this well-deserved accolade. I was proud of my own efforts, struggles and accomplishment. I was exponentially more proud of what Quinn accomplished in guiding me so well, so far and so often, for the very real absolutely astounding requirements of his work, for his joyous passion and his devotion to me. This was his moment more than mine and having a hiking legend call him out for it was all the proof I needed to mark the day and journey a full and historic success.

Pictured: Randy, Quinn and Justin celebrate the finish and Quinn's Golden Biscuit award! Cannon Mt., 2012

The Quest Endures

But there were celebrations and accolades aplenty for me as well. Amusingly I was asked while still atop the summit what I planned next. Prepared for this potential question I quipped: "I think 48 beaches in one summer sounds just about right." The truth is that probably would bore me to tears. That's likely the reason I planned and undertook a 100 mile walk to commemorate the 100th anniversary of the New Hampshire Association for the Blind. Their June Walk for Sight was a 3k awareness and fund raising event. I would try to augment it by walking from their office in Concord, NH to their seacoast office and back again just in time for their walk to commence. Our community building had progressed well enough we managed to reach my goal of 100 people on our team. We also were proud to present each of our supported charities with donations of $10,000 for our second year of work! This additional endurance experience supported the ongoing efforts of 2020 Vision Quest which was growing beyond our initial expectations.

Dina released her movie, "Four More Feet" to highlight our winter quest, and we spent the summer and fall attending showings of the film all over New England. We also managed to add fourteen more peaks to our non-winter hiking accomplishments, leaving us 12 to go for that goal. The movie release turned into a DVD release. As if all her work wasn't enough, Dina also created an "Audio Description" track for the DVD to ensure the sight impaired community will have access to the 48 minute film. Dina generously gave all the rights and earnings from the whole process to our charity. We had tremendous momentum leading into our 3rd annual Peak Potential event, in which my grief over the death of my Dad that very morning could not mitigate the support and success our event provided. I was in awe of the generosity of so many people in our growing community. I felt a mix of pride for the human spirit and amazement as I realized the vision for our charity was succeeding well beyond my initial hopes.

We slipped into the 2013 hiking season while still trying to manage the effect of increasing neuropathy to my legs and hands. While the neuropathy was making some things more difficult I was determined to persevere through the challenges. The first few hikes were all struggles as I learned to hike with the vastly reduced sensation in my feet and legs. Still, something more was amiss and it wasn't until half way through the summer we discovered in a random blood test that I also had contracted Lyme disease, despite never exhibiting the tell-tale bullseye pattern. I was exasperated! I was trying to work through these peaks in principle because that was the original concept. Yet over the winter I lost the feeling below my knees, which challenged my balance and made determining footing drastically more difficult. Now, Lyme disease ensured I felt miserable with no stamina! We were so close to our goal and while Quinn seemed in great health, it felt important to ensure we achieved this goal together. I took my 21 day dose of antibiotics and gritted through several hikes anyhow. I felt good by our final hike on August 24 when we all set out for Mt. Flume. While they had closed the Oseo trail, our intended route, feeling good meant I didn't mind the need to hike over Mt. Liberty to get out to Flume for the success. It was a sweeter celebration because Tracy and John Swenson would join us in completing the non-winter summit of the 48 on Flume.

It's a long steady climb with plenty of hard work but nothing unrealistic for challenge. So when the four of us joined up to walk the final dozen yards together it felt tremendous. John had become a dear friend since this quest started, Tracy and I became husband and wife and Quinn, well, he was already a legend. On the hike back we stopped on Mt Liberty where I'd been several times and Cat Orza took a photo of Quinn laying in the brush wearing his harness, staring with his hallmark devotion directed towards me. She knew when she took it that it was a special photo and as the celebrations faded into photographs and congratulations, the descriptions of that image earned it a designation as my favorite photo of all time.

That would prove to be our final hike together as our fall fell into a flurry of cancer discovery, treatment and eventual comfort care for my beloved boy. We continued to tend all of our work, resting him when he needed and not taxing him with anything unnecessary. He was driven and appreciated having purpose, even if play was his purpose at times. In his passing I wasn't sure how I would continue, though I knew that I would. Just as Ostend's legacy drove me to find my way forward from the wheelchair, I think Quinn's legacy was to give me purpose in my life and much of that purpose was the work of 2020 Vision Quest. Years after his passing I believe it is safe to say we have reached more people than we ever imagined. I've spoken to over 75,000 students in schools, hundreds of corporations/conferences, provided a pair of TED talks and attempted to continually demonstrate the tenets of our mission statement in our outreach.

We try to lead by example and put our focus forward to make a positive difference in the world. We've donated more than one quarter of a million dollars to the organizations we support. We've transformed through the years and our community has changed and grown steadily, as we have ourselves. The New Hampshire Association for the Blind has become Future In Sight and I have been the Chairman of their Board of Directors on my journey. In our quest to always provide the best support, we have also transitioned our charitable funding to Guide Dogs for the Blind who first started me on my Guide Dog journey with Ostend's tremendous care. We remain constant in our drive to live up to our taglines, to achieve a vision beyond our sight, and to strive for and achieve our Peak Potential. In this we are still on a journey forward and upward.

Pictured: Quinn comfortably rests on the summit of Mt. Liberty,
his final hike, and gazes devotedly towards Randy.

Running, Marathons and Mudders

You're tougher than you think you are, and you can do more than you think you can." Brian Powell from his book Relentless Forward Progress

The journey towards Peak Potential is simply a striving to be our personal best. Ironically, for me, this lesson began with running rather than mountains. I spent much of my youth being slower than I wanted or rather, actually allowing my belief that I was slow to limit my speed. All the sports I played while growing up placed an emphasis on quickness and lateral speed more than straight line running. In fact I was generally slow until my 8th grade basketball coach inadvertently called me out. This inspired me to watch the faster students run and practice changes in my technique. Specifically, I sought balance in using my legs to push versus pull me, developed an efficiency of cadence and learned the benefits of striking on the balls of my feet, all leaving me comfortably quick.

By my senior year of high school this new-found quickness shifted into a higher gear still. I found myself leading every fast break on the basketball court, pulling away out of my cuts on the football field and generally being thought of as fast by others. In our physical education class our coach clocked me in the 40 yard dash at 4.4 seconds unofficially and told me I should consider trying to use my speed for more sports there at Nashua High School. Sadly, I already felt regrettably rejected from my new school's athletics program and decided not to pursue anything further for the rest of my senior year.

It wasn't until my time at the University of New Hampshire that I even heard of a road race. As an engineer I understood the metric system for equations and formulas but in practical terms I had no idea how far a kilometer was. I signed up for the Homecoming 10K on a whim. Wearing my everyday Keds sneakers I stepped into the throng with absolutely no idea how to run a race and having not practiced a single distance stride. I'd

Pictured: Randy's bib from his first 10k a handwritten note says 10k 43:57.

always been able to run as long and as far as I needed, driven simply by my passion for the activity. Hours upon hours of relentless running up and down a basketball court seemed all the preparation I needed to run this race. I wasn't trying to win it, just to run in a pack of people and trust their guidance to help me understand what was involved.

I quickly learned that a mile was a long way and 10k was apparently more than 6 miles, which meant I ran too fast for long stretches, slowed dramatically and then pushed myself to run for a slightly shorter stretch. I finished with no awareness of or concern for my time. I had my complimentary race shirt which I gave to my Mom on her next visit and she surprised me by wearing it with pride. We both had fun with the notion of my fifty-something mother suddenly running road races. It was fun and I resolved to run it again next year with a little more preparation and effort. Despite my best intents, the race snuck up on me each year and though I earned my mom her shirt every time I never managed to properly prepare.

In the spring of 1985, when I was a pledge in Phi Kappa Theta Fraternity we pushed hard to compete in the UNH jogging championship. The rules were simple: show up at the track during predetermined times and run as many laps as you can to amass the highest individual or team total possible. My academic schedule was busy but I logged a few laps, using the time to catch up with fraternity brothers. It didn't even feel like running to me, it was just spending time talking with friends while circling the track without pushing towards any particular goal. I delighted in my discovery that this was purely fun, our fraternity won that year and the next two years, setting the stage for me to take up the senior leadership mantle. When my fraternity brother Brent challenged me to follow his lead in bringing home the Phi Kap victory as well as earning the individual crown, it was the first time such a goal resonated with me. I bemoaned my hefty engineering course load when the schedule came out for available track times, but elected to run as often as possible. I pushed my pace a little to be scoring more laps on each visit, and paid attention to my competition. As the final week arrived there were plenty of people vying for the individual prize but I had the lead and was determined not to relinquish it. My feet were a little sore from wearing entirely the wrong shoes. Yet I was so encouraged and excited by the possibility of winning, I attended each open time, even skipping a few classes to run laps continuously until they closed. I watched as the competition slowly lost heart and by the final days it was a sure victory for me and for our fraternity. There was never a burst of intense high pace effort, just a relentless consistent forward progress.

Going blind put running completely out of my mind, with the exception of bursts in various protected activities, nothing purely for the sport of running. I was an entirely unprepared 45 year old when Quinn and I began to undertake the jogging which resulted from our longer and longer walks of conditioning for hiking. Throughout the summer and fall of 2009 I increased the mileage and the terrain in which I ran with Quinn, constantly admiring his decision making prowess. He had an uncanny natural aptitude to adjust pace, alerting me to be cautious of the footing or even pausing when an obstacle could not be avoided and required my full attention. It was March of 2010 when we took our regular jogging sessions for our first official race, the "Irish Legs are Running" 5 miler in Lowell. There, I asked him to follow Carrie McMillen and he managed it all masterfully. Running along the often cracked and broken shoulder and finishing on cobblestone, we didn't push the pace. We paused at each water stop to encouraging him to drink from a cup as well. Quinn made all the decisions for my footing and we worked the pace together but, Carrie ensured we knew the race route properly while providing additional insights into Quinn's well-being. He wanted me to run faster and harder as he was competitive, but I was not ready mentally or physically to run faster just yet. We arrived to the finish line at 52 minutes and in appreciation for Tedy Bruschi chose to cross the finish line at 54 minutes which perplexed the timers. It was my first opportunity to consider timing and the official start of my racing.

With my focus primarily on managing 2020 Vision Quest, preparing for my 2nd degree Black Belt test in Karate and hiking, running, beyond the daily walk/jog sessions, was primarily relegated to an infrequent distraction. This changed with the arrival of Bob Hayes into my world as his passion for hiking the White Mountains barely exceeded his interest in conditioning runs, usually in Mine's Falls Park. As he learned more about Quinn's run guiding he invited us multiple times per week to join him for runs on these gentle trails where his pace was faster than ours, allowing Quinn's competitive drive to steadily help me increase my speed and stamina.

Excited to showcase our increasing proficiency, Bob included us on more races throughout southern NH in the 5k and 10K distances. He kindly adjusted his pace to allow us to challenge ourselves as Quinn learned to use all of a closed road during a race and instantly resume adherence to guide work rules after we finished. These race were pure joy for Quinn and I felt an expanded freedom as well as the improvement to my conditioning. As I improved, Quinn began to challenge me more fervently. If someone passed us, his pace would increase if I allowed it and although I could give him an "easy" to slow down, his preference was clear. Similarly, if someone came into his view ahead, he would become inspired to run faster, determined to overtake them. Bob's competitive nature thrived at encouraging both Quinn and I, resulting in our having a fair bit of success in the races.

I learned strategies for communicating with race directors, founded on my desire to build partnerships and quality relationships.

Many had little to no experience with a sight impaired runner and even less of a chance of understanding the concept of running with a guide dog. In the interest of advocacy, I found phrasing my email or phone call with strength and positivity yielded the best results. "I'm signed up to run your race and I wanted to let you know I'm totally blind and run with my guide dog so that I can understand any concerns you may have and help address them." I wanted to encourage dialog if they felt it was necessary, and frame it with confidence that there was a resolution to any of their concerns.

The most impactful race we ever undertook was the April 14, 2013 Boston Athletic Association 5K Road Race. It was the day before the Boston Marathon and shared the finish line with the legendary race. I was excited to highlight Quinn's incredible work on such a grand stage. Josh Warren coordinated a group known as "Team with a Vision" that brought blind athletes from around the world to run the Boston marathon, and simultaneously support the Massachusetts Association for the Blind. He was interested in my running with Quinn and we agreed to meet at the race. I wore a Go Pro camera on my chest to capture Quinn's work and asked Quinn to follow my friend Jennifer Liang who was a frequent race guide for the two of us that spring.

Jennifer loved everything about the Boston Marathon and her passion for the event was infectious as we lined up for the crowded conditions of the BAA 5k. Taking off from the start Quinn was extra cautious as he avoided runners who were unaware of his low profile in the extremely dense pack. We did more weaving than in most races as he kept me from any collisions and this difficult work required my full focus. When Quinn stepped abruptly to the right in front of me I need to short step whichever leg was moving so I could get the next stride in step with his turn or shift. It was exceedingly reactionary running until we worked through the thickest of the crowds and found a comfortable zone of similar-paced runners.

Jennifer challenged Quinn's competitive streak. When she dashed through a narrow gap of runners where Quinn and I could not fit, he weaved to the left and right, alert for an opportunity for us to burst past the cluster and resume the speedier strides he desired. We crossed the finish line in a literal photo finish that showed him with perhaps a single paw touching the ground, tongue hanging out and sheer joy on his face. I, on the other end of the harness, was a little hunched over and tired from pushing myself to his pace mentally and physically. We had run a great race, collided with none of our fellow runners and I swelled with pride even as Josh caught up to congratulate us on the run and talk about some future work with Team with a Vision.

Jennifer and I joined her husband Robert, and Tracy to celebrate. They stayed in the city to watch the Marathon the next day but we headed home. The next day while they sat on the sidelines watching runners complete the marathon, we shared the incredible B.A.A. official photo of Quinn and I crossing that same finish line with the American flag display in the background. It was a proud moment and popular photo. This joy was shattered as the tragic events of the Boston Marathon Bombing shredded the finish line flag display, so many innocent lives and the entire nation's trust in the expectation of safety. I was concerned for Robert and Jennifer and tremendously relieved to learn of their safety within a few short hours. I was devastated for the many who would never feel such relief.

When people do not learn how to communicate and resolve differences in healthy ways there is a potential for such horrific events. In any situation I always seek enough accountability to understand how it went awry in the hopes of preventing similar events from happening again. I always hope to put the vast majority of my effort towards the things we can change going forward. I think of it as putting my focus forward, and in the case of the Boston Marathon Bombing I knew the response I wanted. I would choose to be part of a community moving forward in hope and positivity. I vowed to run the 2014 Boston Marathon. We were likely to finish our original hiking quest in the summer ahead, so why not pledge to learn how to run a marathon and to qualify for Boston?

Over the next few weeks I came to understand my choice of response was certainly right and reasonable. My belief that I could train for and qualify for the Boston Marathon was possible but daunting beyond my initial understanding. Still, I made the commitment because Boston was a race which didn't just celebrate the elite athlete but celebrated community and the elite human spirit. There are runners undertaking Boston undaunted by a host of challenges. There are runners with varying levels of skill running in support of a person or cause so dear to them they are willing to sacrifice the time, training and pain of the marathon to showcase that support. Then there are the thousands upon thousands of people who line up along the route to give support and this creates an entire Boston Marathon Community of which I was drawn to be a part. I wanted to show that a response to an awful reality was to unite in positive community with determination, resiliency and a choice to celebrate ability awareness.

Quinn and I increased our running but the hiking schedule remained our primary motivation. Although I didn't expect to run Boston with Quinn, I did hope to train with him. Our plans slowly unraveled as Quinn's difficult diagnosis supplanted any thoughts of the marathon. When he took his last breath in my arms on January 20, 2014 I made another promise, to dedicate the year of running ahead to my Mighty Quinn. Our 2020 Vision Quest team joined in this promise by developing the #miles4Quinn program, encouraging all of our community to log as many healthy miles as possible through walking, running, cycling, or hiking to honor his legacy.

I was without my guide and some of the earliest training miles took place on a treadmill at the Nashua YMCA. It took some time and practice to develop comfort placing one of my hands on the side rail so that I would have body awareness of my location on the treadmill. As my pace increased it became more important to keep my focus and awareness sharp in order to ensure my feet stayed centered on the track of the treadmill. In my earliest runs I occasionally clipped the front of the treadmill for a short misstep but the few times my foot struck the side of the treadmill were nearly disastrous as the stagger and stumble it caused brought me close to falling. At least I discovered the tell-tale squeak of seemingly every treadmill if my steps strayed close to the back end. That sound alerted me to pick up my stride and never come close to the certain fall from sliding off the end of the treadmill.

For all of these worries, I was enjoying the physical outlet and escape time I found while running, as I continually worked to deal with my grief over Quinn's death. I was coming to understand, however, why many runners call it the "dreadmill" for the relentless monotony of hours spent running in place. I began social media outreach posts seeking to find human guides to work with me in preparation for my goal to run marathons. Boston was in my sights and that required a qualifying time in a prior marathon. My very first connection came from Christine and Pete Houde who drove all the way from Somersworth, NH on a suddenly snowy day for my inaugural outside run.

I shared instructions for rigid tether guiding with Christine who would be my guide. It was a derivation of the winter hiking approach which had served us very well in the mountains. Here the terrain seemed certain to be smoother and we developed a few basic communication agreements to ensure we could run together. I selected a one piece, shorter blind cane from my wheelchair days. This differed from most blind canes which are collapsible because of their length. The idea was to have Christine hold it in her right hand while I held the opposite end in my left. In this fashion the stick would be parallel to the ground and I would be behind her by about one stride and offset to her right side. On the road, we would run facing on-coming traffic so she could see any drivers and ensure they were reacting appropriately to us. I would be a little more in the road which would protect me from the potential ankle-rolling left edge. If there were potholes or other avoidable obstacles she would adjust her route so I wouldn't have to worry about stepping on them. If it was something unavoidable like a speedbump then she needed to warn me with a simple countdown so I could emphasize a heel strike and sink into my hips, allowing easier reaction to whatever obstacle I might encounter. Turns required a similar countdown warning, especially right turns since they placed her feet directly in front my stride. Left turns are always easier since I can simply follow the direction of the stick without danger of collision.

We set out in the lightly falling snow and determined to run six miles via an easy repeat of a 1 mile loop in my neighborhood. Christine was a natural with a strong voice alerting me for turns and the various rough points in the road. In some ways it was easier than Quinn's guiding because there was no guesswork in the obstacles. She told me if it was a pothole, frost heave, manhole cover or whatever. Despite the clarity, I couldn't help but think longingly of my beloved boy. She told me about her life and running which was great for distraction during the long, for me, run. As the snow began to accumulate at the seeming rate of one inch per mile our feet became heavier and we were suddenly slipping on our turns. This was harder than the treadmill and more work than I anticipated but, as Pete captured a few photos for our finish I beamed with pride for the perseverance, finish and friendship. This new guide system showed enough promise, if only I could find enough of the necessary guides.

My training became more difficult as Autumn arrived on the scene on March 16th. The key to a successful guide dog pairing involves the essential building of a bond and part of that is ensuring time together. I could not leave her for any appreciable amount of time, such as a long outside training run. Thus it was mostly treadmill miles, with Autumn beside me, with very few exceptions until The Great Bay Half Marathon in Newmarket, NH where I took on a very difficult course. The pothole-covered dirt road caught my knee awkwardly. We pushed through but the pace and distance were more than what I was ready to manage despite having run it on the treadmill. One week later though, I joined Laura Mountain for the Moose is Loose Half Marathon in Mine Falls and we used a slower pace to keep me running strong for the entire race. Autumn might suggest it was her dragging Greg Neault to key overlook points of greeting throughout, that formed a major part of my inspiration. At the finish we had conclusive proof the bond was strong, if not her behavior, as Autumn tore free from Greg, ran up to me and leaped all four paws into the air to land wrapped around my chest in an adoring dog hug!

Autumn and I were steadily working on our teamwork for guiding but there was no question she and I could not consider running together on the roads. She had too much demand on her focus to tend her work while running and it wouldn't be safe for either of us to ask her to guide at speed. We did set out on the Nashua Rail Trail to allow her to pick up the pace and see how she felt about running when there were effectively no obstacles or directional choices to challenge her. She loved trotting at a speedy clip for a short burst and then dropped into her normal fast walk pace where she is most comfortable. After a few minutes of this walk break, I invited her to try running again and she enthusiastically agreed but once again only for another five minutes or so before she slowed to her walk pace. This is where she's most happy and I praised her for the steady work and we had a great long walk on the rail trail. I had some disappointment that she wasn't enthusiastic about running with me but my first priority is to choose what works best for us both and I had no disappointment in Autumn herself.

She provided excellent levity at the end of this long walk as we returned to the parking lot at the start of the rail trail. Autumn did not stop at Tracy's car as I anticipated, but rather walked purposefully past where I expected it to be and continued outside the entrance gate. Curious, I let her have the freedom to guide me to whatever had piqued her interest and she guided me to the musical notes of "Turkey in the Straw" then stopped and sat expectantly. There was silence around me but I could sense the presence of people. "An ice cream truck?" I asked and the laughter confirmed my suspicion. A few weeks prior, Autumn and I provided a presentation at the headquarters for WellPet Natural Pet Foods and they hired an ice-cream truck to deliver treats for we humans and frosty paws for the pups. I acquiesced under the pressure of so many other dogs getting the goods and now my girl associated the music of an ice cream truck with her opportunity for a frosty treat. She may not want to run but she is happy to help me carbohydrate load!

Seeking more running guides, I made some connections through a pair of local running clubs, the Greater Lowell Road Runners and Nashua's Gate City Striders. Through one of these posts I met Thor Kirleis who agreed to guide me for my very first marathon, Cox-Providence on May 4, 2014. The problem, as we discussed on our single training run together, was my complete lack of proper preparation. After talking him through the rigid tether training, we set out along the Nashua Rail Trail, a 12.5 mile long bicycle path which only crosses a few roads throughout its completely wooded route. This makes human guiding vastly easier. I shared with him that obeying the time restrictions of Autumn's bonding guidelines had kept my outside runs all at ten miles or less. Even my treadmill miles had topped at 16 and I knew that to be insufficient. He knew it as well but he also understood my Boston qualifying time was 5 hours. Noting my determination and other endurance experiences were significant, he believed we could do this. This would be his 100th marathon and my first if I could finish it. The question would be how much discomfort I was willing to endure on the journey.

As we ran along at a 9:30 minute per mile pace, talking comfortably, he was gauging my conditioning as well as both of us learning a bit about each other. I had signed up for Cox before I learned of Autumn's early arrival and her impact on my training plans. I set a back-up plan to run the Bay State Marathon in Lowell for October but thought forging ahead with this would give me a better understanding and appreciation for running 26.2 miles. I told Thor that despite my intent to learn from this experience I was absolutely committed to the goal of using this race to qualify for

Boston. I was, after all, qualifying for Quinn and that purpose would help me push myself pretty far.

At the four mile mark we crossed a road in Pepperell MA and this required passing through close-set metal pylons which prevent cars from entering the bicycle path. Sometimes at these points a guide may ask me to "Tuck Behind" so that we run in single file. Usually I ask to be alerted for the obstacle on my right or left so I have an idea of when I can relax, knowing the threat is passed. Our guide work on this first training run was so smooth and our conversation so engrossing, I had shifted wider than necessary which allowed us to talk easier as we were closer to side by side. This caught us both less prepared and my right thigh struck the pylon, twisting my body and flipping me forcefully to the ground. Rising slowly I realized I'd been fortunate that my leg was at the ideal angle to ensure my knee hadn't struck the solid object and despite an abrasion on my hand and soreness above my knee, I was effectively fine. Thor was disappointed. I assured him that my choice to enjoy the freedom and wonder of running comes with some risks at times and I wouldn't trade the opportunity for the lack of a few bumps and bruises.

I knew I had drifted and I also quickly understood how, as a first time guide, the rail trail had lulled him into a false sense of security. After several miles of requiring little guide work missing the moment of bringing me in tighter was an easy slip. There was enough room for the both of us if I hadn't drifted and there wasn't a slight turn at just that location. It did provide an opportunity to demonstrate my dedication as we didn't cut the run short but rather continued further out for another mile to ensure we ran the intended 10 miles of our training run. I was mentally ready if not physically and running is 90% mental.

Tracy, Autumn and I met Thor in Providence on Sunday morning, May 4th. I was more nervous than excited. Though ready to turn my attention to my first marathon and give my all, I was quite certain that wasn't going to be nearly enough. It would take the experience and support of Thor's 100 marathons to help me find the way across the finish line. I gave Autumn into Tracy's care and put my trust into Thor as my guide for my very first marathon.

We started toward the back and right away I noticed the difference in his guiding. He was in the zone. Obstacles abounded in the crowded field of runners, small pylons hidden by other runners, potholes, frost heaves and simply old cracked pavement. We set out smoothly striding, my nervousness eased by Thor's competence at guiding and running. I marveled at how many people knew him as we ran by and thought running 100 marathons might just have you crossing paths with a few people along the way. He called out Tracy and Autumn at mile 8 which was an unexpected surprise I loved. My excitement at this surprise sighting suggested my emotions were rising earlier than anticipated. At mile 9 there was a U-turn around a cone which, despite excellent warning, caused a flare-up of my vertigo, staggering me for a few moments. This alarmed Thor until we talked through it and I was able to resume running. When I'm weary it's easier for things to set my balance system into the frenzy which once confined me to a wheelchair. Mostly I control those bouts, but when enough factors align against me, I can slip. Fortunately, I settled my mind and we resumed running. By mile 12 my breathing was too labored and it took no convincing for me to agree to working a few walk sessions into our run, much earlier than I had hoped, but such is the price of being under-trained. At 13.1 miles, half-way, his strategy of mixing running and walking based upon my breathing, was working. I realized that I had now covered a longer distance than I had ever run outside.

When Tracy and Autumn greeted us at mile 18, I was emotionally raw and exposed. Long distance runners often talk about hitting a metaphorical wall, a point where their body physically begins to shut down. I felt as if I was on my third such wall. Teary-eyed, I gave her a hug, gave Autumn a pat and we continued, taking to the bicycle path along the coast, "welcoming" a side wind to challenge my balance more intensely. The next 7 miles were a beautiful ugliness. The support and encouragement of people around us was tremendous. The determination I sought and found again and again was encouraging, but the bond which formed from Thor's unyielding focus, support, coaching, caring, friendship and inspiration was as vast as all the miles he had run in his life. At the end of those seven miles we closed in on the finish and I hurt incredibly. My legs seized near continuously for the last few miles and my mind was exhausted from the concentration of hearing and responding to all of his warnings and requests. Yet the sounds of the finish were near and he told me the final turn was in sight. Somehow, despite all of my struggles we still were well within our goal time to qualify. My eyes welled up one more time, again well past the number of times I could count on this emotional day. I stopped asking him how much further or what time it was and settled in to run steady and slow for the final stretch. As we turned the corner and began the last long straightaway, I heard Tracy announce her presence beside me and then felt Autumn lick and nuzzle my hand. They had stepped onto the course to run beside us in support. It seemed like every step Autumn sprang up to lick my hand and joy surged within me. I forced my focus to Thor's guiding, struggling to hear him over the cacophony of a cheering crowd. I struggled to lift my leaden legs over the timing mat with my arm joining his in the upward thrust of victory! Victory? Absolutely victory. My friend, Richie Blake, provided this powerful quote which resonates well for the reason and potency of running for me: "Only a handful of runners

Pictured: Randy and Thor finish the Cox Providence Marathon 2014

out of hundreds or thousands in each race have the special mix of genetics and hard work to win. It is the rest of us that make the sport what it is, a challenge of body, mind, and spirit. To keep on pushing forward, even when adversity strikes, makes you as much of a winner as the lucky few. "

My bond with Autumn secure, lessons learned and some new guide options available, I began to truly train for the Bay State Marathon. Greg Hallerman became both a coach and a close friend as my weekly mileage escalated with higher paced mid-week runs supporting weekend long runs. Greg was my primary training guide, providing invaluable knowledge and insight. He was, however, unable to guide me on race day. Ron and Meredith Abramson elected to each take half of the double loop course and I was ready to display the results of my hard work and preparation. Ron took the first half and an early strange knee bump proved to not be an error in guiding but a literal bump as the bag of my race nutrition, almond stuffed dates, slipped out of my pouch. This left me at the mercy of Ron's japes regarding trying to find a blind guy a date but otherwise we cruised smoothly through thirteen strong miles, slightly ahead of our race pace goals. Meredith took over and with her enthusiastic start and her generally speedier skillset, we unintentionally picked up the pace. As we crossed the Tyngsboro Bridge at mile 18, I was weary but steady and not feeling my lack of nutrition. Every mile the signs of fatigue increased, but I felt no reason to suspect we wouldn't overcome the lack of fuel. Just after mile 23, my race took a drastic turn. I felt an odd blinking of the world and a sudden bump. I awoke with my head cradled in Meredith's arms, laying on my back in the middle of the road. Nothing hurt but I was confused and disoriented, having blacked out. As I was falling she had somehow helped turn my body and catch my head so it wouldn't strike the pavement. This is all the more impressive since I'm almost double her size! We talked for a moment about how to continue. My disorientation was concerning enough that our conversation slipped into whether we should continue at all, and then unfortunately into choosing a ride to the finish. Was it lack of fuel? There was seemingly no other explanation. My frustration and disappointment was high even as I realized how lucky I was to not be seriously injured.

I went "back to the drawing board": Greg Hallerman's coaching. We taught me to use the readily available race nutrition "gu" options and even how to eat them while running at race pace. I ran hundreds more miles in preparation for my next marathon, which would be the California International Marathon in Sacramento, California. I chose it because the United States Association of Blind Athletes uses it for their National Marathon Championship and I had a chance to be competitive if I could overcome the unfortunate ending of Bay State.

My friend Jose expressed interest in guiding me as he lived in the Pacific Northwest, and although he hadn't ever run a marathon he was willing to dedicate the time to adapt his generally speedier skills to distance training. His first trial had a host of challenging conditions. After suffering through three weeks of pneumonia, I was concerned about pacing, but we still made the decision to compete together.

Tracy, Autumn and I flew across the country. The marathon would be our first stop before a vacation together. I was full of excitement for the many events surrounding the gathering of so many blind athletes, yet especially excited to run with a good friend in a meaningful race. The race starts at Folsom Prison and we started fairly deep in the pack of runners. Running for most is a solo sport, but it is always a team sport for my guide and me. Spirits high, we wove our way steadily through the pack feeling strong in our 9:30 pace.

One of our largest challenges was the clusters of people around pace groups in which a designated runner carried a sign showing the a target finish time, such as 4 hours :40 minutes, This helps many runners find their comfort and not over-run their goals and thus hit "the wall" later in the race. As we started at the back we had to work past a couple of these pace group clusters on our journey. After a lengthy amount of work to pass the 4:15 pace group, we reached the open road for a little running when Jose's stomach gave him enough difficulty to require a bathroom stop. While I waited for him, I heard our hard fought 4:15 pace group as well as the 4:20 behind them pass us by, much to my dismay. Still, this stop eased his challenge, and we were back in stride with each of us having some difficult moments along the route but both of us being there to support the other. We had each trained enough that while not an ideal and smooth run, it was both of our best marathons. We came in at 4:17, good enough as we would learn, to win first place in the B1 National Marathon Championship!

Finally it was time to put my full focus on fulfilling my promise from several years earlier, running the Boston Marathon. Christine and Pete Houde had agreed to each guide me for half of the race. Josh Warren and Team with a Vision invited us into their ranks to help facilitate the race day experience. Greg Hallerman shouldered the bulk of the training. Winter snowstorms made every weekend long run challenging and I quickly came to understand why it is so difficult to train for Boston when living in the Northeast. We ran the course in advance to help me appreciate the journey to and through the Newton hills but race day would be vastly different.

Greg was also qualified and would run alongside us for the entirety of the race, sacrificing his ability to run a much faster race to share the experience with me. Boston, as my friend Tedy Bruschi described it, was the Superbowl of road races, a 26.2 mile home stadium. It was my fourth marathon but the excitement and build-up was magnitudes higher than the others, even the National Marathon Championship. I had numerous TV and radio interviews. Several newspaper articles also highlighted our approach to the race and I once again felt overwhelmed by this epic opportunity. Greg and Pete joined me at the Hopkinton Vision Center just several hundred yards from the start of the race, which they kindly offer to Team with a Vision as a base of operations. It was, of course, rainy and cold with a wind coming off the ocean and into our faces as we waited, feeling the great significance of this event.

The rain was light as we lined up, and before I could fully grasp it, thousands of runners joined us in surging down the hill towards Ashland. It was so tight and crowded Pete had to keep me in close formation while Greg helped find slight clearings through the throng. It was two miles into the race before I could escape the tuck behind and emerge beside Pete to allow myself my full stride. Despite the wind and rain, I felt great. Hearing Greg and Pete's voices in teamwork, eventually settling into an easier race conversation, made everything feel right. I put my focus on my steps, Pete's instructions and staying calm. Greg held our pace back several times as Pete and I had less experience and too much excitement. We connected with another guide team and enjoyed many miles together to Natick and the handoff to Christine. Pete had worked me through the worst of the crowding safely and now Christine needed to keep me strong for the finish. The rain picked up, of course, as we wended our way through the hills but her strength invigorated us all and even the downpour at the base of Heartbreak Hill did not slow our steady pace.

In fact, at the crest of the hill I proudly put my head back and bellowed "I love you Quinn-boy, this hill could never break my heart!" because I had chosen to dedicate every mile to someone who made my life better and this was deliberately Quinn's mile. He was my purpose and I felt that getting to the top of this hill strong was a key for me on the day. After Heartbreak hill, as we ran the haunted mile past the cemetery, Greg began to cramp up but pushed through like the veteran of 10 Boston's he was. Having helped support us through water stops he was perhaps paying the price for the extra efforts. We slowed to stay with him but Greg insisted we keep running our pace and that he would catch up with us. Christine hesitated, asking me for guidance, and I told her to stay steady and trust him. After another half mile of Greg steadily losing ground Christine saw him come to a full stop. Christine hesitated again, giving me pause as well but, I heard him shout keep going. I did not want to leave a part of our team behind. I wanted to run with my friend who gave so much to bring me here, ready to savor this moment in strength. But I chose to trust him and honor the work he put into this day for both of us and we resumed our pace. These were the miles where many runners hit the wall and struggle, slowing, walking, hurting, and Christine had to be vigilant for their unpredictability as we passed runner after runner. I felt some weariness too for sure, but the strength in her voice, her guiding and my own resolve of the past year of dedication for Quinn drove me to keep pace.

Pictured: Randy and Christine finish Randy's first Boston Marathon 2015

We crossed the finish line at 3:50:37, cold and wet but strong and proud. Eagerly we waited in the rain while minutes passed slowly until Christine shouted Greg's name and he too finished, joining us in the raw embrace of achievement and appreciation for our shared experience. I realize that's the crux of all things for me, those moments we experience that bring us together in ways which fill my heart with an appreciation for the human spirit. I felt it with Greg and Christine as I'd felt it with Jose and Thor before them. Though it isn't the finish line, the start line or the race time, it's the point of coming together for having experienced something worthwhile. Boston is special for certain but it was more than Boston we had shared. It was gritty determination to start that first run with Christine in a snowstorm, using a technique we developed but hadn't really put to use in that way. It was struggling through dreadmills, poorly prepared runs, nutrition malfunctions, mornings when I didn't want to run, heat exhaustion, failures, successes and always a relentless drive to keep moving forward to find who I am inside and to reach for and achieve my goals. It was fulfilling a promise to choose the right response to a horrific event. It was a monument of dedication and love to honor my amazing Quinn. It was more than I could do alone and it was all the worthier for doing it with people who bonded so closely with me they understand all those nuances, even the failings, and appreciate the experience shared all the more.

August 23, 2014 provided a perfect, if challenging example of a team coming together in experience: participating in a Tough Mudder event. This extreme 10 mile, mud-laden event is packed with 20 punishing obstacles originally designed to test British special forces. Laura Mountain had first suggested the notion to me, but it was Greg Neault pushing that idea into a plan. "A goal without a plan is just a wish" according to Antoine de Saint-Exupéry. I think I was sufficiently intimidated by the daunting nature of many Tough Mudder obstacles that I was in a holding pattern just outside of the wish range until Greg made it real by presenting the opportunity to tackle the Great Northeast Tough Mudder in Maine with a group of his friends.

Greg previously completed a Mudder earning his "legionnaire" status and thereby had a fair bit of insight to share with us. I was mid-training for the Bay State Marathon and so the distance running of the 10-12 mile course didn't worry me, although the deliberately unreliable terrain provided pause for concern. As a hiker in the White Mountains I knew I could handle virtually any footing with patience and deliberation and presumably boots. The mega-obstacles throughout the course suggested boots wouldn't be ideal and we would need to scheme a different approach for these. We could expect balance beams, underwater ice pits, rope swings, vertical walls, quarter pipes, high jumps and mud beyond mud with a corridor of electric shock wires at the end to reward us for a long day of earnest effort!

A little internet research helped me to learn that a blind man, Darren Fittler, had attempted the Tough Mudder in 2013 in Australia and shared his experience. This provided me two bits of comfort in that there was precedence for possibility, and I wouldn't need to carry the additional burden of being the first, meaning I could fully settle into enjoying the event. Greg had guided me plenty in the White Mountains and I trusted him completely to help me make judgments and execute the challenges. Pete and Christine joined the team as well which provided some additional support for the running between obstacles. I felt comfortable with the rest of the team's eager willingness to give and take support as necessary with an appreciation that my blindness was no small factor in this challenge.

Riding to the event in Greg's jeep I was nervous, pointing out the relatively high risk of rolling my ankle on the terrain and ruining my upcoming marathon. He laughed at me for stating the details we'd already discussed and obviously decided to ignore since we were committed. Weaving through the enthusiastic crowds at check-in, we were shuffled into a large waiting pen where the Tough Mudder team built excitement through inspirational expressions, warm-up drills and crowd interactions. "When is the last time you did something for the first time?!" the MC shouted to us, more as a statement of our choice than a question. We stretched and worked steadily into a bounding frenzy with hundreds of people leaping up and down to charge their quick trigger muscles for the upcoming surge.

There was something different about the crowd, partially in the nature of the encouragement from the MC microphones but mostly in the attitudes present in our fellow Mudders. Nobody expressed frustration at delays or the proximity of our peers. Instead people were enthusiastically encouraging each other and congratulating them for choosing to be there. We were now part of "Mudder Nation" and the camaraderie extended to everyone present. Throughout, we were absolutely encouraged by the MC to understand our mission was not just to finish but to ensure everyone around us finished as well.

The send-off sent us up over a wall which was taller than me but an easy scramble once I assured I wouldn't accidently catch someone beside me with my foot swing. Running across the water-soaked, muddy field, we climbed over hay bales and quickly immersed ourselves into the mud of the mission. I wasn't there for the mud, it didn't entice me in any fashion but I was willing to tolerate it completely in order to feel the exhilarations of overcoming all the obstacles and crossing the finish. We set our pace in waist-high water and knee-deep mud at more of a fast walk than a run. When there was firmer footing the rigid tether made it easy for me to glide along beside my guide. The team soon learned to put another guide to my right when things were tight and my marathon training ensured I had more than enough endurance to keep pace with all the demands. As always, I remained on-guard with my feet. The few times we were in the woods, adding roots and rocks to the mix, we switched from a running to a hiking mentality. Everything went according to plan and as we arrived at "the blades", which were 10' walls at a slight angle towards us, my height and general fitness made it easy for me to scramble over and even give a boost to others. This excited me in ways I didn't expect as I realized I was not a burden but an actual asset. On the exceptionally tall walls it was no different than a scramble in the mountains where my hands on the trail allow me to see and my guides talked me to the destination. My confidence grew steadily.

On an early grand-obstacle I climbed high on a platform with a muddy water pit in front of us. There were rows of these and we simply needed to jump into the water, swim to the other side and climb out. I had jumped from trestle bridges previously and possessed the body awareness to generally keep my feet first. So trusting my team to help me find the platform's edge, I then needed their reassurance any forward jump was safe. Finally confident, I leaped directly and felt the thrill of the moment. Hearing my team call from the far side made it easy to swim out and just like that, one of the harder challenges was past. It isn't that I don't fear heights or even respect them, I have a bit of both, and the imagined height can wreak havoc with me unless my trust and confidence in my guide is higher than my fear. All along our way people were incredibly encouraging, not just to me but to everyone around them, it was an experience beyond what I'd encountered before. Even on this challenge, when Christine struggled and had to climb down, everyone supported her and encouraged her through. They were all the more supportive when she dug deep on her own, built up her courage and went back up and jumped, to thunderous applause for her success.

At every obstacle, my team or other fellow mudders were there to explain the layout enough so I could understand how to approach it. Even the quarter pipe, dubbed "Everest" took me a single speedy surge and leap to the outstretched arms of my companions for us to scramble up in admitted surprise at my first time success. Whether it was the day long supply of adrenaline, the incredible team or astounding Mudder community; I did not falter mentally, emotionally or physically through the entire experience.

When we reached the "Electro-shock Therapy" we held one final regroup to discuss strategy. Electrified wires hang at different heights all through the structure and hay bales crisscross the muddy pit to add difficulty in the crossing. It was loud in there and I would not easily hear anyone on the other side calling to me. The MC had music blaring and called out words of intensity intended to be worthy of an epic finish. To overcome the noise I would need a person to guide me through the path to the finish. A careful person might evade most or possibly all of the wires, but it was far more common for several jolts to buckle the knees of the Mudders working their way through the final obstacle.

Greg got me into this and he would get me out of this: that was the plan. I put my hand on his shoulder and tried my best to follow his guiding precisely. I am, however, a fair bit taller than Greg and his subtle leans were lost in the noise, exhaustion, hay bale scrambles and of course slippery mud footing. The first jolt twisted my shoulder and nearly pulled my grip from Greg. Gritting my teeth I knew I'd passed the shock to him as my hands were tingling as well. Barely one step later another shock caught my ear, then my head and on and on 27 more times while I sank into a resolve as deep as I have known to simply endure the pain, ignore the surprise and stay in step with Greg. Then it was over, we had our finisher headbands and an enthusiastic MC asked us how we did it for all to hear.

The secret is one they already knew, it's choosing to work together. It's surrounding yourself with like-minded people, embracing a common goal to put people first in overcoming obstacles together. Yes we had a plan, and of course our plan adapted as we encountered the reality of each obstacle. I certainly couldn't have done it alone. It was an unrivalled example of teamwork to achieve the euphoria of accomplishment together. By every one of us choosing to give our all to each other and the moment, we took away something greater still. It is the feeling of comradery so intensely unified that each individual success is experienced as an achievement by all. Effectively, every feeling of

Pictured: The Oberto Beef Jerky Tough Mudder Team and
Tough Mudder MC, Mt. Snow Vermont 2015
Photo Credit: Tough Mudder

success is magnified by every member of the group.

This notion of giving your best and receiving more in reward was behind Court Crandall's call to me that winter. Court was a fraternity brother of mine and working on a project called the Oberto Heroes of Summer. He and the Oberto beef jerky company teamed up with Tough Mudder on a campaign based around the slogan "You get out what you put in". He thought my undertaking a Tough Mudder on film would highlight that message powerfully. The plan was to fly me to Los Angeles at the end of March 2015 and produce a film clip highlighting the experience. Given the option to bring one guide I reached out to Greg Neault without hesitation. I was not surprised to discover several more friends wanted to make the additional effort on their own to be out there with us and so Jose, Skye and Loren were added to the team.

Court, Oberto and Tough Mudder were all incredible hosts as we embarked on what I jokingly referred to as my umpteenth experience of a lifetime. How was I so fortunate to be on the positive end of countless incredible experiences? Napoleon was said to select his

262

generals partially by 'choosing the lucky ones.' Luck may often play a role, but I believe in giving it all the help I can through my choices. I think there is something inherent to my approach which has significant influence on the opportunities I encounter. I embrace opportunity or obstacle with an equivalent enthusiasm and try to live up to the philosophy at the heart of the Tough Mudder in supporting our community.

As our team sat in the early morning hours, high on the hill of the motor cross course which would be host for the Tough Mudder in a few hours, I had time to reflect. They filmed us as Court asked various questions to elicit the sound bites they might want for their production. For me though, it was comfortable answers to my outlook on life and the approaches I choose along with the fortunate results I feel come from them. Simply put, I succeed by investing in life, participating mindfully and passionately with people as the primary purpose.

Success on this day was going to be harder to come by as Tough Mudder had created brand new versions of all their obstacles. Everything I thought I knew was going to be a little harder and of course their masterpiece, the King of the Swingers, was there to set the bar literally very high. Every Tough Mudder has the same core staff who travel to each location, and they knew about our success in Maine and about our challenge for the Hero of Summer video today. The MC called out our story as part of the inspiration and invited me to speak to the crowd as we all worked into the frenzied intensity of the start.

Over the wall and off we went, our first challenge was to run up an impossibly steep and long hill. Loose gravel caused many of us to slide back down, sometimes removing all upward progress. I quickly realized the terrain here would be more difficult than in Maine. It was so dry that rocks abounded, endangering my steps. I fervently hoped my guides would remain vigilant. They did, and we eased into a strong confident groove. I was just a couple of weeks away from my first Boston Marathon and my conditioning showed my readiness. Another challenge involved temperatures in the high 90's, a far cry from my snowy and frigid New England training weather. I hoped perhaps the wet obstacles would help cool us down.

It wasn't long before I encountered the new obstacles. First up was Everest 2.0; my initial attempt at the quarter pipe was just short and both Greg and Jose were unable to catch my arms. Crashing into the wall with unexpected force, I slid down the ramp roughly over each seam, sore and disappointed by the failure. The team reminded me it was a few feet taller than the version I had done previously and so I realized I might need to try one more step into the steepness and a harder jump. Skye and Loren each took an arm and guided me for the first few strides of my run approach to ensure I was straight on course. I burst into my top speed. When my last step felt nearly vertical I leapt up and towards the voices of my team which I could barely hear over the shouts and cheers of the crowd along the top of the wall. My left palm struck hard on something soft and my right arm felt nothing until a late grab on my wrist as I started to fall downwards. This caused my body to rotate and I felt my greater weight pull Jose off the wall as he held on for all he was worth. We both slid down together in a tumble of bodies, once again sore, disheartened, and fatigued. Apparently Greg's chin was the soft contact my left hand had found as I had over-jumped and knocked him backwards. Daunted but unwilling to yield, it took two more attempts for me to get the right blend of height, distance and connection for success as tenacity and determination once again won the day!

On the next significant obstacle, my grit would be tested again. The "Funky Monkey II" was upward sloping monkey bars with a twist. At the apex of the climb was a gap in from which hung a short trapeze bar. This meant using the trapeze to swing across and grasp a pole running parallel to the ground for a hand over hand descent. I made the first part with relative ease but the trapeze transition caught me. I grasped the trapeze and swung. Reaching out with one hand to search for the bar, I kept the other hand on the trapeze in case I missed. It was fortunate I did, because in the arc of my swing I simply could not find the bar I needed. Stuck but unwilling to give up I asked Greg who was hanging behind me, to put his feet to my back and kick-push me. He did and with that swing I lunged again but still without success. We repeated this many times in varying ways until both of our arms began to tremble with exhaustion and we were at risk of falling. I determined to make one final attempt and to lunge off the trapeze and either catch it or fall trying. Splat! Arms thoroughly spent, I'd fallen the dozen feet to the muddy water below and climbed out knowing I'd given my all. I learned from my team that my arms were reaching up too much and not out enough as the bar was below my arms on several attempts but hindsight, like our Charity, is 20/20.

Undone by the trapeze I put the disappointment behind me as there was an epic challenge ahead in the King of the Swingers, the challenge I recall at the start of the book. Listening to our team

Pictured: Randy's leap of faith. Tough Mudder. March 2015

describe the various attempts by other mudders was intimidating. Hearing of fall after fall with very few rings of the bell had me concerned. For most, the biggest point of failure was the very first leap and catch of the T-bar trapeze. This would be especially challenging for me, and it was a brilliant suggestion from Greg to have me plan to grab the vertical bar instead and slide down to the handles. Thinking outside of the box and collaborating is the key to untypical success. The rest was about timing, exploiting my long arms better than I had on the Funky Monkey and of course a little bit of luck.

Brian Tracy says "you don't have to be great to start but you have to start to be great!" I spent a little too much time initially thinking about how much pressure there was since any of my failures would be captured on film. While that's certainly true, it's equally accurate any success would be likewise captured, and more importantly the choice to be here immersed in the experience was already a victory. I settled into the moment, feeling an unexpected intensity of emotion. Leap, catch, slide, feel the arc, release, swipe…

Ding! My heart soared with joy as my body plummeted into the muddy depths below. Surging out of the water, fist raised in triumph, I felt like I had won a marathon. I gathered proudly with my team on the sideline, four of us having rung the bell! I felt like we had won something even better. We worked hard through the rest of the course and the congratulations of our fellow mudders never subsided. Our team decided to finish, on Electro Shock Therapy together. The plan was to form one long conga-line with me leading the way. The devastating result of this well-intended choice is that we struck nearly every electrical wire available and shock by shock each member fell off the conga line. Even the painfully bad decision to conga line the electro-shock therapy with me out front tapping my cane could not dampen, for long, the spirits of our team's unimaginable achievements.

We spent hours at the end celebrating with anyone and everyone, most especially each other. When it was over we went back to our hotel for a dinner together. Long after the meal was finished and the final drinks were drained, we still sat together simply not wanting to allow the moment to end. I finally tried to put into words how I felt. I told the team I didn't want to leave the table because once I did the magic would be over. Yes, I'd always feel incredibly bonded to this team. Of course I'd never forget the details of what we accomplished together. When we stepped away from the table the experience would end and we would be unlikely to ever reproduce that moment again. We'd make new moments and all of us would likely have plenty of fantastic experiences with amazing people. Still, I wanted to treasure this group, this moment for as long as possible and to thank them for joining me in this magical thing we created by coming together.

In 2017, Will Deans, the founder of Tough Mudder released his book, "It Takes a Tribe". He dedicated an entire chapter to his perspectives on my particular journey in life and in the Tough Mudder movement. He gets a lot of things right with the tribe he created and with the words he shares. The credit he gives me though, does remind me of something troubling. My friends and teammates are often undervalued and underappreciated by those who focus on me. All too often people outside our group consider me the forefront of our team. I wish more people could be part of the experience with me and see that certainly I do my work and earn my successes, but far more frequently the heroes who carry the day for themselves, for me, for the teams that I'm so proud of; are simply the incredible friends with whom I am fortunate to keep company. I try to celebrate them and so often their subtle support is the larger part of the beauty. If you are not present to see the team come together, then you miss the totality of the experience.

It was with this in mind I shared my last Tough Mudder at Mt. Snow in Vermont in June of 2015. We invited the largest team we could collect to join us and the vast amount of personal triumph on display throughout the day was heartwarming. I even managed to take on the Funky Monkey II and earn my revenge on the elusive challenge which had previously bested me. I watched my wife take on all it had to give, friends rally to support friends, and an epic celebration of success throughout the course. With this massive collection of friends for a final Mudder I've mostly retired my Mudder shoes for my running dreams.

Recalling the joke I'd made at the conclusion of my Winter 48, that I might like 48 beaches in a single summer, I found my running friends celebrating an event called Ragnar Reach the Beach. This was a team run for over 200 miles connecting the mountains I love with New Hampshire's ocean shoreline. It made little sense to include me in this relay team, since the rules allow for only one official runner at a time. As such, either my guide or I did not count but took up space in the relay van. I turned down several offers because I always want everyone to 'count.'

I shared this notion with Pete Houde while we traveled together for the California International Marathon, and he came up with a simple and brilliant solution. "All you need to do, Randy, is get an all-blind team and partner with my running club to be your guides." I loved his idea and wanted to modify it only a little by getting Team with a Vision involved. Suddenly we had two teams and commitments for support from people and places beyond our expectations. Nothing like this had been done before and it was an exciting mix of collaboration and athletic achievement. Instead of the normal 12 person relay team we would employ two 6 person Ultra-relay teams requiring each runner to run between 30-40 miles in six separate legs of running. On September 17, 2016, the Coastal Athletic Association was up to the challenge of running, double duty driving and of course the guide work for 6 visually impaired runners from all over the country. We came together to fill two vans with bad jokes, worse food and a determination to non-stop run from the ski slopes to the sea.

As the resident blind mountain climber and runner I was "gifted" with the first leg which runs literally up the steep ski slope for a mile and then down the tricky terrain of the gravel access 'road.' Pete was my guide of course, and we trudged up the hill reminiscing of hikes and tough mudders together. We were steady and strong but admittedly elated when finally, with our quad muscles burning, we found the turn-off to begin our descent. The road was far more challenging and people began to pass us, Pete had to be extra cautious as a misstep in guiding would result in a tumble to end our run before it had begun. Water bars crossed the road at regular intervals and required precise footing to avoid pitching headlong down the steepness. At the bottom a couple of railroad trail miles allowed us hand the baton to the next team and take our rest in the van.

There was early enthusiasm as each pair of runners took their shift. Most of us were simply eager for another run and excited to celebrate the strength and determination of our fellow runners. The segments grew longer though, and running on roads with narrow shoulders pressures the guides, especially as high speed traffic makes it fairly noisy. We were still strong on our second shift. Our goal was to be steady as I was nursing an achilles injury which would have preferred I not run up or down a mountain to start the race. Still running stride for stride with Pete I had the chance to talk about the journey we shared. He was there the day his wife guided me for my first miles without Quinn and now he was here in an epic endurance experience of impressive teamwork. Our second leg was rolling hills but our third brought us over the hilly terrain of the Ossipee mountain range and my achilles let me know the trip came at a physical cost. At the van we taped up my swollen ankle and calf with a precision learned from one of our blind runner's recent remarkable run across America. It helped, as did the cooler temperatures of our next run in the depth of the night as we ran through cloudbanks around the northern end of Lake Winnipesauke. Here in the dark, our headlamps illuminated our steps for Pete, alerted the cars but at times could not cut through the fog/clouds enough for him to see his own feet to warn either of us of the conditions. He used the reflection of the painted lines, we trusted the feel under our feet and the occasional drift of voices of other runner ahead or behind. It was impossible for me to sleep in the van though some managed a few naps.

By morning we were up for another shift and had to climb yet more mountains, the Belknap range. As we wound back towards the coast our legs were paying the price for running, stiffening in the van and running again. My achilles was still swollen but the tape was holding it together, just as Pete's encouragement did for me. By our final leg, the shortest in the stretch, I felt strong and the team could feel the impending accomplishment. Our teams rallied on the beach for a group run together for the final several hundred yards. Running on beach sand is not the easiest and guiding for it even harder. Having six pairs managing this together might have been a disaster were it not for how comfortable we had all become by the time spent in our vans, at our rest stops, and sharing the pains and struggles of an ultra-run together. Strong connections formed between each guide pair, and for me Pete was already a close friend. This had an interesting feel of a statement run as much as a chance to savor the experience. We were all runners, all athletes in our own right and all giving support to each other throughout, blind and sighted alike. Absolutely our guides take on a monumental task to add guiding to their work. I think they receive a monumental gift as well for the focus guiding requires is often focus taken away from any personal struggle. Similarly the bonds of friendship develop at a depth of teamwork most rarely get to appreciate.

Running with my guides through the years has created some incredible opportunities for me. No success has matched the Christine and Pete Houde 2015 Boston Marathon. No accolade is higher than the B1 National Marathon Championship earned with Jose Acevedo in 2014. No struggle has been greater than my 2016 Boston Marathon when my neurological disorder had attacked anew, causing me to lose consciousness multiple times each day as part of a broken vasovagal system.

It struck in February and through the many attempts at resolution I endured a spinal tap which went awry and a pair of spinal patch procedures, including one the week before the marathon. With my Doctor's support and full understanding Jose guided me for what we feared might be my last marathon if they could not resolve the issue. I passed out 3 times along the course, struggling worse than in my epic run with Thor. It took us 6 hours and 27 minutes to cross the finish line in an experience in which I have as much pride as my fastest time. This is simply because of perseverance and resiliency from both Jose and myself. It also let me experience is the incredible friendship to ease me to the ground in each loss of consciousness, quell the worry while waiting for me to wake and work me through the required slow and steady rising, walking and then running again each time. These are the bonding moments which make it all worthwhile.

Rebecca Dorr guided me for the first 18 miles of the 2017 Boston Marathon in a crowded course with series of challenges resulting in numerous falls and collisions not caused by either of our actions. Bloody-kneed, broken-balanced and frankly frustrated we limped into the transition with her having managed to work me through the toughest crowd guiding anyone has had to experience. All the while, the intensity of her focus and concern for me never wavered. In finishing that race Tom Cassetty, fresh off pneumonia, was handed the cane but not the well-trained runner he guided over the past many months. Instead I was worn down, vertiginous and within half a mile I was tripped up by another runner trying to help by shifting in front of me. Tumbling into a full out somersault, and ever so slowly recovering, I might have quit but for Tom's determination not to allow it. He stabilized me on the side, and worked me slowly and steadily through a painful final 8 miles for one of my ugliest races but one of my most appreciative moments for friends and guides.

It isn't always the marathon goal that drives me, but simply a love of running, likely in remembrance of days when I could

Pictured: Randy and his guide Andy start off fast on an early start of a local 5k, The Hollis Fast 5k, 2018

270

not walk, and the occasional reminder that I am never so far from being unable to run. So I'll speed through a mile and take pride that Rob Webber had guided me to a sub-six minute mile. I'll run with friends for training on the hills, the track or even the trails as it continues to be about the people. In my work with 2020 Vision Quest I wanted to reach more people than peaks. What I've learned in my running, from the guides, the crowds, the clubs and communities is that I believe that the reverse has taken place. I have been reached by more people than I have reached. Along the way I may push the pace or distance in some of the experiences but ultimately I'm always trying to achieve what yet another friend, Dave Salvas, suggests: "What was my time? It was the time of my life!"

Pictured: Randy and Jose run in synch together at the
CIM National Championship 2014.

Ashes Upon Kilimanjaro

"When you arise in the morning, think of what a precious
privilege it is to be alive—to breathe, to think, to enjoy, to love."
Marcus Aurelius

I was physically exhausted. Despite the freezing temperatures my cheeks were wet with the salty, warm tears flowing from my sightless eyes, driven by my deep heaving sobs. My oxygen-deprived muscles ached with the exertions which propelled me to the top of this Pillar of the Earth. I had not slept for two days and three nights, which left exhaustion nearly as complete as my grief. Kneeling on the ground, I took off my glove and flexed my aching hand. It trembled slightly as I slid my index finger through the summit's strange weather-crushed rock, which felt like sand, forming the letters of his name; Q – u – i – n – n. Below his name I pressed my fingers more firmly and deeply to create a hole. Reaching into the chest pocket of my ¾ snow pants I withdrew the pristine bundled handkerchief, so carefully prepared one week earlier.

Tracy and I had entered our meditation room in the back corner of our home in Nashua, NH in solemn preparation. I always feel reverent in this room where the ashes of my three boys are kept in a place of honor for the love, life and joy we shared together. I hold none of my dogs more dearly in my heart than another, for each gave unconditionally and entirely of their being to our partnership. I too gave each my best love and care as I learned both from and with them so many lessons of being a better participant in the journey we shared together.

Tracy held my hand and we paused there beneath a beautiful tapestry of Quinn from our final hike together. Pearls were worked into the piece to provide a braille translation of the quote from Ghandi:

I offer you peace.
I offer you love.
I offer you friendship.
I see your beauty.
I hear your need.
I feel your feelings.
My wisdom flows from
The highest source.
I salute that source in you.
Let us work together
For unity and peace.

I thought briefly on Rachel Morris for applying the quote to our favorite photo of Quinn, and the Gagnons for the creation and gift of the tapestry, but mostly of my Quinn, gone from us for over a year and yet still so powerfully with me in everything I attempt. I unfolded a crisp new white pocket square and both of us reached into Quinn's urn and collected some of his ashes for the journey to Kilimanjaro ahead. I was surprised to feel the bits of bone mingled with the ashes and it pained me for reasons I cannot fully explain. Ever so gently I refolded the handkerchief, his ashes now held within. I tucked this memorial into the chest pocket of my snow pants. This would keep it safe and held over my heart in those pants, likely to be worn only during the frigid temperatures of the summit ascent.

Another deep internal sob shakes me from my reverie and I feel Jose place a comforting hand on my shoulder. I carefully open the handkerchief and ease Quinn's ashes into the hole I have made. I feel the tears flowing steadily and allow the drops to roll off my cheeks and into his honorary grave here atop Kilimanjaro, the tallest stand-alone mountain in the world. I mutter to myself words that may seem barely coherent to Jose on our isolated retreat here on Uhuru peak. "I love you so much my dear sweet Quinn-boy. You gave so much to me. It was you who taught me to fully walk again, it was you who taught me to run and who ever so patiently guided me to learn how to hike. We shared a lot of peaks my beautiful boy and all because you believed in me, encouraged me, supported me with an unrivaled spirit. Of course, you are here with me today too and while I may never reach a higher mountain summit we will forever bound across limitless peaks of love and achievement. A bit of you will always belong here as your love and friendship are the highest summit any of us could ever know."

Then I simply cry until I have no more water for my tears. I hug Jose tightly, loving his friendship even as my heart yearned most for the thick furry body of Quinn to force itself under my arm and against my side as he did so many times in our past. Ever so slowly we turn back to our team gathered around the summit sign for this tallest of Kilimanjaro's peaks. Three volcanos thrust up from the Serengeti plains of Tanzania to form this massive mountain. The ashes of centuries spread from deep within the earth to blanket this landscape. I had added an infinitesimally small amount of ash, but neither the gesture nor the being those ashes represented seemed small to me as I walked to rejoin my companions.

I was still overwhelmed with the massive feel of the mountain and the epic height we had attained. Only an hour or so prior we had paused, already on the rim of the Kibo crater, before making the final somewhat gentle ascent to the highest point. We had paused because the sun was about to rise. The deep black of twilight which accompanied us since the nearly full moon passed beyond a ridge, gave way to midnight blue, purple, red-orange and then those first rays of the dawn burst forth. Its blazingly intense rays assaulted the glacial walls around us. All of this came to me through the inspired descriptions of my friends. I had heard the awe in their voices as they finally understood what it meant to be so high the curvature of the earth was evident on the horizon! Physical exhaustion fueled the emotional intensity as the warmth of the sun ended the long night of our ascent. This had been a goal for several years, intensely so for the most recent year. We had planned, trained and prepared for all of the incredible adventures on our six-day journey to the summit. The intensity of the emotions lifted our weary spirits but only for an all-too-brief series of moments. The oxygen-thin air steadily drained the euphoria of our accomplishment through the process of gathering our team together at the peak. I had already poured all my remaining reserves of emotion and energy into my private tribute to the Mighty Quinn. Our brief moment on top of the world was coming to a close and it was time to end our lofty reflections and begin our descent.

All too often, reaching the summit is viewed as achieving the goal. The reality is that only half of the journey is achieved at the summit. As much work as had gone into the strides and scrambles up, we still had a difficult day ahead returning first to our highest base camp. We would then barely break before working our weary way down to an elevation of only 10,000 feet, a height at which oxygen would surge through us once again. Also, an elevation where sleep would come easily, food would digest, and all would be right once more. This we knew, was all still ahead and the reality was more sobering than any prior summit in my life. I heard the words of Jose sharing a sentiment we all understood so very well: "I've never felt so badly in success." This was because, in part, the victory was not yet fully obtained. It was also simply because the effort and altitude combined to leave us too exhausted and unwell to appreciate the full measure of the marvels captured in our minds for later reflection.

We were on the summit for more than 20 minutes and our guide, Emmanuel, was eager for us to begin the trek downward. The plan for the entire hike was for me to use different friends as guides, so it was time to reach out and find my guide for the next part of the trip. "Who is ready to guide me?" …(silence) …"Who is able to give a little guiding a try?" … (more silence) … There was no panic in me partially because I was too exhausted for panic. I was, however, very concerned. I knew the hike up had proven more taxing than any of us had anticipated. Even as I had adjusted my guiding needs to minimize talking for my oxygen deprived guides, it had been a harrowing and exhausting undertaking for all of us. I thought perhaps I was miscommunicating now in my need, and so inquired if anyone could hear me. A chorus of clear but, weary affirmatives helped me understand the situation was indeed dire.

I asked Emmanuel if he had any suggestions because while the few guides and porters with us were incredibly strong and capable even at this altitude, they had never guided me, and it wasn't part of their expectation or plan. They needed their attention and energy to support the entire team, and not allocated entirely to the unfamiliar task of guiding me. While he was silently mulling it over, either to think of the English translation for my need or to perhaps have other considerations to offer, Rob Webber's frayed voice finally brought hope.

"I'll try." He was ready to give guiding an attempt but knew his stamina would be limited and that our work would require a method similar to our ascent. He would simply walk and choose the route while I used my hand on his pack to glean all the information I could. I would trust my feet to find the right purchase and ease around all the multitude of stumbling blocks the mountain would provide. Our hikes were often livened by playful teasing with the calm, soothing approach of Rob and his voice. Many a "Bob Ross" reference brought smiles and laughter to us all. Now, in this moment his voiced willingness to take those first strides as my guide was pivotal. I was fairly certain I wouldn't be left on the summit, and yet may never properly find words to highlight my appreciation, respect and awe at the inner strength he found that morning.

Thus, began our promised descent. Despite the Diamox, a prescription we took to alleviate the symptoms of altitude sickness, I could feel my head pounding more and more, my sleep deprived brain struggled, and my tired muscles complained as we stepped away. I said a final farewell to Quinn at the Kilimanjaro summit. I silently thanked him for any part his memory or spirit had played in giving Rob the will to guide me again. We stepped away, and while the trail quickly became a sliding scree-laden journey down into more oxygen-rich air, I did not recover.

My stomach was in distress due to absent blood flow redirected to give more oxygen to my legs. My brain needed every bit of concentration to feel out the route from Rob's movements and the feel of the terrain. As a migraine elevated alarmingly I knew it was likely to become one of the longer, more difficult days of my life. Many hours later, with many different guides assisting in the process, my toe-pounded feet were allowed a brief rest back at Barafu camp at just over 15,000 feet. There was still no real rest to be had, and try as I might, my stomach could not hold down the simple food options available. Seven hours of difficult descent still remained, half of which came with my blacking out while trying to walk.

The final stages had guides Emmanuel and Vader each putting a shoulder under my arm and we walked step by slow step with my awareness just this side of consciousness. I don't recall much of the final part of the summit day. I only know that we arrived at our final camp on Kilimanjaro with Tracy helping ease me into our tent. I was in agony and felt sleep closing in immediately. My final thought for the night was that I had truly given absolutely everything to my tribute to Quinn. He gave everything he had for me, guiding me in harness even on the final day of his life because it was what he most wanted to do on that fateful day. Well, perhaps the only thing after play and we had done that with him as well. So, as I slept I dreamt of the playful boy. It was a comforting way to sleep soundly and get the rest I would need for the remainder of the journey ahead.

I did get that rest, and my recovery was swift enough to appreciate our jubilant final descent in the oxygen rich air. This was a springboard for our far less strenuous Serengeti safari. It was, however, the foreshadowing of another neurological episode which overcame me fully several months after our return home. Passing out during a training run with Rob Webber along the Charles River in Boston was somewhat convenient given the proximity of Mass General Hospital. In the emergency room yet another episode of lost consciousness took place and I was admitted directly. These episodes continued to occur multiple times per day with my losing consciousness for periods of roughly 90 seconds each time. A team of doctors studied me for several weeks with the neurologists taking the lead based upon my past history.

In the process we were able to discern that my genome has a pair of unique variants to my Wolfram and Twinkle genes. I didn't even realize I had a twinkle gene! I was told I had an excellent heart for a 20-year-old which is good news for my more than 50 years. More soberingly, we discovered an anomaly in my parasympathetic nervous system relating to the vasovagal response. More commonly known as the "fight or flight" response, something in my broken neurology was triggering me to pass out unpredictably throughout my day. I could detect these coming with a roughly15 second warning, giving me time to lay down safely. Unfortunately travelling alone became entirely unreasonable and so I was under significant restrictions and virtually home bound for almost nine months until we found a medication. Midodrine was prescribed to adjust my blood flow, halting these episodes entirely. A frustrating side effect of this medication increased the frequency of my migraines to nearly 3 per week. It took us several more months to find the balance of additional medications to bring the migraines under control and still allow me the Midodrine I needed.

This year of restriction and medical investigation was an often times painful and continuously frustrating reminder to me of the fragility of my overall neurological ailment. I often downplay the consequences of my condition. But now I was truly afraid while effectively trapped at my home for many weeks worrying about what was happening. I always know it's possible for the wrong nerves to be affected, resulting in gross changes to my personality, loss of body function or even my ultimate death. I also understand very well there is little value in worrying about the aspects of this disorder I cannot control. It is why I put so much effort into learning and understanding the steps I can take for my optimum overall health. None of this knowledge and belief prevents the emotional surges from overwhelming me at times. Certainly, amidst fresh new challenge this is natural and common. The support and encouragement of Tracy, Autumn and a host of friends helps tremendously as I strive to build momentum in a positive direction, from within a single difficult day to the broader planning of my life ahead.

On the mornings when I wake with a bit of struggle I put something encouraging quickly ahead of me. Perhaps by calling Autumn for a quick snuggle or taking her for a walk in a new area which always makes her tail wag with more fervor. Sometimes I choose a five-minute phone call to a fine friend to ask them to share something good in their world to help lift my spirits. Maybe it's as simple as fixing myself a special cup of coffee and sitting out in the backyard to listen to the birdsong while reflecting on a host of past experiences or planning what adventure is next.

Kilimanjaro to the Peruvian Andes, the Grand Canyon to the White Mountains, Marathons, Tough Mudders, Super Bowls, TED Talks, Modi, Ostend, Quinn, Autumn and my dear Tracy are all part of a journey of adventure in life and love, loss and healing along this path. There have been so many epic adventures already in my life. Enough experiences, many of them shared, at least in part with you in the pages just past, to cause some to suggest it is enough. Certainly, to that end I am content with my past despite my many struggles, missteps and lost opportunities. I have come to this point in my journey in full appreciation for who I am. I remain a work in progress ready to learn, grow and change as I discover more of the world ahead.

Once again, as John Lennon rather famously said "Life is what happens while we are busy making other plans." I certainly respect the wisdom in that statement because my own life path was changed dramatically when this neurological disorder altered my life. I think I've learned a few other things of more importance than John's observation. Many suggest a sense of empowerment comes from the realization that we choose how to respond to any adversity we encounter. I'll add my belief the choice we make in how we respond to adversity will have a bigger impact on our lives than the adversity itself. This is why my life is not about my blindness but rather about all the choices I've made since going blind, and the wonderful rewards those choices provide.

Finally referencing Lennon's quote one more time, I think life is more often exactly about the plans we make. A plan is what turns a wish into a reality. People often want to know what is next for me and the difficulty I have is in choosing the answer. There are a few obvious and easy responses, because I always hope to reach more people than peaks and so my presentations to students, organizations and companies will likely continue for quite some time. I cannot emphasize enough how much it helps me to feel I'm helping others. To that extent I will continue to work towards philanthropic endeavors such as giving back to the organizations who helped guide me on such a positive path. There is more, of course, because my adventurous spirit yearns to explore and experience our world.

I believe there are no limits or barriers except those we choose to impose on ourselves. As such, I'll dream big of all the possibilities I might want, prioritize them into what is the reasonable schedule to obtain them, so I can start making the plan. For me that plan almost always includes a good team and a shared dream. So, Tracy and I will sit down with Autumn at our feet getting a pat or two while we exchange ideas. I think the better question is what's next for you? What is your plan? If you are dreaming big and reaching for your peak potential, then we may just see you at the summit!

About the Authors

This book is written with my voice, tells the story of my life yet I'm ostensibly here to tell you about the plural, "authors." Since the rest of the book shares the insights of my life in plenty of detail, I thought to share Tracy's story and her role as co-author. As the Chapter "Hooray Tracy" quite well undertakes the task of introducing her into the story, I want to illuminate the process through which we created this book together.

We are married, sharing our home with our lovely Black and Tan Labrador Retriever, Autumn who also happens to be my guide dog. Our many independent activities come second to our drive to share our lives together. Few experiences have enabled such deep sharing of time, vast amounts of time!, emotion and insights with each other. While certainly it was my entire life in the making, three years of serious intent and the most recent year of absolute dedication to the task. Ours was a dynamic process as we discovered ever improving techniques for streamlining our interactions. Along the way we individually grew in our roles and jointly developed an efficiency of teamwork. The interactions held many cathartic relationship building moments for us. There were stressful times, of course, but more commonly celebrations of working together to create something we both believed worthy.

I typed each chapter through a series of drafts until I felt confident enough I could show it to Tracy. After her initial read we discussed the level of change she thought necessary and some of the details. Often, she would send me back an email with a couple of notes on which areas needed more drastic rework on my part. Quite often, she would draw out more stories from me to breathe life into a section and always she moved me towards improving my writing. Eventually when my draft achieved a level of success we sat together, and she read line by line. We talked about word choices, sentence structure, concepts and the ever-important feel of the story. She edited these into the proper format, including all our adjustments and revisions together for submission to our editor, Gene.

She attended the file management with Gene as we passed through several edit cycles with his insightful comments, questions and alterations. I was impressed but not surprised to note how quickly she incorporated improvements in our approach because of those interactions with Gene. She has read each sentence out loud more times than we care to count as we each worked to suss out the ideal word, phrase, sentence, meaning, emotion and feel. She read more times silently sending draft suggestions for consideration when our discussions were at an impasse. She patiently taught me the words I over use, the words I use improperly and guided me to better ways of expression frequently. As our early reader comments arrived she was a sounding board again, always willing to dig into the finished work and make improvements.

Balancing our lives with the work on the book was frequently complicated. Tracy works full-time and attended college full-time earning a 4.0 in the achievement of her MBA, just as we completed our writing! We jointly founded and manage the charitable organization 2020 Vision Quest while both training for and enjoying a variety of endurance experiences from mountain climbing to marathons. Through all this she also found the balance of when to push me to step back and get a perspective break or dig in and get some writing done. She guided me to reject substandard work and when to allow me to own the final choice with the altruistic grace with which she viewed this as my book. I do not view it as such. This is our book. She has researched and applied incredible amounts of information on layout, publishing and best book practice for marketing. This book would be unlikely to exist without her work outside the creation process. It is, however, for the creation process in which we have joined together as authors. It is the story of my life and like my life, this story would be far less good, far from complete without my other author, Tracy Pierce!

Made in the USA
Middletown, DE
02 November 2018